BEYOND NEURAL CORRELATES OF CONSCIOUSNESS

Drawing on neuroscientific research and metacognitive theory, this groundbreaking volume examines the theoretical implications that are elicited when neural correlates of consciousness (NCC) are identified.

The relationship between consciousness and the brain has concerned philosophers for centuries, yet a tacit assumption in much empirically minded consciousness research seems to be that if we can only develop a map of correlations, no further questions remain to be asked. *Beyond Neural Correlates of Consciousness* starts where others stop, by asking what these correlations may tell us about the nature of consciousness. The book contains chapters considering the upshots of finding the neural correlates of consciousness in light of the most prominent contemporary theories in the field. This illuminates the theoretical consequences of succeeding in the quest for the neural correlates of consciousness from the perspective of global workspace theory, higher-order thought theory, local recurrency theory, and REFCON models, in addition to considering how this quest is shaped by different conscious phenomena, such as dreaming, altered states of consciousness, and different levels of consciousness.

This insightful text features sophisticated theories that goes beyond correlational inferences and neural mapping, and will be of interest to students and researchers of consciousness, particularly those interested in interpreting neural correlates.

Morten Overgaard is Professor of Cognitive Neuroscience at the Center for Functionally Integrative Neuroscience, Aarhus University, Denmark. He is the head of the Cognitive Neuroscience Research Group.

Jesper Mogensen is Professor of Neuroscience at the Department of Psychology at the University of Copenhagen, Denmark. He is the head of the Unit for Cognitive Neuroscience and Director for the Research Center for Brain Injury Rehabilitation.

Asger Kirkeby-Hinrup is Postdoctoral Researcher in Theoretical Philosophy at the Department of Philosophy and Cognitive Science, Lund University, Sweden, and the Center for Functionally Integrative Neuroscience, Aarhus University, Denmark.

Current Issues in Consciousness Research

Series Editor: Morten Overgaard

Current Issues in Consciousness Research is a series of edited books which will reflect the state of the art in areas of current and emerging interest in the psychological and philosophical study of consciousness.

Each volume will be tightly focussed on a particular topic and will consist of from seven to ten chapters contributed by international experts. The editors of individual volumes will be leading figures in their areas and will provide an introductory overview.

Example topics include consciousness and metacognition, consciousness and free will, neural correlates of consciousness, disorders of consciousness, and conscious sensation of movement.

Sensation of Movement
Edited by Thor Grünbaum and Mark Schram Christensen

Transitions between Consciousness and Unconsciousness
Edited by Guido Hesselmann

Beyond Neural Correlates of Consciousness
Edited by Morten Overgaard, Jesper Mogensen and Asger Kirkeby-Hinrup

BEYOND NEURAL CORRELATES OF CONSCIOUSNESS

Edited by
Morten Overgaard
Jesper Mogensen
Asger Kirkeby-Hinrup

Routledge
Taylor & Francis Group

LONDON AND NEW YORK

First published 2021
by Routledge
2 Park Square, Milton Park, Abingdon, Oxon OX14 4RN

and by Routledge
52 Vanderbilt Avenue, New York, NY 10017

Routledge is an imprint of the Taylor & Francis Group, an informa business

British Library Cataloguing-in-Publication Data
A catalogue record for this book is available from the British Library

Library of Congress Cataloging-in-Publication Data
A catalog record has been requested for this book

ISBN: 978-1-138-63799-3 (hbk)
ISBN: 978-1-138-63798-6 (pbk)
ISBN: 978-1-315-20526-7 (ebk)

Typeset in Bembo
by codeMantra

CONTENTS

FIGURES

TABLE

CONTRIBUTORS

Larissa Albantakis, Department of Psychiatry, Wisconsin Institute for Sleep and Consciousness, University of Wisconsin-Madison, USA

Henk P. Barendregt, Faculty of Science, Radboud University, Nijmegen, Netherlands

Alice Barra, Coma Science Group, GIGA-Consciousness, University of Liège, Liège, Belgium; Centre du Cerveau (Centre intégré pluridisciplinaire de l'étude du cerveau, de la cognition et de la conscience), University Hospital of Liège, Liège, Belgium

Manon Carrlère, Coma Science Group, GIGA-Consciousness, University of Liège, Liège, Belgium; Centre du Cerveau (Centre intégré pluridisciplinaire de l'étude du cerveau, de la cognition et de la conscience), University Hospital of Liège, Liège, Belgium

Peter Fazekas, Centre for Philosophical Psychology, University of Antwerp, Belgium; Cognitive Neuroscience Research Unit, CFIN, Aarhus University, Denmark

Asger Kirkeby-Hinrup, Department of Philosophy and Cognitive Science, Lund University, Sweden; Cognitive Neuroscience Research Unit, CFIN, Aarhus University, Denmark

Victor A.F. Lamme, Amsterdam Brain and Cognition (ABC), Department of Psychology, University of Amsterdam, Netherlands

Steven Laureys, Coma Science Group, GIGA-Consciousness, University of Liège, Liège, Belgium; Centre du Cerveau (Centre intégré pluridisciplinaire de l'étude du cerveau, de la cognition et de la conscience), University Hospital of Liège, Liège, Belgium

Charlotte Martial, Coma Science Group, GIGA-Consciousness, University of Liège, Liège, Belgium; Centre du Cerveau (Centre intégré pluridisciplinaire de l'étude du cerveau, de la cognition et de la conscience), University Hospital of Liège, Liège, Belgium

Jesper Mogensen, The Unit for Cognitive Neuroscience (UCN), Department of Psychology, University of Copenhagen, Denmark

Georgina Nemeth, Cognitive Neuroscience Research Unit, CFIN, Aarhus University, Denmark

Morten Overgaard, Cognitive Neuroscience Research Unit, CFIN, Aarhus University, Denmark

Antonino Raffone, Department of Psychology, Sapienza University of Rome, Italy; School of Buddhist Studies, Philosophy and Comparative Religions, Nalanda University, Rajgir, India

BEYOND NEURAL CORRELATES OF CONSCIOUSNESS – AN INTRODUCTION

Why are we conscious? How can it be that information processed in the brains of living creatures is accompanied by subjective experience? In the form of a classical question: Why is there something *it is like* to be consciousness? For centuries, the puzzle of consciousness was mainly the concern of philosophers. However, recent decades have seen a surge of scientific interest within a broad swathe of academic disciplines, and importantly, especially in the empirical sciences. Since the birth of cognitive science in the late 1970s and the later emergence of cognitive neuroscience, the literature on consciousness has expanded vastly.

Significant parts of contemporary consciousness studies are concerned with isolating the neural correlates of consciousness. The idea of a "neural correlate of consciousness", defined as the minimal neural mechanisms jointly sufficient for any one conscious percept, has been around for decades and was probably first used in print by Francis Crick and Christof Koch in 1990. Importantly, such a correlate will always be relative to a certain class of systems and to internal – as well as external – conditions. In an empirical context, it will be the minimal set of properties, described on an appropriate level of neuroscientific analysis that is sufficient to generate a certain conscious content in the mind of the organism. From this definition, the concept of neural correlates of consciousness then can be unpacked in different ways depending on the research context in which it is used. For instance, while the core interest is in *sufficient* conditions, there is likely a set of *necessary* conditions. The necessary conditions may be further broken up into necessary neural conditions, and necessary auxiliary or background conditions (e.g. bloodflow). Another way the concept of neural correlates of consciousness has been developed is by focusing of the *contents* of consciousness. In contrast to the minimal definition that invokes the necessary and sufficient conditions for *any* conscious percept, the content-specific neural correlates of consciousness are conceived of as the neural mechanisms necessary and sufficient for particular phenomenal contents within consciousness (e.g. faces, colors or thoughts). Finally – assuming that any specific content that can become conscious has one or more corresponding content-specific neural correlate (which follows from the statement that the content *can become conscious* combined with the assumption that consciousness is realized in the brain) – we can talk about the *full* neural correlates of consciousness, comprising all the content-specific neural correlates of consciousness.

Experimentally, the way we cash out the NCCs will depend on the area of investigation and the relevant level of analysis and description. In some cases, this means looking for correlations between certain events in the brain – under a certain representation as described on a certain neurobiological level of analysis – and for certain events in the ongoing dynamics of phenomenal experience – under a certain representation, as described by the subject, usually in the everyday terminology of "folk phenomenology". In other cases, it means looking for correlations between the occurrence of events of the first kind – again, as described in neuroscientific terms – and the occurrence of events of the second kind – as only indicated in a nonlinguistic manner by the subject, such as in pushing a button. In yet other cases, it means looking for correlations between states usually associated with being "alert and awake" contrary to other states taken to be associated with a reduced level of consciousness, e.g. the vegetative state.

However, whereas there has been much development in the attempt to find neural correlates of consciousness, there have been surprisingly few attempts to understand or interpret these correlates by the same scientists. Mapping does not mean reduction, and correlation does not mean explanation. This is not to say that consciousness researchers generally believe that the identification of a correlation is an explanation in itself, yet, in practice, the research field often appears as if this is exactly the hypothesis. Certainly, the exact neural implementation of the neural correlates of consciousness (once found) will constrain the kind conceptual inferences and conclusions that can be made from them, and in this way facilitate our interpretation and understanding. But, irrespective of how the pieces fall with respect to their actual neural implementation, there is likely to be substantial theoretical wiggle room with respect to concepts and models deployed to interpret and understand the neural correlates of consciousness. In other words, once strict, fine-grained correlations between brain states and conscious states have been established, a number of theoretical options are still open. Additional constraints therefore will eventually be needed. Important questions are, for example, what is the true nature of these psychophysical correlations? Are we justified in interpreting them as causal relations? What additional constraints would have to be introduced in order to speak of law-like correlations?

To handle this challenge, modern consciousness research is in great need of establishing connections between neural correlates of consciousness and theoretical interpretations. For instance, in case the neural correlates of consciousness indicate that feature F is a key component in conscious experience, this may count in favor of certain ways of thinking about consciousness and count against their competitors. However, to get closer to understanding consciousness and work towards a comprehensive interpretation, we still would need to account for what role exactly F played, how it interacted with other components, whether it may be substituted either synthetically or organically through neural plasticity, how to characterize individuals who lack F, and so on.

In this volume, we have collected recent proposals for the neural correlates of consciousness in a single volume with the essential addition that they will be discussed in relation to their theoretical underpinnings and implications. We have strived to ensure that the major theories on offer in the field are represented, in addition to varies perspectives relevant to current and future debates. It is our hope that this may serve as a catalyst to increased focus on the important connection between empirical findings and theoretical interpretations, in consciousness studies as well as in other fields.

Morten Overgaard
Jesper Mogensen
Asger Kirkeby-Hinrup

1

WILL WE EXPLAIN CONSCIOUSNESS WHEN WE FIND THE NEURAL CORRELATES OF CONSCIOUSNESS?

Morten Overgaard and Jesper Mogensen

When the "science of consciousness" received a resurgence of interest during the last decade of the 20th century, a major concern was how to actually establish this field of research as a "scientific discipline" with a complete research program and an ambition to provide arguments to help solve the metaphysical mind-brain problem (Metzinger, 1995; Chalmers, 1996). Today, some 30 years later, most scientific work is centered around the attempt to isolate neural correlates of consciousness (NCC) and the methodological issues related to that attempt.

To be precise, by consciousness, we are concerned with states of subjective experience or so-called phenomenal consciousness. Conscious states are individuated by their content so that any variation in content (e.g. seeing a cup of coffee vs seeing a glass of wine) means that the conscious state has changed. As debated in more recent literature, conscious states may not be only characterized by the specific representational content, but also its degree (Fazekas & Overgaard, 2018; Lohse & Overgaard, 2019).

"Subjective content" is of course only one relevant meaning of the term "consciousness". We may also speak of a "background state of consciousness" such as being awake, being asleep, being under influence of drugs etc. (Rosenthal, 1993). It is not completely clear how these distinctions should be categorized: In the clinical literature, this is often discussed as differences in degree – e.g. between being in a coma, in a vegetative state, being minimally conscious or awake (Laureys, Owen & Schiff, 2004; Overgaard & Overgaard, 2011). Other distinctions, e.g. the difference between being under hypnosis, dreaming and being awake, may not be a difference in "degree" as much as a difference in "type". Dreams may arguably be as "intense" as normal, awake experiences yet have a different "background feel". Sometimes, such distinctions are characterized as "altered states of consciousness" (Revonsuo, Kallio & Sikka, 2009). It is not generally clear in the consciousness research literature how these different ways to differentiate concepts of consciousness relate. Arguably, however, the notion of subjective content is the most fundamental concept, so that the decision whether a conscious being is in a vegetative or minimally conscious state relates to content. From this perspective, one could not imagine a patient considered as being generally unconscious – as a "background state" – while having clear and vivid subjective content. Or that a subject is in an altered state of consciousness while having completely normal content. At least to some degree, content seems determining – or co-determining – for how we should think of other conceptions of consciousness (Overgaard & Overgaard, 2010).

The rest of this chapter will specifically discuss neural correlates of conscious content as most research has focussed on this conception of consciousness – and as it arguably is the most fundamental conception as well.

Just as the term "consciousness" needs a more precise definition, so does "neural correlates of consciousness". Chalmers (2000, p. 31) suggests that:

> An NCC (for content) is a minimal neural representational system N such that representation of a content in N is sufficient, under conditions C, for representation of that content in consciousness.

Chalmers debates this choice of words, and underlines that the NCC should be a "minimal system". A broad system may correlate with consciousness without correlating with any one specific aspect of consciousness, which suggests that one should attempt to minimize the NCC. One may argue that the entire brain, or the living body, correlates with any conscious content – but in a maximally broad way. The term "sufficient" is used instead of, say, "necessary", as we cannot beforehand know if there is more than one neural correlate of any one conscious state. If that were in fact the case, all these systems could be said to be sufficient for consciousness, while none of them were necessary for consciousness.

Chalmers' view of what is meant by an NCC seems broadly accepted in the scientific community, and is both overall consistent with review and methods articles from now classical papers such as Crick and Koch (1990) to more recent ones, e.g. Koch et al. (2016).

Today, almost 20 years after David Chalmers published his NCC definition, several experiments claim to have found or at least contributed to finding neural activations relevant for subjective experience. Most of these findings converge in a few main clusters of proposals.

Where and when is the NCC?

Several neuroimaging studies that attempt to contrast states of being conscious with comparable non-conscious conditions have found activations in prefrontal areas (Lau & Rosenthal, 2011). Such findings have led to the proposal that prefrontal cortex, or subdivisions hereof, is a candidate for an NCC (Del Cul et al., 2009). Transcranial magnetic stimulation to prefrontal sites has in at least one experiment been shown to modulate reports of subjective experience without modulating the task performance (Rounis et al., 2010) – although similar effects have been found at other neural sites, e.g. the ventral projection streams from V1 (Overgaard, Nielsen & Fuglsang-Frederiksen, 2004).

The proposal is however incongruent with other findings. During REM sleep, prefrontal cortex activity is often low compared to awake states, even though the experienced content may be just as vivid. Similarly, patients undergoing generalized seizures have increased blood flow in prefrontal areas, even though they are considered unconscious. A number of recent highly debated experiments have contrasted experimental conditions where participants were asked to report about consciously seen images contrasted with other conditions where participants were not reporting about the same consciously seen images. Although such so-called no-report paradigms have no methodological control of whether stimuli were in fact consciously seen without the report (Tsuchiya et al., 2015; Overgaard & Fazekas, 2016; Block, 2019), they do provide strong evidence that the frontal activations found in many experiments in fact represent reporting, task preparation and execution rather than the conscious experience per se.

According to several recent reviews, consciousness researchers generally converge towards the position that consciousness is more related to primary sensory cortices – at least in the case of vision – than it is to prefrontal areas (Frässle et al., 2014). This is however still debated.

One recent review by Koch et al. (2016) compared several different experiments using different types of paradigms and conditions to conclude that across conditions and methods, there is most evidence to suggest that the NCC should be located to a temporo-parietal-occipital network rather than fronto-parietal networks. The theoretical proposals that suggest a temporo-parietal-occipital network do not conform to one internally consistent view. To mention a few examples, Victor Lamme argues that all brain regions are unconscious during a feedforward sweep of information, whereas conscious experience happens when information feeds back to occipital regions (Lamme & Roelfsema, 2000). Other views, e.g. the Visual Awareness Negativity hypothesis, make no such claim, but argue that consciousness correlates with activity in the "VAN range" (Koivisto, Kastrati & Revonsuo, 2014). Although the feedback view and the VAN view would localize consciousness within primary sensory regions, they disagree with regards to timing. The feedback view argues that information must first travel through a feedforward sweep before it "returns", whereas the VAN view expects the feedforward sweep to be conscious. Very few experiments have directly attempted to disentangle these views. In one experiment, object substitution masking was used to investigate very early visual processing, showing that the fastest saccadic responses which "escaped" the influence of the mask are associated with some degree of conscious experience (Crouzet, Overgaard & Busch, 2014; Crouzet et al., 2017). This indicates that very early visual processes before reentrant activity are not devoid of experience. In this way, some of the individual models underlying the general idea of a temporo-parietal-occipital network are very much debated.

Another experiment directly compared reports of subjective experience related to two electrophysiological components extensively investigated as candidate NCCs: An early occipital component 130–320 ms after onset of a visual stimulus and late frontal component occurring 320–510 ms after onset (Andersen et al., 2016). The experiment found that occipital sources in the early time range were significantly more accurate in decoding consciousness than frontal sources in both time ranges. Nevertheless, all regions contributed to the decoding model at some point.

This latter point is unsurprising to theoretical accounts that do not insist on one specific neural location as the "one and only NCC", e.g. the REFCON model which does not belong exclusively in either "camp" (Overgaard & Mogensen, 2014).

One (potential) shortcoming of most attempts to localize the NCC (or at least the way such attempts are conceptualized) is that the "final result" is mostly pointing to one or another region of the brain. Regarding attempts to localize (other) cognitive functions, such a strategy has been criticised repeatedly as being insufficient in order to provide a deeper understanding (e.g. Overgaard & Mogensen, 2011; Carandini, 2012; Mogensen & Overgaard, 2018). According to such criticism, it is insufficient to point to a correspondence between a "function" at the mental level and a given structure at the neural level – there is a need for an "intermediate" computational level. Without such a level, there is little or no chance that knowledge about an NCC can inform the understanding of consciousness further. Few of the current models of the NCC come close to pointing to the computational processes. Exceptions may be the Integrated Information Theory (IIT) (e.g. Oizumi, Albantakis & Tononi, 2014) and the REF framework in the form of the REFCON and REFGEN models (e.g. Overgaard and Mogensen, 2014; Mogensen and Overgaard, 2017). In these models the suggested computational processes may point to mechanisms which when further developed can provoke new empirically testable predictions – and thereby contribute to answers in the context of problems of consciousness.

According to REFCON, information that is integrated in the "SAS-network" and is available for action is conscious. From this perspective, there is no specific neural region that as a matter of principle is more related to consciousness than others. This depends on the kind of "neural strategy" – which neural regions that are recruited – in realizing the relevant mental state. A partially related position is expressed in the IIT by Giulio Tononi (2004). According to Tononi, consciousness may be associated with any physical system as determined by the causal properties of this system – and not determined by its exact location in the head.

Will the NCC ever explain consciousness?

Considering that the renewed interest in the mind-body problem gave rise to a great investment in finding NCC, it is surprising how rarely it is debated if and how the NCC can be part of solving the mind-body problem. Intuitively, it seems rather obvious that a complete understanding of consciousness must also involve an understanding of its neural counterparts. However, it is at least not intuitively given that the isolation of an NCC will support any theoretical conclusions about the metaphysical status of consciousness more than any other. It is, in other words, difficult to see how it will bring any more clarity to the debate of *why* and *how* consciousness relates to physical structure to resolve whether, say, visual consciousness correlates with prefrontal or occipital activations.

If one looks closer at the NCC literature, it does in fact contain several claims about how various findings may serve as arguments for a particular mind-body position in different ways.

Explanation by identity

One hypothetical position is that NCC in themselves are explanations without the addition of any theoretical analysis or argument. This position is rarely seen defended or supported by arguments. Nevertheless, the position is not that rarely seen as a kind of implicit idea in consciousness research – and in cognitive neuroscience more broadly. Experimental investigations of NCC are often presented without any discussion of how the findings may contribute to a solution to those questions that motivated consciousness research in the first place (e.g. how subjective experience relates to physical brain structure). The "position" is difficult to maintain for different reasons. One central reason is that the neural activations identified in neuroimaging experiments are identified using measures of subjective experiences in the first place. Obviously, the measure of consciousness in a given experiment is first decided, and whatever neural correlates are identified must be determined by this measure (as they are correlates found in the experiment that have applied this measure). For this reason alone, it is conceptually difficult to claim that those correlates then in and of themselves "explain" the subjective experience any more than the subjective measure would be able to explain consciousness (Overgaard, 2004).

If one were to actually suggest a research program based on this "position" (if it were truly held as an actual position), it would, on the surface of things, likely resemble current cognitive neuroscience a lot. But it would look for correlations as a goal in itself, as a kind of "mapping approach". Scientists would attempt to carve out the contours of the "mental map" and the "brain map", and then simply show which parts related to what counterparts. End of story.

NCC, obviously, are nothing but statistics based on a series of observations of subjective and objective states. Suppose we establish the desired correlation between subjective and objective measures, how will this impact competing theories at the conceptual level? Theories in the conceptual domain predict more or less the same with respect to subjective measures and are silent about objective measures. Objective measures similarly are silent about conceptual theories, and to the extent that subjective measures have anything to say about conceptual theories it is by appeal to how things appear to a single individual through introspection. Such introspective reports have trouble with third-person veri-fication and, somewhat worse, appear arbitrary with respect to the conclusions individuals take them to warrant with respect to conceptual theories. For these reasons, correlations clearly do not serve as – or even give rise to – explanations at a conceptual level.

Explanation by association

Another possible understanding of how correlations relate to explanation is that associations to other functions that are known to have similar correlates as those related to consciousness can help to explain consciousness. It is easy to come up with examples of experiments where this kind of logic could be tempting to apply.

As one example, in the debate about higher-order and first-order theories of consciousness, it could be argued that findings of prefrontal activations related to, e.g., visual consciousness serve as arguments in favour of higher-order the-ory (Lau & Rosenthal, 2011). Variations of higher-order theory of consciousness generally state that consciousness is the consequence of a mental state (typi-cally a thought) that is directed towards (it is "about") an by itself unconscious first-order state (e.g. a visual perception) (Gennaro, 1996). A finding that there are prefrontal correlations to reports of subjective experience could be seen as "explanations" – by association – for higher-order theory based on other findings that relate prefrontal activations to cognitive functions such as working memory and executive control (Odegaard, Knight & Lau, 2017). Obviously, the find-ing that executive functions typically relate to prefrontal areas is not the same as saying that higher-order states (as those discussed in higher-order theory of consciousness) must involve prefrontal regions as well. Neither does it mean that activations of prefrontal regions related to a conscious perception must mean that those activations represent higher-order states that are "about" a first-order perception.

Higher-order theories hypothesize that consciousness generating higher-order thoughts may involve prefrontal activity, but this does not entail that find-ings where conscious subjects do not exhibit significant prefrontal activations is evidence against the higher-order theories. Nevertheless, this argument is fre-quently used (e.g. Kozuch, 2013). Theories of the NCC named "prefrontal theo-ries" referring to a group of theories in the conceptual domain (e.g. higher-order thought theory, global workspace and others) and "local recurrency theory" or "posterior hot zone" (associated with early sensory areas) indicate that somehow the viability of these conceptual theories depend on where in the brain an even-tual discovery locates the NCCs (Lamme, 2006; Bor & Seth, 2012; Ledoux & Brown, 2017; Michel & Morales, 2019). Following the argument above, even if the NCCs are eventually located in the early sensory regions, this does not entail that HOT theory is wrong. Similarly, first-order theories are not automatically wrong, in case the NCCs happen to be in the PFC.

For instance, the HOT theory posits that a mental state, such as a sensation, is conscious when it is the intentional object of another (higher-order) mental state (Lau & Rosenthal, 2011). HOT is similar to first-order theories, in the sense that they both seek to explain consciousness by reference to properties of – or relations between – mental states. However, when it comes to the brain, the notion of mental state does not straightforwardly apply. It is true that neuroscientists may deploy the concept of a mental state; for instance, when referring to representations in the brain incurred by the introduction of a stimulus. However, this usage is merely a proxy referring to a collection of signals and processes propagating through different brain areas. So, while the notion of mental states, conceived of as ontologically distinct entities, is conversationally useful and theoretically harmless, it is, strictly speaking, empirically mistaken. On the neural level, states are *signals* or patterns of neural activation, and this is what we measure empirically. Signals move through brain regions – and patterns unfold – over time. We can trace a signal and its interactions as it propagates through the brain and reaches different stages of processing. And speaking loosely, we may agree that the signal somehow corresponds to, say, a perceptual representation of a visual stimulus. Such loose speak is useful, and for most purposes more than sufficient. But, in virtue of being a general gesture towards an underspecified group of phenomena, loose speak fails to provide a specific answer to what and where the mental state actually is. And this is what matters when we need to individuate a mental state. There is no non-arbitrary way to fixate upon an exact point in time and space to delineate the boundaries of the mental state necessary for individuation (Kirkeby-Hinrup & Overgaard, submitted).

One can have many different opinions about the explanatory strength of "associations". Arguably, however, the most important thing is to be aware of the limitations. Whereas, in the examples above, neural correlates of, say, thinking or metacognition reasonably inspire the idea that if consciousness correlates with prefrontal activity, then that would be empirical support for HOT. However, measures related to one level of description cannot replace measures related to other levels of description. In order to claim that "overlaps" in neural correlates entails "overlaps" in mental states – or vice versa – one would have to also argue for some version of mind-brain identity. All correlational findings in cognitive neuroscience are consistent with the interpretation that correlations represent identity or a 1:1 dependency, but also with multiple realization, i.e. the view that the same conscious states may potentially be realized in different neural substrates. There are arguably good reasons for this idea: If conscious states were identical to neural states, it would be difficult to: (1) consider conscious states subjectively as "the same" over time due to ongoing brain plasticity, or more dramatic changes related to e.g. brain injury, (2) to compare conscious experiences between individuals as no two brains are the same, (3) even more difficult to compare even the simplest experiences such as "vision" or "pain" between species. Accordingly, an "association-driven" approach to the relation between correlation and explanation seems highly speculative.

The NCC is not an explanation

A different approach to the role of NCC in consciousness research would suggest that the NCC in itself does not explain anything. One could argue that an explanation of a theoretical question (i.e. "why are we conscious?") cannot be solved with empirical data on its own (e.g. "42"). An explanation of consciousness from this perspective would involve an understanding of the *nature* of the relation between mind and brain. As there is no necessary relation between any theoretical posits about the nature of the mind-brain relation and specific neural regions, different theoretical perspectives can account for the same correlations (e.g. in the example above regarding multiple realizations), and hence, empirical data seem unable to provide an answer.

Giving up on the idea that the NCC in itself may explain consciousness does however not lead to the conclusion that empirical research has no role in consciousness research. Logically consistent yet mutually exclusive theories about mind-brain relations may in some instances lead to different empirical predictions, which then may shape or even decide the theoretical debate. If we want to truly deploy empirical sciences to establish the NCCs and distinguish between competing theories of consciousness, we must do so on the basis of differing behavioural predictions rather than predicting activation profiles in brain regions. Or, to be clear, if two competing theories have different predictions about neural activations in a neuroimaging experiment but identical predictions about behaviour, it would be difficult to see how the experiment could ever contribute to choose between conceptual theories of consciousness.

Thus, this position does not argue against neural correlates as being an important or even necessary part of explaining consciousness, yet it warns against the temptation to let a perceived similarity in functional characteristics of one process lead to the claim that another process relate to the same brain process. This problem is further aggravated if we allow ourselves to count empirical findings as evidence for or against a conceptual theory simply because some or other brain region is involved.

All things considered, we find the last "type" of position more consistent than attempts to make conclusions about consciousness theories directly on the basis of neural correlations. On this basis, we conclude that consciousness research needs to move "beyond neural correlates", i.e. that the purpose of this research should not be to simply identify neural correlates, but seek to present frameworks of conceptual theory and predictions about behaviour together with NCCs in order to actually contribute to a theoretical debate about consciousness.

Fact is that there is still widespread disagreement about where to even locate the NCCs. This disagreement itself is part of what forms the foundation for the debate in the first place. Some may here object that everyone involved is well aware of this and investigating the competing hypotheses involves exactly making predictions about their location. That is standard scientific practice. It is the testing of these predictions that in the end (sometime far into the future) will allow us to distinguish between the hypotheses empirically and determine the real NCCs and the nature of consciousness.

The extrapolation of topographical regions of interest based on conceived similarity in functional characteristics from data obtained in behavioral paradigms is not *per se* misguided. At least to the extent that this practice merely serves to inform new paradigms. What, however, is misguided is thinking that topographical data obtained through behavioral studies of other phenomena warrants bypassing further behavioral studies when it comes to consciousness, i.e. we cannot let the default be reasoning directly from our (perceived) similarity in functional characteristics of one process to the claim that another process is likely to (or must) reside in the same brain region. This problem is further aggravated if we allow ourselves to count empirical findings as evidence for or against a conceptual theory simply because some or other brain region is involved. If we want to truly deploy empirical sciences to establish the NCCs and distinguish between competing theories of consciousness, we must do so on the bases of differing behavioral predictions rather than predicting activation profiles in brain regions (Kirkeby-Hinrup & Overgaard, submitted).

NCC and the future

Today, many scientific theories of consciousness are not more than collections of mere correlational claims: they only pinpoint those brain processes that co-occur with conscious states. Knowing the correlates of a phenomenon, however, does not contribute to understanding the phenomenon. For a scientific understanding of consciousness, explanatory links between neural mechanisms and features of conscious experiences would be required. Explanatory links move beyond correlational claims by establishing a connection between characteristic features of correlating phenomena on the basis of functional or structural similarities. Via such connections, explanatory links between neural processes and conscious experiences would allow for the transfer of explanations of the neural features in question to the realm of consciousness, thereby accounting for features of consciousness.

An explanatory link is indeed "explanatory" only if it relates to theory that actually informs about how we are to logically conceive of the mind-brain relation. This requires for the theories to have different predictions for the outcome of behavioural experiments. If two theories, e.g. higher-order and first-order theory, have different predictions for the NCC but the same predictions for the behavioural results in the same experiment, those neural correlates would do little work to provide evidence for which theory is more correct. This is so because the mere geography of the NCC says little or nothing about whether it suggests higher-order or first-order theory (or any other theory) as more correct. For that reason, experiments must be designed to give different behavioural predictions in order to establish functional connections between consciousness and brain states.

One such example is whether mental states relate to physical states in a 1:1 fashion, or whether "the same" mental state can be realized in different substrates, e.g. between individuals or within individuals over time. Any evidence leaning towards one or the other view will not in itself, according to this understanding of an NCC, be explanatory, yet they will feed into theoretical positions such as identity theory or functionalism as arguments that could not have been provided without empirical data.

We believe that the analysis above leads to the conclusion that research into NCC is still a meaningful endeavour, yet not in and of itself. Thus, the NCC should change its status from being a "research goal" to an element or "part of an argument" for a theoretical position. From this perspective, the NCC may answer certain specific questions relating to more general conceptual questions, but specific neural geography or types of processing will never work as a direct window to decide how we should conceive of mind-brain relations.

References

Andersen, L.M., Pedersen, M.N., Sandberg, K. & Overgaard, M. (2016): Occipital MEG activity in the early time range (<300 ms) predicts graded changes in perceptual consciousness, *Cerebral Cortex, 26,* 6, 2677–2688.

Block, N. (2019): What is wrong with the no-report paradigm and how to fix it, *Trends in Cognitive Sciences, 23,* 1003–1013.

Bor, D. & Seth, A. (2012): Consciousness and the prefrontal parietal network: insights from attention, working memory, and chunking, *Frontiers in Psychology, 12.* https://www.frontiersin.org/articles/10.3389/fpsyg.2012.00063/full.

Carandini, M. (2012): From circuits to behavior: a bridge too far? *Nature Neuroscience, 15,* 507–509.

Chalmers, D.J. (1996): *The Conscious Mind,* Oxford University Press, New York, US.

Chalmers, D.J. (2000): What is a neural correlate of consciousness?, in: T. Metzinger (ed): *Neural Correlates of Consciousness,* MIT Press, Cambridge, US, 17–39.

Crick, F. & Koch, C. (1990): Towards a neurobiological theory of consciousness, *Seminars in Neuroscience, 2,* 263–275.

Crouzet, S., Kovalenko, L., del Pin, S., Overgaard, M. & Busch, N. (2017): Early visual processing allows for selective behavior, shifts of attention, and conscious visual experience in spite of masking, *Consciousness and Cognition, 54,* 89–100.

Crouzet, S., Overgaard, M. & Busch, N. (2014): The fastest saccadic responses escape visual masking, *PLoS ONE, 9,* 2, 1–6.

Del Cul, A., Dehaene, S., Reyes, P., Bravo, E. & Slachevsky, A. (2009): Causal role of prefrontal cortex in the threshold for access to consciousness, *Brain, 132,* 2531–2540.

Fazekas, P. & Overgaard, M. (2018): A multi-factor account of degrees of awareness, *Cognitive Science, 42,* 1833–1859.

Frässle, S., Sommer, J., Jansen, A., Naber, M. & Einhäuser, W. (2014): Binocular rivalry: frontal activity relates to introspection and action but not to perception, *Journal of Neuroscience, 34,* 1738–1743.

Gennaro, R. (1996): *Consciousness and Self-Consciousness: A Defense of the Higher Order Thought Theory of Consciousness,* John Benjamins, Amsterdam, NL.

Lau, H. & Rosenthal, D. (2011): Empirical support for higher-order theories of consciousness, *Trends in Cognitive Science, 15,* 8, 365–373.

Laureys, S., Owen, D. & Schiff, N. (2004): Brain function in coma, vegetative state, and related disorders, *The Lancet Neurology, 3,* 9, 537–546.

Koch, C., Massimini, M., Boly, M. & Tononi, G. (2016): Neural correlates of consciousness: progress and problems, *Nature Reviews Neuroscience, 17*, 307–321.

Kirkeby-Hinrup, A. & Overgaard, M. (submitted): Finding the NCCs will not solve all our problems, *Philosophy and the Mind Sciences*.

Koivisto, M., Kastrati, G. & Revonsuo, A. (2014): Recurrent processing enhances visual awareness but is not necessary for fast categorization of natural scenes, *Journal of Cognitive Neuroscience, 26*, 223–231.

Kozuch, B. (2013): Prefrontal evidence against higher order theories of consciousness, *Philosophical Studies, 167*, 721–746.

Lamme, V.A.F. (2006). Towards a true neural stance on consciousness. *Trends in Cognitive Sciences, 10*, 11, 494–501.

Lamme, V. & Roelfsema, P. (2000): The distinct modes of vision offered by feedforward and recurrent processing, *Trends in Neuroscience, 23*, 571–579.

LeDoux, J.E. & Brown, R. (2017). A higher-order theory of emotional consciousness. *Proceedings of the National Academy of Sciences, 114*, 10, E2016–E2025.

Lohse, M. & Overgaard, M. (2019): Emotional priming depends on the degree of conscious experience, *Neuropsychologia, 128*, 96–102.

Metzinger, T. (1995): *Conscious Experience*, Imprint Academic, Schöningh, DE.

Michel, M. & Morales, J. (2019): Minority reports: consciousness and the prefrontal cortex, *Mind and Language*, 1–21. DOI: 10.1111/mila.12264.

Mogensen, J. & Overgaard, M. (2017): Reorganization of the connectivity between elementary functions – a model connecting conscious states to neural connections, *Frontiers in Psychology: Consciousness Research, 8*, 1–21.

Mogensen, J. & Overgaard, M. (2018): Neural connections and mental states: the need for a neurocognitive framework, *EC Neurology, 10*, 180–194.

Odegaard, B., Knight, R. & Lau, H. (2017): Should a few null-findings falsify prefrontal theory of conscious perception? *Journal of Neuroscience, 37*, 9593–9602.

Oizumi, M., Albantakis, L. & Tononi, G. (2014): From the phenomenology to the mechanisms of consciousness: integrated information theory 3.0, *PLoS Computational Biology, 8*, e1003588.

Overgaard, M. (2004): Confounding factors in contrastive analysis, *Synthese, 141*, 2, 217–231.

Overgaard, M. & Fazekas, P. (2016): Can no-report paradigms extract true neural correlates of consciousnesss? *Trends in Cognitive Sciences, 20*, 4, 241–242.

Overgaard, M. & Mogensen, J. (2011): A framework for the study of multiple realizations: the importance of levels of analysis, *Frontiers in Psychology, 2*, 79, 1–10.

Overgaard, M. & Mogensen, J. (2014): Conscious perception: a representational, nonreductionistic, level-dependent approach, *Philosophical Transactions of the Royal Society of London – Series B: Biological Sciences, 369*, 20130209.

Overgaard, M., Nielsen, J.F. & Fuglsang-Frederiksen, A. (2004): A TMS study of the ventral projection streams from V1 with implications for the finding of neural correlates of consciousness, *Brain and Cognition, 54*, 1, 58–64.

Overgaard, M. & Overgaard, R. (2010): Neural correlates of states and levels of consciousness, *Frontiers in Psychology: Consciousness Research, 1*, 1–3.

Overgaard, M. & Overgaard, R. (2011): Measurements of consciousness in the vegetative state, *The Lancet, 6736*, 11, 61224–61225.

Revonsuo, A., Kallio, S. & Sikka, P. (2009): What is an altered state of consciousness? *Philosophical Psychology, 22*, 187–204.

Rosenthal, D. (1993): State consciousness and transitive consciousness, *Consciousness and Cognition, 2*, 4, 355–363.

Rounis, E., Maniscalco, B., Rothwell, J.C., Passingham, R.E. & Lau, H. (2010): Theta-burst transcranial magnetic stimulation to the prefrontal cortex impairs metacognitive visual awareness, *Cognitive Neuroscience, 1*, 165–175.

Tononi, G. (2004): An information integration theory of consciousness, *BMC Neuroscience, 2*, 42.

Tsuchiya, N., Wilke, M., Frässle, S. & Lamme, V. (2015): No-report paradigms: extracting the true neural correlates of consciousness, *Trends in Cognitive Sciences, 19*, 757–770.

2

FROM UNCONSCIOUS TO CONSCIOUS

A spectrum of states

Alice Barra, Manon Carrière,
Steven Laureys and Charlotte Martial

Introduction

Over the last three decades, researchers have shown an increasing interest in the so-called altered states of consciousness (ASCs). The classification of ASCs includes a broad spectrum of experiences or conditions, notably including coma, disorders of consciousness (DOCs), hypnosis, anaesthesia, or near-death experiences (NDEs). This chapter presents some of those most intriguing instances that science attempts to describe and understand as well as the current knowledge of their underlying neural basis.

Consciousness

Currently, it is widely accepted that being conscious means to subjectively experience something (e.g., seeing an image, hearing a sound, feeling an emotion; Koch, Massimini, Boly & Tononi, 2016). In clinical setting, consciousness can be considered as a multifaceted concept that can be explained by the simultaneous emergence of two main components: wakefulness and awareness (Laureys, 2005). The level of wakefulness (i.e., arousal) is manifested by eye-opening. At a neuroanatomical level, wakefulness is mediated mainly by the brainstem (Damasio & Meyer, 2009; Lin, 2000; Schiff, 2008). Awareness, the second component of consciousness, refers to the content of experience, behaviourally manifested by self-awareness and the presence of interactions with the environment. This component can be further divided in two subcomponents: *internal* (i.e., of self; that can be pictured as the little voice inside our heads; anatomically related to a mesial fronto-parietal brain network) and *external awareness* (i.e., of the environment; related to a lateral fronto-parietal brain network; Vanhaudenhuyse, Demertzi, Schabus, Noirhomme, Bredart & Boly, 2011). Internal and external

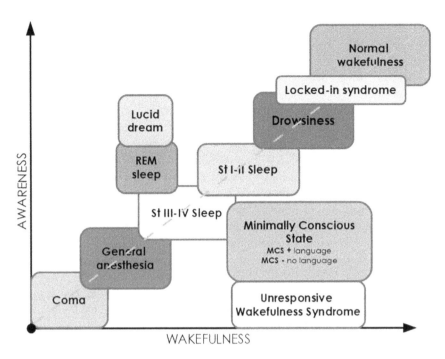

FIGURE 2.1   Illustration of the two main components of consciousness: wakefulness and awareness (adapted from Laureys, 2005) in "normal" physiological states (in which both components are generally positively correlated) and in states in which a disrupted relationship between both components exists.

awareness usually behave in an anti-correlated manner: when one increases, the other decreases (Boly, Balteau, Schnakers, Degueldre, Moonen & Luxen, 2007; Smallwood & Schooler, 2006), switching their dominance at an average frequency of 0.05 Hz (Vanhaudenhuyse et al., 2011). While wakefulness and awareness usually correlate one another, "dissociated states" of consciousness may also happen (i.e., conditions in which a disrupted relationship between wakefulness and awareness exists; e.g., unresponsive wakefulness syndrome – UWS – in which individuals are awake but lack any behavioural evidence of "voluntary" response; see Figure 2.1). These states can be characterized by behavioural, cognitive and electrophysiological changes, and offer researchers and clinicians a unique opportunity to investigate consciousness and its underlying neural correlates.

Neuroimaging and electrophysiological techniques to study brain activity

This section briefly presents the techniques that have been developed to study the neural substrates of the ASCs treated below. In neuroscience research, two main types of techniques are frequently adopted to investigate the neural correlates of consciousness: hemodynamic and metabolic measurements (e.g., Positron Emission Tomography – PET, Magnetic Resonance Imaging – MRI) and electrical measurements (e.g., Electroencephalogram – EEG).

The PET, among the most used methods, interestingly allows to analyse different metabolic activities happening in the body using radioisotopes. Essentially, a radiotracer is injected into the bloodstream and eventually reaches the body part of interest through blood circulation. A large variety of radioisotopes exists, each one used to map different metabolic aspects of the body. Among these, the fluorodeoxyglucose tracer (FDG-PET) permits to visualize glucose uptake in brain regions. The radioactivity measured by the detectors included in PET scanners is processed by a computer using sophisticated mathematical algorithms in order to create multi-dimensional images showing the distribution of the radiotracer in the brain. Even if data from FDG-PET are highly reliable since they are directly associated to neural glucose consumption, this technique is limited by its relatively poor temporal resolution (up to one minute) and spatial resolution (up to one centimetre; Vaquero & Kinahan, 2015). Importantly, the main drawback of this technique is that it involves the exposure to small amounts of radiation.

Another method that avoids exposing subjects to radiations and has better temporal and spatial resolution is the MRI. Within this method, two techniques can be distinguished: structural and functional. The first one is morphologically based and helps detecting brain lesions as well as preserved and impaired regions following cerebral injuries. The second one generates dynamic representations of brain activity through Blood Oxygenation Level Dependent (BOLD) signal, offering observations about the functional activity of the brain. Indeed, functional MRI (fMRI) relies on the fact that cerebral blood flow and neuronal activation are coupled.

The EEG is another non-invasive measure of cerebral activity, permitting to record spontaneous electrical brain activity through electrodes placed on the scalp. Since it is a non-invasive, non-painful and easy-to-use technique, this method is widely used in both research and clinical settings to examine healthy and damaged brain electrical activity patterns. However, one drawback is that standard EEG montages have poor spatial resolution. High-density EEG attempts to overcome this issue by providing a larger number of electrodes (up to 256), thus covering more precisely the whole scalp. Coupled with Transcranial Magnetic Stimulation (TMS), this method can be used to observe the cortical response following triggered stimulations. TMS is a non-invasive tool, used in clinical practice for almost 30 years, allowing to stimulate specific regions of the brain (a brief stimulation with a coil placed near the scalp) to explore their integrity and modulate their functions. By modulating the stimulation parameters (e.g., intensity, frequency, duration of stimulation), this tool can activate, inhibit, or induce short- or long-term changes of activity in targeted cortical regions.

These different advanced neuroimaging methods offer the possibility to measure the spread of a lesion and to observe the brain's activity at rest, but also during active task or passive stimulation. These techniques are promising approaches to address the continuum from coma to "normal" waking state of consciousness.

Disorders of consciousness

Since the middle of the 20th century, neurosurgery and resuscitation techniques have progressed so much that the number of brain-injured survivors has grown considerably. DOCs refer to medical conditions resulting from severe brain injury after a period of coma. Coma is defined by the absence of the two components of consciousness mentioned above (Laureys & Boly, 2008): wakefulness and awareness. One could distinguish between injury-related and medically induced coma: the former is a direct consequence of the brain injury itself (due to structural or metabolic lesions of the brainstem reticular system or to widespread bilateral cerebral damage; Laureys, Owen & Schiff, 2004), while the latter is induced by sedatives in order to allow the brain and the body to rest. Comatose patients will not open their eyes despite strong stimulations (Plum & Posner, 1983) nor show behavioural evidence of interaction with the environment. Coma is also characterized by a lack of sleep-wake cycles (Teasdale & Jennett, 1974) and must persist for at least one hour, contrarily to other transient states of unconsciousness such as syncope. A prolonged injury-related coma is relatively rare and, in general, patients begin to awaken after two to four weeks. Following this awakening, different scenarios are possible (Laureys et al., 2004) and are outlined in this section.

After a severe brain injury (often of traumatic or hypoxic aetiologies), some patients may recover rapidly, while others may have a more dramatic outcomes and evolve to a state of brain death or develop an unresponsive wakefulness state (UWS; formerly called "vegetative state"; Laureys, Celesia, Cohadon, Lavrijsen, León-Carrión & Sannita, 2010) before partially or fully recovering awareness. Brain death refers to a complete and irreversible loss of neural functions and is defined by specific criteria (see Laureys & Fins, 2008; The Quality Standards Subcommittee of the American Academy of Neurology: Practice Parameters for Determining Brain Death in Adults, 1995). By contrast, if the patient opens his/her eyes but shows no awareness, he/she is in what we now call the UWS. Patients with UWS show reflexive movements such as blinking to threat, auditory startle, or withdrawal from pain stimulation, but no sign of voluntary conduct is present. When the syndrome persists for more than one month, it is defined as *persistent* UWS, whereas a *permanent* UWS diagnosis (i.e., non-reversibile; American Congress of Rehabilitation Medicine, 1995; Jennett & Plum, 1972) is given three months after injury for non-traumatic brain aetiologies and one year after injury for traumatic injuries. Unfortunately, these two additional terms are confusing, sometimes increasing the risk of patients with a *persistent* UWS being denied certain therapies. Hence, for reasons of prudence, clinicians may rather prefer to simply mention the cause and duration of the UWS. As soon as a patient manifests clear and reproducible behaviours indicating conscious perception of self or the environment, he or she is no longer said to be in a UWS, but in a minimally conscious state (MCS; Giacino, Ashwal, Childs, Cranford, Jennett & Katz, 2002). Within this diagnostic category, a distinction can be made between MCS *minus* (MCS−) and MCS *plus* (MCS+) (Bruno, Majerus, Boly, Vanhaudenhuyse,

Schnakers & Gosseries, 2012; Bruno, Vanhaudenhuyse, Thibaut, Moonen, & Laureys, 2011). MCS− shows signs of consciousness considered as low-level purposeful behaviours such as visual pursuit, object manipulation, or localization of painful stimulation (Wannez, Gosseries, Azzolini, Martial, Cassol & Aubinet, 2017a), while MCS+ shows additionally more complex behaviours such as reproducible or systematic (evidencing that the action is intentional) responses to command, non-functional communication, or intelligible verbalization (Bruno et al., 2011; Wannez et al., 2017a). This distinction seems to reflect language-related abilities: MCS+ patients appear to have relatively preserved language cognitive functions, whereas MCS− patients show signs of consciousness that do not imply preserved language functions (Aubinet, Larroque, Heine, Martial, Majerus & Laureys, 2018; Bruno et al., 2012). Nevertheless, both types of patients are able to consciously interact at some level with their environment and this is the main feature distinguishing them from UWS patients. MCS is the endpoint of patients' improvement or a temporary condition towards recovery of consciousness. In some cases, the patient may evolve and regain the ability to functionally communicate (i.e., appropriate answers when asked autobiographical/contextualized questions, either with a verbal or gestural code) and/or appropriately use objects; the patient is therefore said to have emerged from the MCS (EMCS; Giacino et al., 2002).

In marked contrast with the previously described conditions, the defining feature of the locked-in syndrome (LIS) is the relative preservation of cognition (intact sensations, full awareness of their environment; Laureys, Pellas, Van Eeckhout, Ghorbel, Schnakers & Perrin, 2005). Although LIS is not considered as a DOC, it is nevertheless worth to be mentioned here as it is sometimes difficult to distinguish LIS from coma, UWS, or MCS (American Congress of Rehabilitation Medicine, 1995). Patients with LIS have a complete paralysis of the body resulting from lesions in the brainstem and have to use eye movements to communicate with others. In rare cases, all voluntary muscles are impaired, including extrinsic eye muscles, and the syndrome is called *complete* LIS (Laureys et al., 2005).

Although the neuroimaging techniques described in the previous section can objectively indicate how different from normal the patient's brain activity is, bedside assessments are the "gold standard" in establishing a proper DOC diagnosis (Giacino, Schnakers, Rodriguez-Moreno, Kalmar, Schiff & Hirsch, 2009). In intensive care units, the Glasgow Coma Scale (GCS; Teasdale & Jennett, 1974) is the most common scale to evaluate neurological state of patients. This scale includes a short sequence of items that aim to evaluate the level of consciousness in the acute setting. Although very useful in acute phases such as at hospital admittance and before or after surgery, the GCS presents some limitations when used in a chronic condition: this scale is not sensitive to differential diagnosis between consciousness and unconsciousness and its predictive value for outcome seems to be limited (Balestreri, Czosnyka, Chatfield, Steiner, Schmidt & Smielewski, 2004). More recently, the Coma Recovery Scale-Revised (CRS-R) was developed by Giacino, Kalmar and Whyte (2004) and is now considered to be the gold standard tool (Seel, Sherer, Whyte, Katz, Giacino & Rosenbaum, 2010), especially to distinguish UWS and MCS patients. It investigates auditory, visual, motor, oromotor functions and the presence of communication and wakefulness. The scale is composed of 23 items and 6 subscales, the lowest items on each subscale representing reflexive activity and the highest cognitively mediated behaviours. Scores are given according to a standardized protocol and is based on the presence or absence of behavioural responses to specific sensory stimuli. As soon as one cognitively mediated behaviour is observed, the patient is no longer considered as being in an UWS. It is important to note that the CRS-R must be administered repetitively to increase its sensitivity due to major fluctuations in responsiveness and wakefulness in these patients. According to Wannez and colleagues (2017b), a minimum of five CRS-R assessments is needed to have an accurate and reliable diagnosis.

Neural correlates of disorders of consciousness

These patients are a very challenging population regarding diagnosis, treatment and prognosis. Previous studies (e.g., Andrews, Murphy, Munday & Littlewood, 1996; Schnakers, Vanhaudenhuyse, Giacino, Ventura, Boly & Majerus, 2009) showed that from 37% up to 43% of minimally conscious patients are misdiagnosed and erroneously considered unconscious. For example, it can be the case that a patient, due to motor or language impairment resulting from the accident, cannot express behavioural signs of consciousness, but can nevertheless be (partially) conscious. For this reason, behavioural evaluations are usually coupled with neuroimaging exams to offer a cross-modal approach and establish a proper diagnosis based on the results of all exams.

After several decades of neuroimaging research on DOC, studies suggest that consciousness may be underpinned by internally and externally awareness-related networks encompassing fronto-parietal associative cortices, precuneus, thalamus and cingulate gyrus (see Figure 2.2; Laureys et al., 2004; Vanhaudenhuyse et al., 2011; Vanhaudenhuyse, Noirhomme, Tshibanda, Bruno, Boveroux & Schnakers, 2010). Using FDG-PET, it has been shown that awareness does not seem to be specifically related to a different global glucose consumption, but rather to the modification of the regional distribution of this consumption (Laureys, Lemaire, Maquet, Phillips, Franck, 1999). Furthermore, a large fronto-parietal network and its connections with thalamic nuclei appear to be crucial (Laureys, Goldman, Phillips, Van Bogaert, Aerts & Luxen, 1999; Figure 2.2). This was notably suggested by the recovery of thalamo-cortical activity in patients with UWS who recovered consciousness (Laureys et al., 1999). In addition, MCS patients showed a partial preservation of this large-scale associative fronto-parietal network (Laureys et al., 2004). Interestingly, studies in other fields also highlight the key role of an extensive fronto-parietal associative cortex in the emergence of awareness, such as for loss of consciousness during seizures

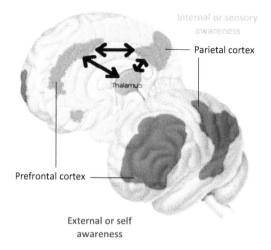

Internal or sensory awareness

Parietal cortex

Thalamus

Prefrontal cortex

External or self
awareness

FIGURE 2.2 Consciousness may be underpinned by internally and externally awareness-related networks encompassing frontoparietal associative cortices,
precuneus, thalamus, and cingulate gyrus. A large fronto-parietal network and its connections with thalamic nuclei appear to be crucial.

(Blumenfeld, McNally, Vanderhill, Paige, Chung & Davis, 2004; Salek-Haddadi,
Lemieux, Merschhemke, Friston, Duncan & Fish, 2003) or somnambulism (Bassetti, Vella, Donati, Wielepp & Weder, 2000). Currently, FDG-PET remains the
most sensitive neuroimaging technique to detect changes in brain function related to residual consciousness in patients with DOC (Stender, Gosseries, Bruno,
Charland-Verville, Vanhaudenhuyse & Demertzi, 2014). This method has also
been used to predict long-term recovery of patients with UWS (Stender, Kupers,
Rodell, Thibaut, Chatelle, Bruno & Gejl, 2015).

When individual bedside assessments do not allow observing any sign of consciousness, notably because of motor disabilities (e.g., hemiplegia, spasticity),
fMRI active tasks can be used. Notably, an active paradigm has been developed
by Owen and colleagues (2006) to detect the preservation of awareness in behaviourally unresponsive patients consisting in two imagery tasks: a motor task
in which patients are instructed to imagine playing tennis and a spatial task in
which they are asked to imagine walking through their home. During these two
established tasks, five patients (out of 54) were able to reliably and repeatedly
modulate their brain responses, reflecting preserved awareness. Distinct activation patterns of the appropriate cortical regions were detected for each task, consisting mainly of the supplementary motor area when imagining playing tennis
and of the parahippocampal gyrus when imagining navigating into the house.
Thus, in the case where an activation is observed in the regions typically associated with one of the two tasks, it may be speculated that patients understood
and executed the command (Monti, Vanhaudenhuyse, Coleman, Boly, Pickard &
Tshibanda, 2010). However, for two of these patients, no voluntary behaviour
could be detected at the bedside – even after the fMRI responses were observed

(Monti et al., 2010). Yet, it is important to note that the absence of command-related brain activity does not permit to conclude that the patient is unconscious. Monti and colleagues (2010) went one step further by using these two imagery tasks to test patients' communication. Only one patient was able to answer to several binary questions (responding adequately "yes" or "no") using these mental imagery tasks. Clearly, this type of active paradigms is not adequate for patients with aphasia. In such cases, fMRI resting state paradigms might be a possibility, this approach being particularly advantageous since it does not require any specific collaboration from the patients. The resting state paradigm is based on the principle that the spontaneous variations in the concentrations of the oxy- and deoxyhemo-globin (BOLD signal) are different between conscious and unconscious patients. Overall, resting state fMRI studies suggest that the connectivity of the default mode network (DMN) decreases in severely brain-injured patients as a function of their level of consciousness (Vanhaudenhuyse et al., 2011). In patients with DOC, a correlation can be found between the clinical severity showed at bedside and the functional disconnection within thalamo-cortical and cortico-cortical regions of the DMN (Fernandez-Espejo, Soddu, Cruse, Palacios, Junque & Vanhauden-huyse, 2012; Vanhaudenhuyse et al., 2010). Furthermore, a preserved functional connectivity between frontal and parietal DMN regions might be a predictor of the recovery from coma at three months (Silva, De Pasquale, Vuillaume, Riu, Loubinoux & Geeraerts, 2015). In line with this, connectivity in the posterior cingulate cortex (PCC) is relatively preserved in MCS patients while significantly reduced in UWS patients (Vanhaudenhuyse et al., 2010). Additionally, recent findings showed decreased positive correlations within the DMN in patients with UWS and MCS, while negative correlations between the DMN and the external network completely disappear, to finally reappear in EMCS patients (Di Perri, Bahri, Amico, Thibaut, Heine & Antonopoulos, 2016).

The DMN is not the only network to attract scientific attention in the study of DOC. Demertzi and colleagues (2015) found that system-level resting state fMRI showed consciousness-dependent breakdown not only for the DMN, but also for five other networks (fronto-parietal, salience, auditory, sensorimotor and visual). A correlation was observed between functional connectivity in key regions of each network and CRS-R total scores. All networks had a high rate of discrimination (>80%) between UWS and MCS patients, but the auditory network was found the most sensitive for accurately classifying patients in either category (Demertzi et al., 2015).

In the same vein of guiding diagnostic assessment, researchers have more recently been interested in using structural MRI. Lutkenhoff and colleagues (2015) suggested that awareness and wakefulness might be respectively associated with damage in the thalamus and in the basal ganglia. Specifically, structural differences have been highlighted between UWS and MCS patients, with less damage in the ventromedial prefrontal cortex and the precuneus/PCC in MCS patients (Guldenmund, Soddu, Baquero, Vanhaudenhuyse, Bruno & Gosseries, 2016). The importance of thalamo-cortical connections for consciousness has also been stressed thanks to the diffusion tensor imaging technique allowing accurate descriptions of the white matter and eventual damages in the connections (Zheng, Gao, Wang, Wang, Yang & Wang, 2016). Finally, a recent study, investigating brain volumetry at the single-subject level, identified regions in the DMN and subcortical gray matter regions as the most important to distinguish levels of consciousness, but also white matter regions involved in long-range connectivity (Annen, Frasso, Heine, Di Perri, Martial & Antonopoulos, 2018).

Just as fMRI, EEG can be used in DOC patients to assess residual cognitive function and to provide means of communication without motor output. Overall, the electrophysiology of patients with DOC is characterized by a global slowdown and an increase of delta slow waves (Lehembre, Bruno, Vanaudenhuyse, Chatelle, Cologan & Leclercq, 2012; León-Carrión, Martin-Rodriguez, Damas-Lopez, Barroso y Martin & Dominguez-Morales, 2008). In resting conditions, diffuse delta or theta appears, and these bands are usually associated with slow sleep stages in healthy individuals. A recent study suggested that relative theta and alpha power could discriminate MCS from UWS (Sitt, King, El Karoui, Rohaut, Faugeras & Gramfort, 2014). Moreover, they highlighted that the stability between trials and the average of EEG complexity increases monotonically when moving from UWS to full consciousness. More recently, Piarulli and colleagues (2016) employed long-duration EEG recordings and demonstrated that patients in MCS (but not those in UWS) were characterized by spectral entropy fluctuations with a cyclicity of about 70 minutes. Interestingly, this periodicity appears to resemble those reported in awake healthy people, thus suggesting the presence of vigilance/awareness fluctuations in those patients. Approaches applying complex network analyses to resting-state EEG of patients have also recently emerged, such as the work of Chennu and colleagues (2017) showing that key quantitative metrics (e.g., participation coefficient, median connectivity) correlate with the level of consciousness (ranging from UWS to EMCS) as well as with brain metabolism as assessed with FDG-PET.

Finally, EEG combined with TMS can be particularly useful to explore the level of consciousness of DOC patients, as this method does not rely on individual's ability to follow instructions. In healthy subjects, the TMS produces an EEG evoked potential in the brain that has a specific shape, timing and time course. Moreover, this response moves from the stimulated area towards connected regions (Sarasso, Rosanova, Casali, Casarotto, Fecchio & Boly, 2014). In patients with UWS, the response to TMS is dramatically different and rather resembles the one observed during anaesthesia (Ferrarelli, Massimini, Sarasso, Casali, Riedner & Angelini, 2010) or deep sleep (Massimini, Ferrarelli, Sarasso & Tononi, 2012). Those patients present either no response or a simple response and a local EEG response, suggesting an impairment of effective connectivity (Ragazzoni, Pirulli, Veniero, Feurra, Cincotta & Giovannelli, 2013; Rosanova, Gosseries, Casarotto, Boly, Casali & Bruno, 2012). By contrast, patients with MCS have more complex EEG activations involving different cortical areas. An empirical measure of brain complexity, called the *Perturbational Complexity Index*

(PCI), has been developed in order to quantify the level of consciousness (Casali, Gosseries, Rosanova, Boly, Sarasso & Casali, 2013). This index permits to measure the amount of information included in the integrated TMS response. The PCI appears to be above 0.31 when consciousness is present (e.g., normal wakefulness, under Ketamine, rapid-eye movement (REM) sleep, in patients with LIS) and below 0.31 when consciousness is absent (e.g., under Propofol). Importantly, this index allows to distinguish between UWS (presenting a PCI below 0.31) and MCS (presenting a PCI above 0.31) at a single-subject level (Casali et al., 2013). Hence, TMS seems to be a promising tool in the establishment of a proper diagnosis of patients with DOC.

Anaesthesia

Anaesthesia is a medical process that involves the administration of sedative agents to an individual in order to temporarily modify his or her level of awareness and at the same time, induce a loss of sensations. Anaesthesia can be divided in three subcategories: general anaesthesia, sedation and regional/local anaesthesia. We will here mainly focus on general anaesthesia that refers to "a drug-induced, reversible condition that includes specific behavioural and physiological traits – unconsciousness, amnesia, analgesia, and akinesia – with concomitant stability of the autonomic, cardiovascular, respiratory, and thermoregulatory systems" (Brown, Lydic & Schiff, 2010; Evers & Crowder, 2006).

Conceptions on mechanisms underlying the loss of consciousness induced by anesthesia have evolved considerably since the first hypotheses were made several decades ago. If we take a step back, it seems that researchers have evolved from a rather holistic explanation to a more targeted and specific effect of the anesthetic agents (Bonhomme, Boveroux, Bricant, Laureys & Boly, 2012).

Neural correlates of anaesthesia

Initially, anesthesia was thought to cause a global depression of brain function, based on several studies demonstrating that most of the anesthetic agents reduced global metabolism and had a depressive effect on the EEG activity (Alkire, Haier, Shah & Anderson, 1997; Alkire, Pomfrett, Haier, Gianzero, Chan & Jacobsen, 1999; Newberg, Milde & Michenfelder, 1983). However, this view has considerably changed today. Indeed, it has been now demonstrated that anesthetic agents exert dose-dependent specific effects on particular brain systems sustaining internal consciousness and perception of the environment.

Considering its key role in sleep and sensory perception, the thalamus has highly attracted the researchers interested in anesthesia. Alkire and associates (2000) have developed the idea of the "thalamic consciousness switch" (i.e., the thalamus serving as an on/off switch for anesthetic state). According to this model, anesthetic-induced unconsciousness would be caused by a hyper-polarization of this area that would lead to a switch from tonic to burst firing, thus preventing sensory stimuli from reaching the cortex (Mashour, 2016). But later on, notably by analogy with the physiology of sleep (Steriade, McCormick & Sejnowski, 1993), a disruption of functional interactions between the thalamus and cortex (thalamocortical-corticothalamic loops) has been further hypothesized to be important in general anesthetic-induced unconsciousness (e.g., Boveroux, Vanhaudenhuyse, Bruno, Noirhomme, Lauwick & Luxen, 2010;). This thalamo-cortical connectivity has however not been consistently identified as impaired in anesthetic-induced unconsciousness, thereby leading to the conclusion that this connectivity is not sufficient to entirely explain loss of consciousness.

The alteration of consciousness produced by anesthesia might be associated with a loss of information and/or integration due to a breakdown of large-scale cerebral connectivity (Alkire et al., 2000). The anesthetic agents would have a dose-dependent effect on cortical networks involved in consciousness, with consequences on cortico-subcortical interactions and subcortical structures activity. These assumptions are supported by several studies using various neuroimaging and neurophysiological techniques and different anesthetics (e.g., Deshpande, Kerssens, Sebel & Hu, 2010; Dueck, Petzke, Gerbershagen, Paul, Hesselmann & Girnus, 2005; Ferrarelli et al., 2010; Heinke & Koelsch, 2005; Martuzzi, Ramani, Qiu, Rajeevan & Constable, 2010; Ramani, Qiu & Constable, 2007). Notably, Boveroux and collaborators (2010) showed that, at the point of loss of responsiveness, propofol induces a dose-dependently reduced connectivity in the DMN and external network.

Very recently, a few studies have used an intriguing method called the isolated forearm technique, in order to detect consciousness under general anaesthesia. In this procedure, the patient may potentially respond to verbal instructions with the "isolated" forearm that remains non-paralyzed. This technique consists in inflating a tourniquet on one arm (above the systolic blood pressure) in an anesthetized person before the administration of the muscle relaxant, which allows a potential movement of the "isolated" arm in response to a verbal instruction. It seems that up to 40% of patients may report responsiveness using this technique under general anesthesia and that these events are rarely followed by explicit recall postoperatively (Gaskell, Hight, Winders, Tran, Defresne & Bonhomme, 2017; Sanders, Tononi, Laureys & Sleigh, 2012). Gaskell and colleagues (2017) have further shown that those events, suggesting a minimum of consciousness, can occur even in the presence of the frontal alpha-delta-dominant EEG pattern (typically considered to be a marker of anaesthetic-induced unconsciousness) under general anaesthesia. However, findings from electrophysiological studies using this technique are still mixed, but undoubtedly question existing knowledge on network changes related to anaesthetic-induced unconsciousness. Indeed, this kind of study illustrates that we are far from fully understanding anaesthesia and its underlying neural mechanisms. The process of characterizing brain changes during general anaesthesia is therefore still ongoing.

Hypnosis

Although the word *hypnosis* finds its roots in ancient Greek where the original meaning was "put to sleep", hypnosis is far from being a sleeping state. Hypnosis refers to "a procedure during which a health professional or researcher suggests that a patient or subject experience changes in sensations, perceptions, thoughts, or behaviour" (The Executive Committee of the American Psychological Association – Division of Psychological Hypnosis, 1994). In this process, the subject undergoes inner absorption and concentration with disengagement from extraneous stimuli and a reduction in spontaneous thoughts (Vanhaudenhuyse, Laureys & Faymonville, 2014). Overall, there are three main components of hypnosis: absorption, dissociation and suggestibility (Cardeña & Speigel, 1991). Absorption refers to the degree to which one subject is fully focused on a mental experience, while dissociation concerns the mental separation from the environment (McGeown, Mazzoni, Venneri & Krisch, 2009; Oakley & Halligan, 2009; Rainville & Price, 2003; Vanhaudenhuyse et al., 2014). Suggestibility relates to the individual degree of responsiveness to hypnotic suggestions, involving a suspension of critical judgment and spontaneous thoughts (Vanhaudenhuyse et al., 2014). Individuals' hypnotisability can be measured through standardized scales administered before, during or after the session (e.g., the Stanford Hypnotic Susceptibility Scale; Weitzenhoffer & Hilgard, 1962). In addition, some authors recently proposed three self-assessment scales evaluating absorption, dissociation and time perception to more quickly and directly assess the level of hypnotisability (Vanhaudenhuyse, Ledoux, Gosseries, Demertzi, Laureys & Faymonville, 2019).

Neural correlates of hypnosis

For some years now, clinicians and researchers have sought to understand hypnosis and its neural signature, notably because it is increasingly used during surgical operating room in some hospitals (e.g., Faymonville, Mambourg, Joris, Vrijens, Fissette & Albert, 1997). In hypnosis research, two main approaches can be found: "intrinsic" research trying to understand the nature of hypnosis itself; and "instrumental" research in which hypnotic induction is used to produce targeted effects of interest (Cox & Bryant, 2008; Jensen, Jamieson, Lutz, Mazzoni, McGeown & Santarcangelo, 2017; Oakley & Halligan, 2009; Reyher, 1962). Even though significant research has been conducted in the past two decades suggesting that hypnosis leads to objectively measurable brain changes, the obtained results seem rather dishomogeneous and controversial (see Landry, Lifshitz & Raz, 2017; Vanhaudenhuyse et al., 2014, for recent reviews). It is likely that the mixed results obtained in the literature can be partially explained by differences in the suggestion instructions used to induce hypnosis (e.g., using the recall of pleasant autobiographical memories versus neutral hypnosis) or in the experimental design (Vanhaudenhuyse et al., 2014).

Scholars have been notably interested in individual differences to respond to hypnotic suggestions (Oakley & Halligan, 2009, 2010, 2013). For example, McGeown and colleagues (2009) used fMRI to highlight a greater selective reduction of resting state medial prefrontal cortex activity in individuals scoring high on a measure of hypnotic suggestibility than those scoring low. Other studies focused on neural correlates directly associated with the subjective changes in response to suggestion (e.g., Cojan, Waber, Schwartz, Rossier, Forster, & Vuilleumier, 2009; Demertzi et al., 2015; Kosslyn, Thompson, Costantini-Ferrando, Alpert & Spiegel, 2000). Pain perception under hypnosis and comparison between hypnosis and mental imagery have mostly been studied. Notably, Demertzi and colleagues (2015) were interested to quantify how external and internal awareness is related to a modified subjective state induced by hypnosis. They showed enhanced self-oriented processing, parallel to an increased dissociation from the environment. Moreover, self-awareness and external awareness brain-related components showed a tendency to anti-correlate less in a hypnotic state as compared to rest (Demertzi et al., 2015). In general, hypnosis-induced modulation of resting state fMRI networks appears to conduct in a reduced "extrinsic" lateral fronto-parietal cortical connectivity, possibly reflecting a decreased sensory awareness (e.g., Demertzi, Soddu, Faymonville, Bahri, Gooseries & Vanhaudenhuyse, 2011; Demertzi et al., 2015). In parallel, in this state, the DMN show increased connectivity in its lateral parietal and middle frontal areas, but reduced connectivity in its posterior midline and parahippocampal structures (e.g., Demertzi et al., 2011). However, other studies observed opposite results with increased activity in posterior regions of the DMN as compared to decreased metabolic activity in anterior DMN areas (Lipari, Baglio, Griffanti, Mendozzi, Garegnani & Motta, 2012; Oakley, 1999).

Overall, several brain regions are recurrently reported as playing an important role in hypnotic state. Notably, increased activation of the anterior cingulate cortex (ACC; e.g., Faymonville, Laureys, Degueldre, DelFiore, Luxen & Franck, 2000; Rainville, Duncan, Price, Carrier & Bushnell, 1997; Rainville, Hofbauer, Bushness, Duncan & Price, 2002) and of a large cortical and subcortical network (encompassing prefrontal cortex, insular cortex, thalami, brainstem; e.g., Faymonville et al., 2000; Faymonville, Roediger, DelFiore, Delgueldre, Phillips & Lamy, 2003; Rainville et al., 1997, 2002; Rainville, Hofbauer, Paus, Duncan, Bushnell & Price, 1999) have been reported in PET studies. Very recently, based on the current literature, including a large number of empirical data, Landry and associates (2017) have suggested a general framework to understand the neural correlates of hypnotic phenomena, specifying the functions of three relevant large-scale intrinsic brain systems: the DMN, the central executive network (encompassing the dorsolateral prefrontal cortex) and the salience network (including the ACC and the anterior insula). In short, during hypnotic states, the central executive network may be related to the sustained attention towards relevant mental representations and strategies. The salience network would be involved in particular in changes in awareness. Finally, self-related components experienced during hypnosis would be more directly related to modulations of the DMN. Their meta-analysis highlighted the key role of these three networks in hypnotic susceptibility and induction, and response to hypnotic suggestions.

Near-death experiences

Among the various ASCs in which humans can be, NDEs are today one of the most intriguing and debated instances. When facing a (real or subjectively felt as) life-threatening situation, some people will later report having lived various phenomenological experiences (known in the current scientific literature as *features*; e.g., seeing a bright light and/or a tunnel, having the sensation of leaving the physical body, encountering deceased relatives) that are intriguing by their paranormal appearance. These complex subjective experiences that occur in critical contexts (e.g., traumatic accident, cardiac arrest, near-drowning) are usually associated with an ASC. NDE can be considered as a series of mental events with self-related, emotional, mystical and spiritual aspects, resulting in a complex phenomenon. Interestingly, similar phenomenological experiences, termed *NDEs-like*, have also been reported in situations where there was no genuine threat to the individuals' life (e.g., during intense grief, syncope, anxiety, meditation; Charland-Verville, Jourdan, Thonnard, Ledoux, Donneau & Quertermont, 2014; Facco & Agrillo, 2012; Kelly, 2001; Lempert, Bauer & Schmidt, 1994a, b). In either case (i.e., "classical" NDE or NDE-like), the level of wakefulness and awareness appears to change from "normal" awareness. Nonetheless, it is an arduous task to determine where NDE could be placed on the Figure 2.1 of this chapter. Indeed, it is still unclear when exactly the NDE phenomenology appears (i.e., determining the exact level of wakefulness and awareness). Yet, it seems likely that NDEs are conditions in which there is a disrupted relationship between the two components of consciousness described above, wakefulness and awareness. In fact, although being in an ASC, the phenomenology of the experience reported subsequently seems to be very rich (Martial, Cassol, Antonopoulos, Charlier, Herosa & Donneau, 2017a) and deeply encoded in memory (Martial, Charland-Verville, Cassol, Didone, Van Der Linden & Laureys, 2017b; Moore & Greyson, 2017; Thonnard, Charland-Verville, Brédart, Dehon, Ledoux & Laureys, 2013). Moreover, NDE experiencers usually report having lived a clear sensorium and an intense illusion of reality (i.e., similar phenomenological sense of certainty that accompanies the everyday perception; Dell'Olio, 2010; Schwaninger, Eisenberg, Schechtman & Weiss, 2002).

Insofar as there is no universally accepted definition of the phenomenon itself, the identification of NDE experiencers is rather tricky. Currently, this identification is based on the number of features subsequently reported as well as the experienced intensity of each feature. A few years ago, to minimize the potential complications caused by scholars adopting different definitions, some chose to build and validate standard scales, including threshold scores. Among them,

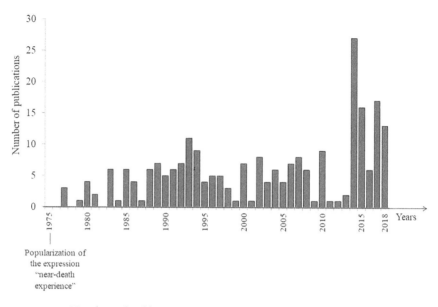

FIGURE 2.3 Number of publications per year on NDEs (for a total of 295 publications). Medline search performed in September 2018 with the keyword *"near-death experience"* and *"near-death experiences"*.

Greyson (1983) developed the Greyson NDE Scale, which is a standardized multiple choice tool that provides a cut-off score (i.e., 7 out of 32) for identifying NDEs.

While the scientific community appears to acknowledge the existence of the phenomenon as a clearly identifiable psychological and physiological reality, its origin is still a matter of debate. Actually, the number of scientific publications about NDEs is relatively limited, in contrast to non-scholarly and non-peer-reviewed works which are abundant. In addition, while the scientific literature contains a predominance of opinion and review papers, there is a lack of empirical investigations trying to understand the phenomenon and its particularities (Sleutjes, Moreira-Almeida & Greyson, 2014). When looking at publications about NDEs in PudMed (a free search engine indexing primarily the Medline database of peer-reviewed references and abstracts on life sciences and biomedical topics), only a total of 295 publications is obtained (see Figure 2.3). It is however worth noting that an increased number of publications in the last five years can be observed.

Neural correlates of near-death experiences

In attempts to explain the whole phenomenon of NDEs or certain distinct feature of the experience, various explanatory theoretical approaches have been proposed. Among these, there are neurobiological theories accounting for the NDE phenomenology in terms of brain and physiological function. While a very large number of theories have been proposed, they can be separated into three (non-mutually exclusive) categories: levels of blood gases; endorphins and other neurotransmitters; and dysfunction in temporal lobes.

Several models have highlighted the potential implication of disturbed levels of blood gases in the NDE phenomenon. Hypercarbia (i.e., abnormal high levels of carbon dioxide in the blood) appear to produce some NDE features such as out-of-body experiences (OBEs) or bright lights (Klemenc-Ketis, Kersnik, & Grmec, 2010; Meduna, 1950; Sabom, 1982). It has also been advanced that cerebral anoxia (e.g., Robin, 1980) or hypoxia (e.g., Els, Kassubek, Kubalek & Klisch, 2004; Lempert et al., 1994a, b) might cause the NDE phenomenology. Particularly, syncopal hallucinations resulting from transient cerebral hypoxia appear to present some similarities with NDEs (Lempert et al., 1994a). Lempert and collaborators (1994a, b) were amongst the first to report that syncopes (induced through hyperventilation and forceful attempted exhalation against a closed airway, a method called *Valsalva manoeuvre*) in healthy people can provoke NDE-like phenomena (including, e.g., an intense feeling of peace, OBE). Since then, it has been postulated that impaired cerebral oxygen levels (in contexts, ranging from the "simple" syncope to more serious impairments such as cardiac arrests) can result in a disruption of the physiological balance between the conscious and unconscious states, causing a state similar to the one experienced during REM sleep (Nelson, Mattingly, Lee & Schmitt, 2006). In this regard, the REM intrusion can disturb wakefulness in the form of visual hallucinations and give an impression of being dead (Nelson et al., 2006). Interestingly, a cohort of NDE experiencers have been assessed as particularly sensitive to REM sleep intrusions and sleep paralysis associated with hypnagogic and hypnopompic states (Britton & Bootzin, 2004; Nelson et al., 2006). Other authors have considered a neuronal disinhibition in the visual cortex (Blackmore, 1993, 1996; Saavedra-Aguilar & Gómez-Jeria, 1989; Woerlee, 2005). More specifically, Blackmore (1996) argued that the perception of bright lights and a tunnel vision might be related to a random excitation in the organization of cells (devoted to the centre or the periphery of the visual field) in the visual cortex, associated with anoxia. In line with this hypothesis, based on previous clinical neuroimaging data, one can envisage that resuscitated patients reporting NDEs have transient ischemic and/or hypoxic lesions or interferences with bilateral occipital cortex and the optic radiation (Ammermann, Kassubek, Lotze, Gut, Kaps & Schmidt, 2007; Els et al., 2004; Owens, Cook & Stevenson, 1990). However, although it is admissible, this assumption needs to be read with caution because no neurological data support it. More recently, Borjigin and colleagues (2013) conducted an electrophysiological study investigating cardiac arrest in rats. Their findings demonstrated evidence of a transient and global surge of synchronized gamma oscillations, exhibiting increased interregional connectivity, during cardiac arrests in rats. This study may lead to the hypothesis that NDEs could be caused by transient organized brain activity and neurophysiologic states at near-death. However, there is a need for clear empirical evidence.

In parallel, theories based upon naturally occurring or drug-induced neurotransmitter releases have been suggested. Notably, endorphin release has been considered to account for different aspects of NDEs (Carr, 1981). In particular, Saavedra-Aguilar and Gómez-Jeria (1989) stated that because of increased stress, endorphin release may be responsible for pleasant and blissful feelings occurring during NDEs. Other authors have suggested the implication of serotonin to specifically account for OBEs (Morse, Venecia & Milstein, 1989). Jansen's (1989, 1997, 2001) theory supplies a convincing framework by suggesting a blockade of the glutamate N-methyl-D-aspartate (NMDA) receptors to account for the NDE phenomenology (Curran & Morgan, 2000). He developed his model based on the observation that most of the core NDE features (e.g., seeing a bright light, experiencing a tunnel) appear to emerge during the administration of Ketamine. This dissociative aesthetic drug can produce NDE-like symptoms and is a potent NMDA antagonist. Similarly, in conditions that appear to precipitate NDEs (e.g., decreased brain oxygen, blood flow), an increased level of glutamate is released to prevent neuronal damage. In turn, it stimulates the release of a Ketamine-like neurotoxin (Jansen, 1997). Other psychedelic substances appear to induce phenomenological experiences that seem to closely resemble "classical" (i.e., reported after a life-threatening situation) NDEs. In addition, Timmermann and colleagues (2018) suggested recently that subjective experiences closely resembling NDEs may be induced in healthy volunteers by administering the classic serotonergic psychedelic N,N-Dimethyltryptamine (DMT). Interestingly, we did not observe significant differences when comparing the phenomenological features reported by their participants and those reported by a sample of "classical" NDE experiencers (i.e., individuals who have reported a NDE after having been in a critical situation of impending death). Obviously, although this type of experiments appears to show striking similarities between the phenomenology of "classical" NDEs and laboratory-induced experiences, it must be kept in mind that these latter ones are thought to be only a mere reflection of what is really happening during an "authentic" NDE. Nonetheless, the fact that some NDE features can emerge in non-NDE contexts (i.e., NDE-like phenomenon) is interesting in itself, and might provide direct evidence for particular theories by showing significant overlap between both ASCs. To a certain extent, studying the phenomenology of psychedelic experiences and NDEs may permit to use one neurobiological or psychological phenomenon to model the other one, still bearing in mind that only limited conclusions can be drawn. To date, it is not yet clear which pharmacological cerebral mediators or hallucinogenic agents underlie NDE features.

In parallel to the two above-presented theoretical fields, other models have considered a significant implication of temporal lobe dysfunctions (Blanke, Landis, Spinelli & Seeck, 2004; Blanke & Mohr, 2005; Blanke, Ortigue, Landis & Seeck, 2002; Britton & Bootzin, 2004; Hoepner, Labudda, May, Schoendienst, Woermann & Bien, 2013). Interestingly, both direct cortical stimulation (e.g., Blanke et al., 2002, 2004; Penfield, 1958) and altered functioning (e.g., due to damage or seizures; Hoepner et al., 2013) of this brain region appear to produce similar NDE-like features (e.g., OBEs; Britton & Bootzin, 2004) or other mystical experiences (Daly, 1975; Devinsky, Feldmann, Burrowes & Bromfield, 1989; Penfield, 1955). It is worth mentioning that this area is sensitive to anoxia, and that its seizure threshold can be lowered by an endorphin release (Frenk, McCarty & Liebeskind, 1978). Stimulating the specific area of the right temporo-parietal junction enables the production of OBE that would result from a deficient multisensory integration in this area (Blanke et al., 2002, 2004; De Ridder, Van Laere, Dupont, Menovsky & Van de Heyning, 2007). Studies in neurological patients appear to corroborate this observation. Patients with epilepsy or migraine have reported a similar phenomenology after focal electrical stimulation protocols (Blanke et al., 2002; Jasper & Rasmussen, 1958). Several authors have suggested that hypoxia and/or stress occurring during life-threatening conditions might hypersensitise neurons and lower seizure thresholds, especially in the temporal lobe (Benveniste, Drejer, Schouseboe & Diemer, 1984; Britton & Bootzin, 2004). Interestingly, Britton and Bootzin (2004) found more temporal lobe epileptiform activity and symptoms in NDE experiencers as compared to matched non-experiencers.

Overall, these theories can account for some specific components of NDEs, but there is no consensual or satisfying scientific explanation for the whole experience. Another interesting field of research concerns the assessment of NDE experiencers' cognitive and personality traits. Although little empirical study has been done in this regard, some investigations support the view that individuals' traits might influence the appearance of such phenomena. Notably, Greyson (2000) observed that NDE experiencers more easily experience common and non-pathological dissociation states, such as daydreaming, than matched people who came close to death but did not report a NDE phenomenology. More recently, Martial and colleagues (2018) observed particularly strong engagement in fantasy and imagination by individuals reporting NDEs-like as well as a significant relationship between fantasy proneness and richness (i.e., the number of reported features and their intensity) of the NDE phenomenology reported by experiencers. In addition, by assessing their memory formation, a recent study suggests that NDE experiencers present less efficient monitoring abilities (i.c., difficulty to identify the origin of memories) than matched people who came close to death but did not report a NDE (Martial, Charland-Verville, Dehon & Laureys, 2017c). However, the retrospective and correlational design of these studies does not permit to draw any conclusions about the causal pathway. To conclude, it seems probable that several factors might trigger a NDE, with each above-stated factor being just one of them (Blackmore, 1996). Although the basis of NDEs remains conjectural at this time, the few available data support the presence of specific neural correlates associated with each NDE features, integrated in a broader biopsychosocial phenomenon.

Conclusion

Humans go hand in hand with consciousness. This idea is nicely summarized in Descartes' expression "Cogito ergo sum", meaning "I think therefore I am". Yet, although technology is expanding extremely rapidly and gives a unique opportunity to observe human brain activity, there is to date no consensus regarding the objective and measurable signature of consciousness. Current research has repeatedly shown that awareness might not be unequivocally related to a specific brain area nor to the whole grey matter, but is way more complex than that.

Research on consciousness and ASC tells us that there is a wide range of states and experiences (associated with specific phenomenology and brain activity) within a continuum from unconscious states to conscious states. Some of them appear to involve a correlation between both wakefulness and awareness, whereas others seem to display a disrupted relationship between the two components. Uniquely, the latter enables scientists to determine the necessary and sufficient conditions for conscious cognition to happen. Consciousness is not an all-or-nothing phenomenon (Wade, 1996; Wade & Johnston, 1999). On the contrary, the boundaries between the different states are not often clear-cut, suggesting overlaps and intermediary transitions between them. From a neuroscientific perspective, studies on the different ASCs may enrich our current understanding of the emergence of the conscious mind.

Shared first authorship

Alice Barra and Manon Carrière contributed equally to this work.

References

Alkire, M.T., Haier, R.J., & Fallon, J.H. (2000). Toward a unified theory of narcosis: brain imaging evidence for a thalamocortical switch as the neurophysiologic basis of anesthetic-induced unconsciousness. *Consciousness and Cognition* 9: 370–386.

Alkire, M.T., Haier, R.J., Shah, N.K., & Anderson, C.T. (1997). Positron emission tomography study of regional cerebral metabolism in humans during isoflurane anesthesia. *Anesthesiology* 86: 549–557.

Alkire, M.T., Pomfrett, C.J., Haier, R.J., Gianzero, M.V., Chan, C.M., Jacobsen, B.P., et al. (1999). Functional brain imaging during anesthesia in humans: effects of halothane on global and regional cerebral glucose metabolism. *Anesthesiology* 90: 701–709.

American Congress of Rehabilitation Medicine (1995). Recommendations for use of uniform nomenclature pertinent to patients with severe alterations of consciousness. *Archives of Physical Medicine and Rehabilitation* 76: 205–209.

Ammermann, H., Kassubek, J., Lotze, M., Gut, E., Kaps, M., Schmidt, J., et al. (2007). MRI brain lesion patterns in patients in anoxia-induced vegetative state. *Journal of the Neurological Sciences* 260: 65–70.

Andrews, K., Murphy, L., Munday, R., Littlewood, C. (1996). Misdiagnosis of the vegetative state: retrospective study in a rehabilitation unit. *BMJ* 313(7048): 13–16.

Annen, J., Frasso, G., Heine, L., Di Perri, C., Martial, C., Antonopoulous, G., et al. (2018). Regional brain volumetry and brain function in severely brain-injured patients. *Annals of Neurology* 83(4): 842–853.

Aubinet, A., Larroque, S., Heine, L., Martial, C., Majerus, S., Laureys, S., et al. (2018). Clinical subcategorization of minimally conscious state according to resting functional connectivity. *Humain Brain Mapping* 39(11): 4519–4532..

Balestreri, M., Czosnyka, M., Chatfield, D.A., Steiner, L.A., Schmidt, E.A., Smielewski, P., et al. (2004). Predictive value of Glasgow Coma Scale after brain trauma: change in trend over the past ten years. *Journal of Neurology, Neurosurgery, and Psychiatry* 75: 161–162.

Bassetti, C., Vella, S., Donati, F., Wielepp, P., & Weder, B. (2000). SPECT during sleepwalking. *Lancet* 356(9228): 484–485.

Benveniste, H., Drejer, J., Schouseboe, A., & Diemer, H. (1984). Elevation of extracellular concentrations of glutamate & aspartate in rat hippocampus during cerebral ischaemia monitored by microdialysis. *Journal of Neurochemistry* 43: 1369–1374.

Blackmore, S. (1993). *Dying to Live: Science and Near-death Experience*. London: Grafton.

Blackmore, S. (1996). Near-death experiences. *Journal of the Royal Society of Medicine* 89(2): 73–76.

Blanke, O., Landis, T., Spinelli, L., & Seeck, M. (2004). Out-of-body experience and autoscopy of neurological origin. *Brain* 127: 243–258.

Blanke, O., & Mohr, C. (2005). Out-of-body experience, heautoscopy, and autoscopic hallucination of neurological origin. Implications for neurocognitive mechanisms of corporeal awareness and self-consciousness. *Brain Research Reviews* 50(1): 184–199.

Blanke, O., Ortigue, S., Landis, T., & Seeck, M. (2002). Stimulating illusory own-body perceptions. *Nature* 419: 269–270.

Blumenfeld, H., McNally, K.A., Vanderhill, S.D., Paige, A.L., Chung, R., Davis, K., et al. (2004). Positive and negative network correlations in temporal lobe epilepsy. *Cerebral Cortex* 14(8): 892–902.

Boly, M., Balteau, E., Schnakers, C., Degueldre, C., Moonen, G., Luxen, A., et al. (2007). Baseline brain activity fluctuations predict somatosensory perception in humans. *Proceedings of the National Academy of Sciences of the United States of America* 104(29): 12187–12192.

Bonhomme, P., Boveroux, P., Brichant, J, F., Lawley, S., & Boley, M. (2012). Neural correlates of consciousness during general anesthesia using functional magnetic resonance imaging (fMRI). *Archives Italiennes de Biologie* 150: 155–162.

Borjigin, J., Lee, U., Liu, T., Dinesh, P., Huff, S., Klarr, D., et al. (2013). Surge of neurophysiological coherence and connectivity in the dying brain. *Proceedings of the National Academy of Science* 110: 14432–14437.

Boveroux, P., Vanhaudenhuyse, A., Bruno, M.A., Noirhomme, Q., Lauwick, S., Luxen, A., et al. (2010). Breakdown of within- and between-network resting state functional magnetic resonance imaging connectivity during propofol-induced loss of consciousness. *Anesthesiology* 113: 1038–1053.

Britton, W.B., & Bootzin, R.R. (2004). Near-death experiences and the temporal lobe. *Psychological Science* 15(4): 254–258.

Brown, E.N., Lydic, R., & Schiff, N.D. (2010). General anesthesia, sleep, and coma. *New England Journal of Medicine* 363(27): 2638–2650.

Bruno, M.-A., Majerus, S., Boly, M., Vanhaudenhuyse, A., Schnakers, C., Gosseries, O., et al. (2012). Functional neuroanatomy underlying the clinical subcategorization of minimally conscious state patients. *Journal of Neurology* 259(6): 1087–1098.

Bruno, M.-A., Vanhaudenhuyse, A., Thibaut, A., Moonen, G., Laureys, S. (2011). From unresponsive wakefulness to minimally conscious PLUS and functional locked-in syndromes: recent advances in our understanding of disorders of consciousness. *Journal of Neurology* 258: 1373–84.

Cardeña, E., & Spiegel, D. (1991). Suggestibility, absorption, and dissociation: an integrative model of hypnosis. In J.F. Schumaker (Ed.), *Human Suggestibility: Advances in Theory, Research and Applications* (pp. 93–107). New York: Routledge.

Carr, D.B. (1981). Endorphins at the approach of death. *Lancet* 1(8216): 390.

Casali, A.G., Gosseries, O., Rosanova, M., Boly, M., Sarasso, S., Casali, K.R., et al. (2013). A theoretically based index of consciousness independent of sensory processing and behavior. *Science Translational Medicine* 5: 198ra105. doi:10.1126/scitranslmed.3006294.

Charland-Verville, V., Jourdan, J.-P., Thonnard, M., Ledoux, D., Donneau, A.-F., Quertermont, E., et al. (2014). Near-death experiences in non-life-threatening events and coma of different etiologies. *Frontiers in Human Neuroscience* 8: 203.

Chennu, S., Annen, J., Wannez, S., Thibaut, A., Chatelle, C., Cassol, H., et al. (2017). Brain networks predict metabolism, diagnosis and prognosis at the bedside in disorders of consciousness. *Brain* 140: 2120–2132.

Cojan, Y., Waber, L., Schwartz, S., Rossier, L., Forster, A., & Vuilleumier, P. (2009). The brain under self-control: modulation of inhibitory and monitoring cortical networks during hypnotic paralysis. *Neuron* 62: 862–875.

Cox, R.E., & Bryant, R.A. (2008). Advances in hypnosis research: methods, designs, and contributions of intrinsic and instrumental hypnosis research. In M.R. Nash, & A.J. Barnier (Eds.), *The Oxford Handbook of Hypnosis: Theory, Research, and Practice* (pp. 311–336). Oxford: Oxford University Press.

Curran, H.V., & Morgan, C. (2000). Cognitive, dissociative and psychotogenic effects of ketamine in recreational users on the night of drug use and 3 days later. *Addiction* 95(4): 575–590.

Daly, D. (1975). Ictal clonical manifestations of complex partial seizures. In D.D. Daly (Ed.), *Advances in Neurology: Complex Partial Seizures and Their Treatment* (pp. 89–127). New York: Raven.

Damasio, A., & Meyer, K. (2009). Consciousness: an overview of the phenomenon and of its possible neural basis. In S. Laureys, & G. Tononi (Eds.), *Neurology of Consciousness: Cognitive Neuroscience and Neuropathology* (pp. 3–14). San Diego, CA: Elsevier Academic Press Inc.

Dell'Olio, A.J. (2010). Do near-death experiences provide a rational basis for belief in life after death? *Sophia* 49: 113–128.

Demertzi, A., Soddu, A., Faymonville, M.E., Bahri, M.A., Gosseries, O., Vanhaudenhuyse, A., et al. (2011). Hypnotic modulation of resting state fMRI default mode and extrinsic network connectivity. :E. J.W. Van Someren, Y. D. Van Der Werf, P. R. Roelfsema, H. D. Mansvelder, & F. H. Lopes Da Silva (Eds.), *Progress in Brain Research* (Vol. 193, pp. 309–322). Amsterdam: Elsevier.

Demertzi, A., Vanhaudenhuyse, A., Noirhomme, Q., Faymonville, M. E., & Laureys, S. (2015). Hypnosis modulates behavioural measures and subjective ratings about external and internal awareness. *Journal of Physiology-Paris* 109(4–6): 173–179.

De Ridder, D., Van Laere, K., Dupont, P., Menovsky, T., & Van de Heyning, P. (2007). Visualizing out-of-body experience in the brain. *The New England Journal of Medicine* 357(18): 1829–1833.

Deshpande, G., Kerssens, C., Sebel, P.S., & Hu, X. (2010). Altered local coherence in the default mode network due to sevoflurane anesthesia. *Brain Research*, 1318: 110–121.

Devinsky, O., Feldmann, E., Burrowes, K., & Bromfield, E. (1989). Autoscopic phenomena with seizures. *Archives of Neurology* 46: 1080–1088.

Di Perri, C., Bahri, M.A., Amico, E., Thibaut, A., Heine, L., Antonopoulos, G., et al. (2016). Neural correlates of consciousness in patients who have emerged from a minimally conscious state: a cross-sectional multimodal imaging study. *Lancet Neurology* 15: 830–842.

Dueck, M.H., Petzke, F., Gerbershagen, H.J., Paul, M., Hesselmann, V., Girnus, R., et al. (2005). Propofol attenuates responses of the auditory cortex to acoustic stimulation in a dose-dependent manner: a FMRI study. *Acta Anaesthesiologica Scandinavica* 49: 784–791.

Els, T., Kassubek, J., Kubalek, R., & Klisch, J. (2004). Diffusion-weighted MRI during early global cerebral hypoxia: a predictor for clinical outcome? *Acta Neurologica Scandinavica* 110: 361–367.

Evers, A., & Crowder, M. (2006). Cellular and molecular mechanisms of anesthesia. In P.G. Barash, B.F. Cullen, R.K. Stoelting, M. Cahalan, & M.C. Stock (Eds.), *Clinical Anesthesia* (Vol. 6, pp. 95–114). New York: Lippincott Williams & Wilkins.

Facco, E., & Agrillo, C. (2012). Near-death-like experiences without life-threatening conditions or brain disorders: a hypothesis from a case report. *Frontiers in Psychology* 3: 490.

Faymonville, M.E., Laureys, S., Degueldre, C., DelFiore, G., Luxen, A., Franck, G., et al. (2000). Neural mechanisms of antinociceptive effects of hypnosis. *Anesthesiology* 92(5): 1257–1267.

Faymonville, M.E., Mambourg, P.H., Joris, J., Vrijens, B., Fissette, J., Albert, A., et al. (1997). Psychological approaches during conscious sedation. Hypnosis versus stress reducing strategies: a prospective randomized study. *Pain* 73(3): 361–367.

Faymonville, M.E., Roediger, L., Del Fiore, G., Delgueldre, C., Phillips, C., Lamy, M., et al. (2003). Increased cerebral functional connectivity underlying the antinociceptive effects of hypnosis. *Cognitive Brain Research* 17(2): 255–262.

Fernandez-Espejo, D., Soddu, A., Cruse, D., Palacios, E.M., Junque, C., Vanhaudenhuyse, A., et al. (2012). A role for the default mode network in the bases of disorders of consciousness. *Annals of Neurology* 72(3): 335–343.

Ferrarelli, F., Massimini, M., Sarasso, S., Casali, A.G., Riedner, B., Angelini, G., et al. (2010). Breakdown in cortical effective connectivity during midazolam-induced loss of consciousness. *Proceedings of the National Academy of Sciences of the United States of America* 107(6): 2681–2686.

Frenk, H., McCarty, B.C., & Liebeskind, J.C. (1978). Different brain areas mediate the analgesic and epileptic properties of enkephalin. *Science* 200: 335–337.

Gaskell, A.L., Hight, D.F., Winders, J., Tran, G., Defresne, A., Bonhomme, V., et al. (2017). Frontal alpha-delta EEG does not preclude volitional response during anaesthesia: prospective cohort study of the isolated forearm technique. *British Journal of Anaesthesia* 119(4): 664–673.

Giacino, J.T., Ashwal, S., Childs, N., Cranford, R., Jennett, B., Katz, D.I., et al. (2002). The minimally conscious state: definition and diagnostic criteria. *Neurology* 58(3): 349–353.

Giacino, J.T., Kalmar, K., Whyte, J. (2004). The JFK coma recovery scale-revised: measurement characteristics and diagnostic utility. *Archives of Physical Medicine and Rehabilitation* 85(12): 2020–2029.

Giacino, J.T., Schnakers, C., Rodriguez-Moreno, D., Kalmar, K., Schiff, N., & Hirsch, J. (2009). Behavioral assessment in patients with disorders of consciousness: gold standard or fool's gold? S. Laureys, N.D. Schiff, & A. M. Owen (Eds.) *Progress in Brain Research* (Vol. 177, pp. 33–48). Oxford: Elsevier.

Greyson, B. (1983). The near-death experience scale. Construction, reliability, and validity. *Journal of Nervous and Mental Disease* 171: 369–375.

Greyson, B. (2000). Dissociation in people who have near-death experiences: out of their bodies or out of their minds? *The Lancet* 355: 460–463.

Guldenmund, P., Soddu, A., Baquero, K., Vanhaudenhuyse, A., Bruno, M.-A., Gosseries, O., et al. (2016). Structural brain injury in patients with disorders of consciousness: a voxel-based morphometry study. *Brain Injury* 30(3): 343–352.

Heinke, W., & Koelsch, S. (2005). The effects of anesthetics on brain activity and cognitive function. *Current Opinion in Anesthesiology*, 18: 625–631.

Hoepner, R., Labudda, K., May, T.W., Schoendienst, M., Woermann, F.G., Bien, C.G., et al. (2013). Ictal autoscopic phenomena and near death experiences: a study of five patients with ictal autoscopies. *Journal of Neurology* 260(3): 742–749.

Jansen, K. (1989). Near death experience and the NMDA receptor. *British Medical Journal* 298(6689): 1708.

Jansen, K. (1997). The ketamine model of the near-death experience: a central role for the N-methyl-D-aspartate receptor. *Journal of Near-Death Studies* 16(1): 5–26.

Jansen, K. (2001). *Ketamine: Dreams and Realities*. Sarasota, FL: Multidisciplinary Association for Psychedelic Studies.

Jasper, H.H., & Rasmussen, T. (1958). Studies of clinical and electrical responses to deep temporal stimulation in man with some considerations of functional anatomy. *Association for Research in Nervous and Mental Disease* 36: 316–334.

Jennett, B., & Plum, F. (1972). Persistent vegetative state after brain damage. A syndrome in search of a name. *Lancet* 1(7753): 734–737.

Jensen, M.P., Jamieson, G.A., Lutz, A., Mazzoni, G., McGeown, W.J., Santarcangelo, E.L., et al. (2017). New directions in hypnosis research: strategies for advancing the cognitive and clinical neuroscience of hypnosis. *Neuroscience of Consciousness* 3: nix004.

Kelly, E.W. (2001). Near-death experiences with reports of meeting deceased people. *Death Studies* 25: 229–249.

Klemenc-Ketis, Z., Kersnik, J., & Grmec, S. (2010). The effect of carbon dioxide on near-death experiences in out-of-hospital cardiac arrest survivors: a prospective observational study. *Critical Care* 14(2): R56.

Koch, C., Massimini, M., Boly, M., & Tononi, G. (2016). Neural correlates of consciousness: progress and problems. *Nature Reviews Neuroscience* 17(5): 307–321.

Kosslyn, S.M., Thompson, W.L., Costantini-Ferrando, M.F., Alpert, N.M., & Spiegel, D. (2000). Hypnotic visual illusion alters color processing in the brain. *The American Journal of Psychiatry* 157: 1279–1284.

Landry, M., Lifshitz, M., & Raz, A. (2017). Brain correlates of hypnosis: a systematic review and meta-analytic exploration. *Neuroscience & Biobehavioral Reviews*, 81: 75–98.

Laureys, S. (2005). The neural correlate of (un)awareness: lessons from the vegetative state. *Trends in Cognitive Sciences* 9(12): 556–559.

Laureys, S., Boly, M. (2008). The changing spectrum of coma. *Nature Clinical Practice Neurology* 4(10): 544–546.

Laureys, S., Celesia, G., Cohadon, F., Lavrijsen, J., León-Carrión, J., Sannita, W.G., et al. (2010). Unresponsive wakefulness syndrome: a new name for the vegetative state or apallic syndrome and the European Task Force on Disorders of Consciousness. *BMC Medicine* 8: 68.

Laureys, S., Fins, J.J. (2008). Are we equal in death? Avoiding diagnostic error in brain death. *Neurology* 70(4): e14–e15.

Laureys, S., Goldman, S., Phillips, C., Van Bogaert, P., Aerts, J., Luxen, A., et al. (1999). Impaired effective cortical connectivity in vegetative state: preliminary investigation using PET. *NeuroImage* 9(4): 377–382.

Laureys, S., Lemaire, C., Maquet, P., Phillips, C., & Franck, G. (1999). Cerebral metabolism during vegetative state and after recovery to consciousness. *Journal of Neurology, Neurosurgery, and Psychiatry* 67(1): 121.

Laureys, S., Owen, A.M., & Schiff, N.D. (2004). Brain function in coma, vegetative state, and related disorders. *Lancet Neurology* 3(9): 537–546.

Laureys, S., Pellas, F., Van Eeckhout, P., Ghorbel, S., Schnakers, C., Perrin, F., et al. (2005). The locked-in syndrome: what is it like to be conscious but paralyzed and voiceless? *Progress in Brain Research* 150: 495–511.

Lin, J.S. (2000). Brain structures and mechanisms involved in the control of cortical activation and wakefulness, with emphasis on the posterior hypothalamus and histaminergic neurons. *Sleep Medicine Reviews* 4(5): 471–503.

Lipari, S., Baglio, F., Griffanti, L., Mendozzi, L., Garegnani, M., Motta, A., et al. (2012). Altered and asymmetric default mode network activity in a "hypnotic virtuoso": an fMRI and EEG study. *Consciousness and Cognition* 21(1): 393–400.

Lehembre, R., Bruno, M.-A., Vanhaudenhuyse, A., Chatelle, C., Cologan, V., Leclercq, Y., et al. (2012). Resting-state EEG study of comatose patients: a connectivity and frequency analysis to find differences between vegetative and minimally conscious states. *Functional Neurology* 27(1): 41–47.

Lempert, T., Bauer, M., & Schmidt, D. (1994a). Syncope and near-death experience. *The Lancet* 344(8925): 829–830.

Lempert, T., Bauer, M., & Schmidt, D. (1994b). Syncope: a videometric analysis of 56 episodes of transient cerebral hypoxia. *Annals of Neurology* 36(2): 233–237.

León-Carrión, J., Martin-Rodriguez, J., Damas-Lopez, J., Barroso y Martin, J.M., & Dominguez-Morales, M.R. (2008). Brain function in the minimally conscious state: a quantitative neurophysiological study. *Clinical Neurophysiology* 119: 1506–1514.

Lutkenhoff, E.S., Chiang, J., Tshibanda, L., Kamau, E., Kirsch, M., Pickard, J.D., et al. (2015). Thalamic and extrathalamic mechanisms of consciousness after severe brain injury. *Annals of Neurology* 78: 68–76.

Martial, C., Cassol, H., Antonopoulos, G., Charlier, T., Herosa, J., Donneau, A.-F., et al. (2017a). Temporality of features in near-death experience narratives. *Frontiers in Human Neuroscience* 11: 311.

Martial, C., Cassol, H., Charland-Verville, V., Merckelbach, H., & Laureys, S. (2018). Fantasy proneness correlates with the intensity of near-death experience. *Frontiers in Psychiatry* 9: 190.

Martial, C., Charland-Verville, V., Cassol, H., Didone, V., Van Der Linden, M., & Laureys, S. (2017b). Intensity and memory characteristics of near-death experiences. *Consciousness and Cognition* 56: 120–127.

Martial, C., Charland-Verville, V., Dehon, H., & Laureys, S. (2017c). False memory susceptibility in coma survivors with and without a near-death experience. *Psychological Research* 82(4): 1–13.

Mashour, G.A. (2016). Consciousness and anesthesia. In S. Laureys, O. Gosseries, & G. Tononi (Eds.), *The Neurology of Consciousness, Second Edition* (pp. 139–152). San Diego, CA: Elsevier.

Massimini, M., Ferrarelli, F., Sarasso, S., & Tononi, G. (2012). Cortical mechanisms of loss of consciousness: insight from TMS/EEG studies *Archives Italiennes de Biologie* 150(2012): 44–55.

Martuzzi, R., Ramani, R., Qiu, M., Rajeevan, N., & Constable, R.T. (2010). Functional connectivity and alterations in baseline brain state in humans. *NeuroImage* 49: 823–834.

McGeown, W.J., Mazzoni, G., Venneri, A., & Kirsch, I. (2009). Hypnotic induction decreases anterior default mode activity. *Consciousness and Cognition* 18: 848–855.

Meduna, L.T. (1950). *Carbon Dioxide Therapy: A Neurophysiological Treatment of Nervous Disorders*. Springfield, IL: Charles C. Thomas.

Monti, M.M., Vanhaudenhuyse, A., Coleman, M.R., Boly, M., Pickard, J.D., Tshibanda, L., et al. (2010). Willful modulation of brain activity in disorders of consciousness. *The New England Journal of Medicine* 362(7): 579–589. Epub 2010 Feb 3.

Moore, L.E., & Greyson, B. (2017). Characteristics of memories for near-death experiences. *Consciousness and Cognition* 51: 116–124.

Morse, M.L., Venecia, D., & Milstein, J., (1989). Near-death experiences: a neurophysiologic explanatory model. *Journal of Near-Death Studies* 8(1): 45–53.

Nelson, K.R., Mattingly, M., Lee, S.A., & Schmitt, F.A. (2006). Does the arousal system contribute to near death experience? *Neurology* 66(7): 1003–1009.

Newberg, L.A., Milde, J.H., & Michenfelder, J.D. (1983). The cerebral metabolic effects of isoflurane at and above concentrations that suppress cortical electrical activity. *Anesthesiology* 59: 23–28.

Oakley, D.A. (1999). Hypnosis and conversion hysteria: a unifying model. *Cognitive Neuropsychiatry* 4(3): 243–265.

Oakley, D.A., & Halligan, P.W. (2009). Hypnotic suggestion and cognitive neuroscience. *Trends in Cognitive Sciences* 13: 264–270.

Oakley, D.A., & Halligan, P.W. (2010). Psychophysiological foundations of hypnosis and suggestion. In S.J. Lynn, J.W. Rhue, & I. Kirsch (Eds.), *Handbook of Clinical Hypnosis* (pp. 79–177). Washington, DC: American Psychological Association.

Oakley, D.A., & Halligan, P.W. (2013). Hypnotic suggestion: opportunities for cognitive neuroscience. *Nature Reviews Neuroscience* 14: 565–576.

Owen, A.M., Coleman, M.R., Boly, M, Davis, M.H., Laureys, S., & Pickard, J.D. (2006). Detecting awareness in the vegetative state. *Science* 313(5792): 1402.

Owens, J.E., Cook, E.W., & Stevenson, I. (1990). Features of "near-death experience" in relation to whether or not patients were near death. *The Lancet* 336(8724): 1175–1177.

Penfield, W. (1955). The twenty-ninth Maudsley lecture: the role of the temporal cortex in certain psychical phenomena. *Journal of Mental Science* 101: 451–465.

Penfield, W. (1958). *The Excitable Cortex in Conscious Man*. Liverpool: Liverpool University Press.

Piarulli, A., Bergamasco, M., Thibaut, A., Cologan, V., Gosseries, O., & Laureys, S. (2016). EEG ultradian rhythmicity differences in disorders of consciousness during wakefulness. *Journal of Neurology* 263(9): 1746–1760.

Plum, F., Posner, J.B. (1983). *The Diagnosis of Stupor and Coma*, 3rd edn. Philadelphia, PA: FA Davis.

Ragazzoni, A., Pirulli, C., Veniero, D., Feurra, M., Cincotta, M., & Giovannelli, F. et al. (2013). Vegetative versus minimally conscious states: a study using TMS-EEG, sensory and event-related potentials. *PloS One* 8(2): e57069.

Rainville, P., Duncan, G.H., Price, D.D., Carrier, B., & Bushnell, M.C. (1997). Pain affect encoded in human anterior cingulate but not somatosen-sory cortex. *Science* 277(5328): 968–971.

Rainville, P., Hofbauer, R.K., Bushnell, M.C., Duncan, G.H., & Price, D.D. (2002). Hypnosis modulates activity in brain structures involved in the regulation of consciousness. *Journal of Cognitive Neuroscience* 14(6): 887–901.

Rainville, P., Hofbauer, R.K., Paus, T., Duncan, G.H., Bushnell, M.C., & Price, D.D. (1999). Cerebral mechanisms of hypnotic induction and suggestion. *Journal of Cognitive Neuroscience* 11(1): 110–125.

Rainville, P., & Price, D.D. (2003). Hypnosis phenomenology and the neurobiology of consciousness. *International Journal of Clinical and Experimental Hypnosis* 51(2): 105–129.

Ramani, R., Qiu, M., & Constable, R.T. (2007). Sevoflurane 0.25 MAC preferentially affects higher order association areas: a functional magnetic resonance imaging study in volunteers. *Anesthesia & Analgesia* 105: 648–655.

Rosanova, M., Gosseries, O., Casarotto, S., Boly, M., Casali, A.G., & Bruno, M.A., et al. (2012). Recovery of cortical effective connectivity and recovery of consciousness in vegetative patients. *Brain* 135(Pt 4): 1308–1320.

Reyher, J. (1962). A paradigm for determining the clinical relevance of hypnotically induced psychopathology. *Psychological Bulletin* 59: 344–352.

Robin, E.D. (1980). Of men and mitochondria: coping with hypoxic dysoxia. *The American Review of Respiratory Disease* 122: 517–531.

Saavedra-Aguilar, D.J.C., & Gómez-Jeria, L.J.S. (1989). A neurobiological model for near-death experiences. *Journal of Near-Death Studies* 7(4): 205–222.

Sabom, M. (1982). *Recollections of Death: A Medical Investigation*. New York: Harper & Row.

Salek-Haddadi, A., Lemieux, L., Merschhemke, M., Friston, K.J., Duncan, J.S., & Fish, D.R. (2003). Functional magnetic resonance imaging of human absence seizures. *Annals of Neurology* 53(5): 663–667.

Sanders, R.D., Tononi, G., Laureys, S., & Sleigh, J.W. (2012) Unresponsiveness ≠ unconsciousness. *Anesthesiology* 116: 946–959.

Sarasso, S., Rosanova, M., Casali, A.G., Casarotto, S., Fecchio, M., Boly, M., et al. (2014). Quantifying cortical EEG responses to TMS in (un) consciousness. *Clinical EEG and Neuroscience* 45(1): 40–49.

Schiff, N.D. (2008). Central thalamic contributions to arousal regulation and neurological disorders of consciousness. *Annals of the New York Academy of Sciences* 1129: 105–118.

Schnakers, C., Vanhaudenhuyse, A., Giacino, J., Ventura, M., Boly, M., Majerus, S. et al. (2009). Diagnostic accuracy of the vegetative and minimally conscious state: clinical consensus versus standardized neurobehavioral assessment. *BMC Neurology* 9: 35.

Schwaninger, J., Eisenberg, P., Schechtman, K., & Weiss, A. (2002). A prospective analysis of near-death experiences in cardiac arrest patients. *Journal of Near Death Studies* 20: 215–232.

Seel, R.T., Sherer, M., Whyte, J., Katz, D.I., Giacino, J.T., Rosenbaum, A.M., et al. (2010). Assessment scales for disorders of consciousness: evidence-based recommendations for clinical practice and research. *Archives of Physical Medicine and Rehabilitation* 91: 1795–813.

Silva, S., De Pasquale, F., Vuillaume, C., Riu, B., Loubinoux, I., Geeraerts, T., et al. (2015). Disruption of posteromedial large-scale neural communication predicts recovery from coma. *Neurology* 85: 2036–2044.

Sitt, J.D., King, J.R., El Karoui, I., Rohaut, B., Faugeras, F., Gramfort, A., et al. (2014). Large scale screening of neural signatures of consciousness in patients in a vegetative or minimally conscious state. *Brain* 137: 2258–2270.

Sleutjes, A., Moreira-Almeida, A., & Greyson, B. (2014). Almost 40 years investigating near-death experiences: an overview of mainstream scientific journals. *Journal of Nervous and Mental Disease* 202(11): 833–836.

Smallwood, J., & Schooler, J.W. (2006). The restless mind. *Psychological Bulletin* 132(6): 946.

Stender, J., Gosseries, O., & Bruno, M-A, Charland-Verville, V., Vanhaudenhuyse, A., Demertzi, A., et al. (2014). Diagnostic precision of PET imaging and functional MRI in disorders of consciousness: a clinical validation study. *Lancet* 384: 514–22.

Stender, J., Kupers, R., Rodell, A., Thibaut, A., Chatelle, C., Bruno, M.A., et al. (2015). Quantitative rates of brain glucose metabolism distinguish minimally conscious from vegetative state patients. *Journal of Cerebral Blood Flow & Metabolism* 35(1): 58–65.

Steriade, M., McCormick, D.A., & Sejnowski, T.J. (1993). Thalamocortical oscillations in the sleeping and aroused brain. *Science* 262: 679–685.

Teasdale, G., & Jennett, B. (1974). Assessment of coma and impaired consciousness: a practical scale. *Lancet* 304(7872): 81–84.

The Executive Committee of the American Psychological Association – Division of Psychological Hypnosis (1994). Definition and description of hypnosis. *Contemporary Hypnosis* 11, 142–162.

The Quality Standards Subcommittee of the American Academy of Neurology (1995). Practice parameters for determining brain death in adults (summary statement). *Neurology* 45(5): 1012–1014.

Thonnard, M., Charland-Verville, V., Brédart, S., Dehon, H., Ledoux, D., & Laureys, S. (2013). Characteristics of near-death experiences memories as compared to real and imagined events memories. *PloS One* 8: e57620.

Timmermann, C., Roseman, L., Willimans, L., Erritzoe, D., Martial, C., Cassol, H., et al. (2018). DMT induces features of near-death experiences in healthy volunteers. *Frontiers in Psychology* 9: 1424.

Vaquero, J.J., & Kinahan, P. (2015). Positron emission tomography: current challenges and opportunities for technological advances in clinical and preclinical imaging systems. *Annual Review of Biomedical Engineering* 17: 385–414.

Vanhaudenhuyse, A., Demertzi, A., Schabus, M., Noirhomme, Q., Bredart, S., & Boly, M. (2011). Two distinct neuronal networks mediate the awareness of environment and of self. *Journal of Cognitive Neuroscience* 23(3): 570–578.

Vanhaudenhuyse, A., Laureys, S., & Faymonville, M.E. (2014). Neurophysiology of hypnosis. *Clinical Neurophysiology* 44, 343–353.

Vanhaudenhuyse, A., Ledoux, D., Gosseries, O., Demertzi, A., Laureys, S., & Faymonville, M.-E. (2019). Can subjective ratings of absorption, dissociation, and time perception during "neutral hypnosis" predict hypnotizability? An exploratory study. *International Journal of Clinical and Experimental Hypnosis* 67(1): 28–38.

Vanhaudenhuyse, A., Noirhomme, Q., Tshibanda, L.J., Bruno, M.-A., Boveroux, P., Schnakers, C., et al. (2010). Default network connectivity reflects the level of consciousness in non-communicative brain-damaged patients *Brain* 133(1), 161–171.

Wade, D.T. (1996). Misdiagnosing the persistent vegetative state. Persistent vegetative state should not be diagnosed until 12 months from onset of coma [letter; comment]. *BMJ* 313(7062): 943–944.

Wade, D.T., & Johnston, C. (1999). The permanent vegetative state: practical guidance on diagnosis and management. *BMJ* 319(7213): 841–844.

Wannez, S., Gosseries, O., Azzolini, D., Martial, C., Cassol, H., Aubinet, C., et al. (2017a). Prevalence of coma-recovery scale-revised signs of consciousness in patients in minimally conscious state. *Neuropsychological Rehabilitation* 11: 1–10.

Wannez, S., Heine, L., Thonnard, M., Gosseries, O., Laureys, S., & Coma Science Group collaborators. (2017b). The repetition of behavioral assessments in diagnosis of disorders of consciousness. *Annals of Neurology* 81(6): 883–889.

Weitzenhoffer, A.M., & Hilgard, E.R., 1962. *Stanford Hypnotic Susceptibility Scale, Form C* (Vol. 27). Palo Alto, CA: Consulting Psychologists Press.

Woerlee, G.M. (2005). *Mortal Minds: The Biology of Near-Death Experiences.* Amherst, NY: Prometheus Books.

Zheng, Y., Gao, L., Wang, G., Wang, Y., Yang, Z., Wang, X., et al. (2016). The influence of unilateral contraction of hand muscles on the contralateral corticomuscular coherence during bimanual motor tasks. *Neuropsychologia* 85: 199–207.

3

MULTIDIMENSIONAL DEGREES OF CONSCIOUSNESS

Qualities of experiences during wakeful perception, working memory tasks, mental imagery, mind wandering and dreaming

Peter Fazekas and Georgina Nemeth

Introduction

In contemporary cognitive neuroscience, the two major issues related to consciousness concern (1) the neural correlates of consciousness, i.e. what the neural underpinnings of having conscious experiences might be, and (2) the graded versus dichotomous nature of conscious experience, i.e. whether consciousness is an all-or-nothing kind of phenomenon or it comes in degrees. This paper focuses on the relation between these two issues. We defend the view that conscious experience is gradual (*gradual view*, for short) and show how it is reflected in the neural correlates of consciousness. In doing so, we bring different threads of empirical research (focusing on perception, attention, working memory, mental imagery, mind wandering and dreaming) together to illustrate that the body of evidence that has been accumulating from these fields uniformly supports the gradual view.

In the bigger picture, this paper fits into the recent trend of trying to move beyond mere correlational claims with respect to conscious experiences. For a scientific understanding of consciousness, over and above identifying neural correlates of consciousness, explanatory links between neural mechanisms and features of conscious experiences would be required (Seth, 2009, 2010). According to an influential account, such explanatory links between a target and a base phenomenon (consciousness and neural activity in our case, respectively) are typically established by first proposing hypothetical correspondence relations between features of the two phenomena (Bechtel & McCauley, 1999; Fazekas, 2009; Fazekas & Kertesz, 2011; McCauley & Bechtel, 2001). If this initial mapping can be extended to include further feature-pairs, then the explanatory schemes provided by the scientific theories describing the base phenomenon, in our particular case, a mechanistic understanding of neural processes, can be transferred to the target phenomenon leading to an account of features of consciousness in neural terms. From this perspective, our aim here is to propose and explore the viability of hypothetical correspondence relations between certain characteristics of conscious experiences and their neural basis.

Moving beyond mere correlational claims: qualities of experiences and features of underlying neural representations

To introduce and motivate the specific correspondence relations that are proposed to establish explanatory links between consciousness and its neural substrate, and to provide a novel framework to understand the gradual nature of conscious experiences, first it needs to be clarified how the central notion of this proposal – the quality of experiences – is related to other key notions of the literature.

Gradual experiences clarified: states, levels, degrees and qualities of consciousness

Global states of consciousness, like alert wakefulness, dreaming, mind wandering, sedation, hypnosis, minimally conscious state, vegetative state etc., characterise an organism's overall conscious condition. Traditionally, different global states of consciousness have been compared and ordered relative to each other on the basis of (i) how rich the content of awareness can be and (ii) what level of wakefulness or arousal characterises the state in question (Laureys, 2005). Such an ordering is manifest in claims, according to which patients in minimally conscious state have a higher level of consciousness than patients in vegetative state and people in alert wakefulness have higher level of consciousness than those having dream experiences (Bayne, Hohwy, & Owen, 2016a). Recently, however, it has been argued that this is a too simplified picture and global states of consciousness are, in fact, to be characterised in terms of a multi-dimensional feature space, including such dimensions as the *gating* of conscious content (i.e. the range of contents that can enter consciousness) and the *accessibility* of conscious content (which cognitive processes can access the contents entering consciousness) (Bayne et al., 2016a). To amend this picture, we have previously argued that the way the contents entering consciousness *appear* in a conscious experience – what we call the *quality* of the experience – is also a crucial factor (Fazekas & Overgaard, 2016, 2018a), as the neural features that underpin the quality of experiences are constrained by global states of consciousness (Nemeth & Fazekas, 2018).

The emerging picture is a gradual view, in the sense that the different dimensions along which global states of consciousness can be compared have multiple values and some are even continuous: an individual in one global state of consciousness can be more or less conscious than someone in another global state depending on the level of gating, the level of accessibility and the level of quality characteristic of the global states in question. Since at least some dimensions are probably independent, no uniform ordering of global states follows from this gradual view. That is, one global state of consciousness might very well be characterised with a higher level along one dimension while being at a lower level along a different dimension than another global state (Bayne et al., 2016a).

In what follows, we shall focus on the gradual nature of the quality dimension. As mentioned above, the term 'quality of experience' is meant to capture how specific content elements appear in an experience. In fact, the quality of an experience is itself a feature family, as it can be characterised along multiple dimensions. The *subjective intensity* of an experience is determined by how salient the content of the experience is. For example, a less salient or less intense content element of an experience stands out from the perceived background to a lesser degree. The *subjective specificity* of an experience is determined by how distinguishable a content element is from other content elements: a less specific experience of a content element is more generic, more vague, more ambiguous, i.e. the content element is less distinguishable from other similar content elements. The *subjective stability* of an experience is determined by how long a content element is present in the experience. Less stable content elements occur in an experience only for a shorter period of time (Fazekas, Nemeth, & Overgaard, forthcoming; Fazekas & Overgaard, 2018a; Nemeth & Fazekas, 2018).

This characterisation of experiences can, of course, reflect features of the external objects perceived, like in the case of blurry images (less specific experiences) or rapidly presented stimuli (low stability experiences), but can also capture the characteristics of object-independent modulations of percepts, for instance how attention structures experiences (highly intense, highly specific, highly stable attended elements; less intense, less specific, less stable unattended elements; see Fazekas & Nanay, 2018; Watzl, 2017).

The neural underpinnings of the quality of experiences

How attention modulates the appearance of certain stimuli is informative with regard to the possible neural underpinnings of the quality – i.e. intensity, specificity and stability – of conscious experiences (Fazekas & Overgaard, 2018a). For instance, allocating attention to a stimulus (compared to allocating attention elsewhere) can increase the subjective intensity of the corresponding conscious experience: it increases the apparent contrast of a Gabor patch (Carrasco, Ling, & Read, 2004) or the level of saturation of a colour patch (Fuller & Carrasco, 2006). We also know that attention achieves this effect via inducing an increase in the amplitude of the response function of the corresponding populations of neurons, i.e. via increasing the *intensity* of the neural representations coding for the specific properties in question (Carrasco, 2011; Fazekas & Nanay, 2018).

Similarly, allocating attention to a specific non-spatial feature, say, to the colour crimson, in a visual search task results that the colour of crimson objects enter consciousness in a more specific form, i.e. with less ambiguity between different shades of red. It is known that feature-based attention is able to sharpen the population response function (i.e. decrease its variance), and thus increase the *precision* of the population code (Martinez-Trujillo & Treue, 2004; Maunsell & Treue, 2006), thereby providing more unique neural representations coding for the feature in question (Carrasco, 2011; Fazekas & Nanay, 2018).

These findings point towards a correspondence relation between properties of the neural representation encoding a specific feature and properties of the quality (appearance) of the content element in the matching conscious experience. On these and similar grounds, in a previous work we have proposed that the neural underpinnings of subjective intensity, specificity and stability are the intensity, precision and maintenance of the underlying neural population codes, respectively (Fazekas et al., forthcoming; Fazekas & Overgaard, 2018a, 2018b), and argued that thinking about the quality of conscious experiences in terms of the interplay between these different factors helps account for a multitude of findings reporting reduced awareness (Asplund, Fougnie, Zughni, Martin, & Marois, 2014; Lavie, 2006; Lavie, Beck, & Konstantinou, 2014; Overgaard, Fehl, Mouridsen, Bergholt, & Cleeremans, 2008; Windey, Gevers, & Cleeremans, 2013).

These correspondence relations further strengthen the gradual view, as there are well-known mechanisms that can gradually change the proposed neural underpinnings of the different aspects of the quality of conscious experiences, and hence can gradually modulate the quality of experiences. The different forms of attentional influence (affecting intensity and precision) briefly introduced above are only one group of such mechanisms – prior expectations, prior experiences, context, mental imagery and possibly other mechanisms can also influence the formation and features of relevant neural representations (Fazekas & Overgaard, 2018b), and thus play a role in eliciting gradual changes in the quality of conscious experiences.

Supporting findings

In what follows, our aim is to explore the viability of the proposed correspondence relations and the gradual view itself by systematically reviewing recent findings with regard to the quality of conscious experiences in different global states of consciousness ranging from alert wakefulness to dreaming.

Quality of experiences and the perceptual awareness scale

The Perceptual Awareness Scale (PAS) has been developed for the specific purpose of providing a measure of the gradation of consciousness (Ramsøy & Overgaard, 2004; Sandberg & Overgaard, 2015; Sandberg, Timmermans, Overgaard, & Cleeremans, 2010). It offers four categories that had been constructed to reflect and generalise subjects' own descriptions of how to differentiate between degrees of awareness of a stimulus. These categories are: 'no experience', when subjects have no impression of the stimulus; 'weak glimpse', when subjects have a feeling that something has been shown but cannot specify any features of the stimulus; 'almost clear experiences', when subjects have an ambiguous experience of the stimulus with more vivid impressions of some stimulus aspects and less vivid impression of others; and 'clear experience', when subjects have a clear, specific, unambiguous experience of the stimulus.

Using PAS ratings in masking paradigms, it has been demonstrated that there is a continuous transition between clearly seen and not seen stimuli, such that in intermediate cases subjects, although report having experiences but only in a dim or unclear form, are less certain about or even have no knowledge of the identity of the stimuli (Christensen, Ramsøy, Lund, Madsen, & Rowe, 2006; Overgaard, Feldbæk Nielsen, & Fuglsang-Frederiksen, 2004; Overgaard, Rote, Mouridsen, & Ramsøy, 2006; Ramsøy & Overgaard, 2004; Sandberg, Bibby, Timmermans, Cleeremans, & Overgaard, 2011; Sandberg & Overgaard, 2015; Sandberg et al., 2010). As one moves along this continuum from clearly seen stimuli towards not seen stimuli, the experiences subjects report get more and more degraded, their content becomes less intense and less specific up until a point where subjects, although still confident that they are perceiving something, are not able to discern any kind of detail in their experience.

That is, although the terminology used to describe the different PAS scores indicates that they measure the *clarity* of consciousness, this clarity is, in fact, what we call here the *quality* of the experience. The degrees of consciousness PAS measures thus are the gradation in the quality of the conscious experiences – how the content appears in the experience ('no experience': no content appears; 'weak glimpse': only dull non-specific content appears; 'almost clear experience': the content was somewhat intense and specific; 'clear experience': fully intense and specific content). Therefore, the experiments that aim to uncover the neural correlates of the conscious experiences labelled by different PAS scores are informative with regard to the correspondence relations proposed above between the perceived qualities of subjective intensity, subjective specificity and subjective stability, and the neural features intensity, precision and maintenance.

In an fMRI-based study of processing masked stimuli, Christensen and colleagues, using a 3-point scale (clear experience, vague glimpse-like experience, no experience) investigated the neural activity correlating with different quality conscious experiences (Christensen et al., 2006). Their results showed that the increase in the quality of experiences correlated with an increase in the intensity of the neural activity pattern throughout several regions of the brain that are usually implicated as the neural substrate of the Global Workspace (Dehaene & Naccache, 2001): a significantly higher level of brain activity was detected when clear experiences were reported than in the case of vague experiences (both in a direct comparison and in comparisons to no experiences).

More recent studies further confirm the link between the intensity of the neural activity and the quality of the conscious experience. Moreover, they improve the accuracy of the localisation of the neural activity relevant for the content of a conscious percept both in time and in space. For instance, Andersen and colleagues have managed to decode the different degrees of the quality of experiences of simple geometrical figures reported by subjects using the PAS scale from MEG signals from the occipital lobe within the Visual Awareness Negativity (VAN) time window using multivariate classification algorithms (Andersen, Pedesen, Sandberg, & Overgaard, 2016). Findings of other groups have provided further support for the specific link between the strength of neural signals and the PAS-measured quality of corresponding experiences and also for the claim that the VAN activity reflects graded visual phenomenal awareness (Fu et al., 2017; Tagliabue, Mazzi, Bagattini, & Savazzi, 2016).

Quality of experiences during working memory tasks

The proposed correspondence relation between the quality of experience and the features of the underlying neural code – especially the link between the specificity of a conscious experience and the precision of the associated neural population code – is further supported by recent studies on working memory.

In an attempt to explore the features of the neural representations that underlie the information maintained in working memory during a delay period, Ester and colleagues recorded fMRI signals from areas V1 and V2 of subjects who were asked to report the orientation of a square-wave grating by turning a probe grating after a 12-second delay interval (Ester, Anderson, Serences, & Awh, 2013). Relying on a forward encoding model of orientation selectivity (Brouwer & Heeger, 2009, 2011), a set of orientation selective response functions – tuning profiles – were generated. These tuning profiles represented the intensity of the activity of orientation-sensitive neural populations as a function of orientation, and they peaked around the orientation stored in working memory. According to the main finding, the mean recall error of the participants, i.e. the difference between the orientation reported and the orientation of the stimulus, correlated well with the precision (but not with the intensity) of the tuning profiles. That is, less precise neural representations were associated with greater mean recall error, while more precise neural representations predicted smaller mean recall error (Ester et al., 2013; D'Esposito & Postle, 2015), establishing a link between the precision of the neural representation underlying information maintenance in working memory and the specificity of the mental representation of the content of working memory that is assumed to support the recall performance (Postle, 2015).

As keeping a target orientation in mind is standardly conceived of as a conscious effort and many consider working memory representations to be conscious (Dehaene, Changeux, Naccache, Sackur, & Sergent, 2006; Dehaene & Naccache, 2001), the specificity of the mental representations of the content of working memory can be seen as the subjective specificity of the accompanying conscious experience. Given this interpretation, the findings of Ester and colleagues provide support for the hypothetical correspondence relation between the precision of neural representations and subjective specificity. Note however that whether the content of working memory is conscious is actively debated in contemporary literature (see e.g. Jacobs & Silvanto, 2015; Persuh, LaRock, &

Berger, 2018; for work specifically on unconscious working memory representations, see e.g. Bergström & Eriksson, 2018; King, Pescetelli, & Dehaene, 2016).

Quality of experiences in mental imagery

Even if there is no direct information about the conscious experiences accompanying actively storing items during the working memory tasks discussed above, there is another tightly linked strand of research that can provide the relevant kind of information. As recent studies show, mental imagery and visual working memory share common representations in early visual areas, and it has even been claimed that mental imagery is the dynamic component of visual working memory (Albers, Kok, Toni, Dijkerman, & de Lange, 2013; Tong, 2013).

In the context of studying mental imagery, the quality of conscious experiences, called 'vividness' in the mental imagery literature (see Fazekas et al., forthcoming), is often directly evaluated. Different approaches to study the vividness of mental imagery – from questionnaire-based methods measuring mental imagery vividness at the trait level (i.e. how vivid someone's mental imagery usually is) to different methods to assess mental imagery vividness at the level of trial-by-trial variations (i.e. how vivid a particular mental imagery experience is) – found converging evidence of a strong correlation between the level (intensity) of brain activity in relevant content-specific regions and the vividness of the conscious experience that accompany mental imagery tasks.

For instance, in visualisation tasks using the Vividness of Visual Imagery Questionnaire (Marks, 1973), in which subjects had to rate (on a 5-point scale where 5 is 'no image at all' and 1 is 'perfectly clear and as vivid as normal vision') how vivid their visual imagery usually was, higher activity in the visual cortex was found during mental imagery in individuals who reported more vivid imagery. More precisely, the reported vividness of mental imagery correlated with the average of the relative visual cortex signal measured by fMRI (Amedi, Malach, & Pascual-Leone, 2005; Cui, Jeter, Yang, Montague, & Eagleman, 2007).

At the level of trial-by-trial variations, binocular rivalry studies showed that the vividness of mental imagery correlated with the strength of the priming effect of mental imagery on the dominant stimulus in a succeeding binocular rivalry presentation (Bergmann, Genç, Kohler, Singer, & Pearson, 2016; Pearson, Rademaker, & Tong, 2011; Rademaker & Pearson, 2012). As this strength of the priming effect can be seen as an indicator of the quality (intensity, precision, maintenance) of the neural code underlying the imagined content (James, Humphrey, Gati, Menon, & Goodale, 2000; Pearson & Brascamp, 2008; Pearson, Clifford, & Tong, 2008; Wiggs & Martin, 1998), it offers support for the hypothetical correspondence relations between phenomenal characteristics and neural features.

Even more direct support can be found in experimental paradigms investigating the moment-to-moment changes in experienced vividness. For instance, when subjects were asked to rate the vividness of their mental imagery (on a

4-point scale: 1 – not vivid at all; 4 – very vivid) after each trial of an imagery task, experimenters found that the moment-to-moment variations in the
vividness of visual imagery correlated with changes in the intensity of the simultaneously recorded fMRI signal in a series of posterior brain regions. More
concretely, correlations were found between the vividness of imagery and the
intensity of brain activity in early visual cortex, the precuneus, the right parietal
cortex and the medial frontal cortex (Dijkstra, Bosch, & van Gerven, 2017).
Similar positive correlations were reported between imagery vividness (judged
image by image) and the level of activity in the precuneus, the posterior cingulate and higher order visual association cortex (Fulford et al., 2017).

Alternative interpretations and future directions

The findings reviewed so far support the correspondence relations proposed between the subjective intensity and subjective specificity of conscious experiences
and the intensity and precision of the underlying neural representations, and
also demonstrate that – with gradual changes in these qualities of experiences –
consciousness does, indeed, come in degrees. In this section, we will review our
previous suggestions regarding how relying on these correspondence relations
might shed new light on what is known about conscious experiences occurring in mind wandering (Fazekas et al., forthcoming) and dreaming (Fazekas,
Nemeth, & Overgaard, 2019).

Quality of experiences in mind wandering

While in the course of mental imagery tasks subjects intentionally construct
a mental image, during mind wandering conscious experiences occur spontaneously, relatively unconstrained by automatic mechanisms and deliberation
(Christoff, Irving, Fox, Spreng, & Andrews-Hanna, 2016). The generation of
the contents of mind wandering is neither determined top-down by cognitive
control mechanisms nor is driven by stimulus salience in a bottom-up manner.
It is rather under the influence of a part of the so-called default mode network,
which shows increased activity during tasks when externally oriented cognitive
efforts are not required (Raichle, 2015; Raichle et al., 2001). According to a
recent proposal, a subsystem of the default mode network, which includes the
hippocampal formation, parahippocampal cortex, retrosplenial cortex, ventral
medial prefrontal cortex and the posterior inferior parietal lobule, is responsible
for the variability in the content of mind wandering (Christoff et al., 2016).

Although the most characteristic type of content in mind wandering is
thought-like (Perogamvros et al., 2017), still a significant proportion of spontaneous mental activity unfolds in the form of mental images (Andrews-Hanna
et al., 2013; Chou et al., 2017; Delamillieure et al., 2010). Even if the primary
sensory areas are characteristically decoupled from the default more network during mind wandering (Schooler et al., 2011), higher order sensory association areas

are highly active subserving the occurrence of perception-like content elements (Andrews-Hanna, Irving, Fox, Spreng, & Christoff, 2018; Fox, Nijeboer, Solomonova, Domhoff, & Christoff, 2013; Fox, Spreng, Ellamil, Andrews-Hanna, & Christoff, 2015).

This overlap between the probable neural substrate of perception-like content elements in mind wandering and in other forms of online and offline conscious experiences, as we have recently proposed (Fazekas et al., forthcoming), allows us to reevaluate the standard interpretation of a now classical study regarding mind wandering.

In a groundbreaking experiment, Mason and colleagues found that the self-reported frequency of mind wandering positively correlated with greater activity in regions, including the medial prefrontal cortex, the anterior cingulate, the posterior cingulate, the precuneus, the left angular gyrus, the insula and areas in the superior and middle temporal gyri (Mason et al., 2007; for a recent confirmation by a meta-analytic review, see Fox et al., 2015). Mason and colleagues contrasted the fMRI-measured brain activity in conditions which did and did not support the frequent occurrence of episodes of mind wandering (practised working memory task requiring little cognitive effort versus novel tasks requiring more cognitive effort), and compared the results with a questionnaire-based score (Singer & Antrobus, 1972) of the subjects' general mind wandering proclivity. According to the original interpretation, the increased neural activity in these areas track with the subjects' mind wandering frequency, i.e. with how often subjects find themselves being engaged in mind wandering (Mason et al., 2007).

However, the brain areas implicated in these experiments include regions, the activity of which have been associated with imagery vividness – and thus with the quality of the conscious experience – in mental imagery studies (Dijkstra et al., 2017; Fulford et al., 2017; see section **'Quality of experiences in mental imagery'**). On the basis of this, we have proposed that the elevated activity in these regions during mind wandering might not be directly linked to the high frequency of the occurrence of mind wandering, but rather reflects the more intense vividness of the content of mind wandering. That is, the minds of those subjects who, on the basis of questionnaire-based self-reports, appear to have low mind wandering proclivity might still wander just as often as those who report high frequency mind wandering. The difference, instead of how often episodes of mind wandering occur, might be in the subjective intensity of the associated conscious experiences.

Mason and colleagues already acknowledge that the questionnaire-based measure of the frequency of mind wandering might assess subjects' meta-awareness regarding their mind wandering episodes rather than their propensity to engage in such episodes. The picture suggested by our interpretation is compatible with this view: more vivid, more intense experiences are more salient, capture attention to a greater extent and therefore elicit a higher level of meta-awareness, and thus ultimately are easier to remember. We think that this interpretation is more in agreement with the general idea that mind wandering is a psychological base-line emerging when the brain is otherwise unoccupied (Mason et al., 2007). The original interpretation of the findings suggested that it happens less often is some cases (when self-reported frequency is low). According to our interpretation, the mind does return into this baseline state automatically – it is only that in the case of certain individuals the intensity of the accompanying experiences are usually lower, which results in less robust memories about these states that are then re-flected in their negative answers to retrospective questionnaires.

Investigating the activity of content-specific areas during individual episodes of mind wandering might be able to provide more information with regard to the viability of the interpretation proposed above. Although this kind of study is not in the focus of current research on mind wandering, relevant data have been provided by recent work on dreaming.

Quality of experiences in dreaming

Although bottom-up, perception-like views (Antrobus, 1991; Hobson, Pace-Schott, & Stickgold, 2000) had significant influence on how to think about dream experiences, top-down approaches have recently become increasingly popular and started to dominate the field (Domhoff, 2011, 2018; Domhoff & Fox, 2015; Foulkes, 1990, 1999; Foulkes & Domhoff, 2014; Fox et al., 2013). Supported by various lines of evidence, these top-down approaches see an inher-ent connection between dreaming, mind wandering and mental imagery (Dom-hoff, 2018; Nir & Tononi, 2010).

For instance, it has been found that a significant number of the core nodes of the default mode network are also active and functionally connected during REM sleep. The level of activity detected in the medial prefrontal cortex, the hippocampus, the parahippocampus, the entorhinal cortex and temporo-parietal junction was even more elevated in REM sleep than in mind wandering (Fox et al., 2013, 2015). Increased activity and stable connectivity of key default mode network areas have been demonstrated at sleep onset and in NREM 2 sleep as well.

Similarly, it is well documented that damage in or near the temporo-parieto-occipital junction that results in a cessation of dreaming (Murri, Massetani, Si-ciliano, Giovanditti, & Arena, 1985; Solms, 2000) also leads to problems with mental imagery in wakefulness (Kerr & Foulkes, 1981; Kosslyn, 1994; Kosslyn, Ganis, & Thompson, 2001). Furthermore, the ability of dream recall correlates with the ontogenesis of mental imagery and visual-spatial skills (Casey, Tot-tenham, Liston, & Durston, 2005; Piaget & Barbel, 1966), and dream recall frequency correlates with a greater capacity for visualisation in wakefulness (His-cock & Cohen, 1973; Okada, Matsuoka, & Hatakeyama, 2000; Watson, 2003).

Given all these findings, it is not surprising that connections between dream-ing and mental imagery have been uncovered explicitly with respect to the qual-ity of the conscious experiences subjects undergo during these states as well. For instance, mental imagery vividness has been associated with the quality of dream experiences (Watson, 2003).

Interesting findings with regard to the visual qualities of dream experiences come from a classical strand of studies that developed different varieties of visual scales based on variations of a single photograph, where each variation was reduced along one or more dimensions like brightness, contrast, colour saturation, figure clarity, background clarity, overall hue etc. (Antrobus, Hartwig, Rosa, Reinsel, & Fein, 1987; Antrobus, Kondo, Reinsel, & Fein, 1995; Antrobus & Wamsley, 2009; Fosse, 2000; Kerr, 1993; Rechtschaffen & Buchignani, 1983, 1992). Subjects had to find that element of a set of manipulated photographs that best matched the appearance of a preceding dream experience. It was found that REM dreams, in general, were more intense (higher brightness and contrast) and more specific (higher clarity) than NREM mentations (Antrobus, 1991; Kerr, 1993; Rechtschaffen & Buchignani, 1992). Additionally, better quality dream experiences were reported from phasic than from tonic periods of REM sleep (Foulkes & Pope, 1973; Kahn, Pace-Schott, & Hobson, 1997; Molinari & Foulkes, 1969; Pivik, 1991; Rechtschaffen & Buchignani, 1992). Importantly, from our present perspective, it has also been implicated that enhanced quality dream experiences were underlain by increased neural activity (Antrobus, Kondo, & Reinsel, 1995; Nielsen, 2017; Rechtschaffen & Buchignani, 1992).

Utilising the connection between the subjective intensity of experiences and the intensity of the underlying neural representations, we have recently amended this picture by arguing that not just dream experiences from different stages of sleep, but individual dream experiences reported from the same state (REM or NREM sleep; phasic or tonic period) differ in quality as well (Fazekas et al., 2019). We relied on a recent study that by utilising hd-EEG and a serial awakening paradigm, provided both content and neural activity-specific data with high spatial resolution for the first time (Siclari et al., 2017). Although the study did not directly evaluate the vividness of reported dreams, it did investigate the EEG signal comparing cases where subjects (i) could report the content of their dreams (contentful dreams), (ii) were sure that they had a dream experience but couldn't specify any content (white dreams) and (iii) denied having any pre-awakening experience (no dream experience). Proposing an alternative interpretation of the original findings, we argued that in the case of white dreams (compared to no dream experiences) the high-frequency component of the EEG signal showed a local increase over posterior content-specific regions (similar to the ones implicated in the mental imagery studies of Dijkstra et al., 2017; Fulford et al., 2017, see above), which was smaller than the local increase that was found in the case of contentful dreams (Fazekas et al., 2019). Since it is known that higher intensity population codes can be inferred from local increases in the high-frequency component of EEG signals (Le Van Quyen et al., 2010; Masuda & Doiron, 2007; Panzeri, Macke, Gross, & Kayser, 2015), we concluded that the intensity of the neural codes encoding experienced dream content during white dreams was lower than during contentful dreams. This, given the link between subjective intensity and the intensity of the underlying neural activity then means that dream experiences during white dreams are less intense than during contentful dreams. Finally, the fact that both white and contentful dreams are reported from the same sleep stages (Siclari et al., 2017; Siclari, LaRocque, Postle, & Tononi, 2013) indicates that the subjective intensity of dreams fluctuates, i.e. changes on (at least) a dream-by-dream basis – similar to how mental imagery vividness and probably the subjective intensity of the content of mind wandering change on a trial-by-trial basis (see sections **'Quality of experiences in mental imagery'** and **'Quality of experiences in mind wandering'**, respectively).

Conclusion

We have proposed correspondence relations between features of conscious experiences like their intensity, specificity and stability, and the intensity, precision and maintenance of the underlying neural representations. Accumulating evidence from wakeful perception, working memory tasks, mental imagery, mind wandering and dreaming support these correspondence relations and demonstrate that conscious experiences can come in degrees along the different dimensions defined by these characteristics of the quality of experiences. Beyond directly supporting the gradual view of consciousness, the framework presented here establishes links between the neural and the subjective level which are tighter than mere correlational claims.

The findings reviewed suggest that the subjective intensity and the subjective specificity of conscious experiences change together with the intensity and precision of the neural representations that are formed in posterior, content-specific regions of the brain. Note however that this issue is independent of the question whether the seat of consciousness is in the back or in the front of the brain (Boly et al., 2017; Koch, Massimini, Boly, & Tononi, 2016; Odegaard, Knight, & Lau, 2017; Storm et al., 2017), and also of the related question whether local recurrence (Block, 2011; Lamme, 2006) or global availability (Dehaene et al., 2006; Dehaene & Naccache, 2001) or some higher-order state (Lau & Rosenthal, 2011) is responsible for the occurrence of conscious experience (see Fazekas & Nemeth, 2018). No matter what processes make the contents encoded in these posterior regions conscious, gradual changes in the content of consciousness renders the experiences themselves gradual – very similar to how a gradual degradation of the symbols utilised to create a map results in less and less map-like objects (cf. Bayne, Hohwy, & Owen, 2016b).

References

Albers, A. M., Kok, P., Toni, I., Dijkerman, H. C., & de Lange, F. P. (2013). Shared representations for working memory and mental imagery in early visual cortex. *Current Biology, 23*, 1427–1431.

Amedi, A., Malach, R., & Pascual-Leone, A. (2005). Negative BOLD differentiates visual imagery and perception. *Neuron, 48*(5), 859–872.

Andersen, L. M., Pedesen, M., Sandberg, K., & Overgaard, M. (2016). Occipital MEG activity in the early time range (<300 ms) predicts graded changes in perceptual consciousness. *Cerebral Cortex, 26*, 2677–2688.

Andrews-Hanna, J., Irving, Z. C., Fox, K. C. R., Spreng, R. N., & Christoff, K. (2018). The neuroscience of spontaneous thought: An evolving, interdisciplinary field. In K. C. R. Fox & K. Christoff (Eds.), *The Oxford Handbook of Spontaneous Thought*. New York: Oxford University Press.

Andrews-Hanna, J., Kaiser, R., Turner, A., Reineberg, A., Godinez, D., Dimidjian, S., & Banich, M. (2013). A penny for your thoughts: Dimensions of self-generated thought content and relationships with individual differences in emotional wellbeing. *Frontiers in Psychology, 4*, 900.

Antrobus, J. (1991). Dreaming: Cognitive processes during cortical activation and high afferent thresholds. *Psychological Review, 98*(1), 96–121.

Antrobus, J., Hartwig, P., Rosa, D., Reinsel, R., & Fein, G. (1987). Brightness and clarity of REM and NREM imagery: Photo response scale. *Sleep Research, 16*, 240.

Antrobus, J., Kondo, T., & Reinsel, R. (1995). Dreamin in the late morning: Summation of REM and diurnial cortical activation. *Consciousness and Cognition, 4*, 275–299.

Antrobus, J., Kondo, T., Reinsel, R., & Fein, G. (1995). Dreaming in the late morning: Summation of REM and diurnial cortical activation. *Consciousness and Cognition, 4*, 275–299.

Antrobus, J., & Wamsley, E. J. (2009). Sleep mentation in REM and NREM: A neurocognitive perspective. In L. R. Squire (Ed.), *Encyclopedia of Neuroscience* (pp. 1021–1026).Cambridge, MA: Academic Press.

Asplund, C. L., Fougnie, D., Zughni, S., Martin, J. W., & Marois, R. (2014). The attentional blink reveals the probabilistic nature of discrete conscious perception. *Psychological Science, 25*(3), 824–831.

Bayne, T., Hohwy, J., & Owen, A. (2016a). Are there levels of consciousness? *Trends in Cognitive Sciences, 20*, 405–413.

Bayne, T., Hohwy, J., & Owen, A. (2016b). Response to Fazekas and Overgaard: Degrees and levels. *Trends in Cognitive Sciences, 20*(10), 716–717.

Bechtel, W., & McCauley, R. (1999). Heuristic identity theory (or back to the future): The mind-body problem against the background of research strategies in cognitive neuroscience. In M. Hahn & S. C. Stones (Eds.), *Proceedings of the Twenty-First Meeting of the Cognitive Science Society* (pp. 67–72). Mahwah, NJ: Erlbaum.

Bergmann, J., Genç, E., Kohler, A., Singer, W., & Pearson, J. (2016). Smaller primary visual cortex is associated with stronger, but less precise mental imagery. *Cerebral Cortex, 26*(9), 3838–3850.

Bergström, F., & Eriksson, J. (2018). Neural evidence for non-conscious working memory. *Cerebral Cortex, 28*(9), 3217–3228.

Block, N. (2011). Perceptual consciousness overflows cognitive access. *Trends in Cognitive Sciences, 15*(12), 567–575.

Boly, M., Massimini, M., Tsuchiya, N., Postle, B., Koch, C., & Tononi, G. (2017). Are the neural correlates of consciousness in the front or in the back of the cerebral cortex? Clinical and neuroimaging evidence. *The Journal of Neuroscience, 37*(40), 9603–9613.

Brouwer, G. J., & Heeger, D. J. (2009). Decoding and reconstructing color from responses in human visual cortex. *Journal of Neuroscience, 29*, 13992–14003.

Brouwer, G. J., & Heeger, D. J. (2011). Cross-orientation suppression in human visual cortex. *Journal of Neurophysiology, 106*, 2108–2119.

Carrasco, M. (2011). Visual attention: The past 25 years. *Vision Research, 51*, 1484–1525.

Carrasco, M., Ling, S., & Read, S. (2004). Attention alters appearance. *Nature Neuroscience, 7*(3), 308–313.

Casey, B. J., Tottenham, N., Liston, C., & Durston, S. (2005). Imaging the developing brain: What have we learned about cognitive development? *Trends in Cognitive Sciences, 9*(3), 104–110.

Chou, Y.-h., Sundman, M., Whitson, H. E., Gaur, P., Chu, M.-L., Weingarten, C. P., … Chen, N.-k. (2017). Maintenance and representation of mind wandering during resting-state fMRI. *Scientific Reports, 7*, 40722.

Christensen, M. S., Ramsøy, T. Z., Lund, T. E., Madsen, K. H., & Rowe, J. B. (2006). An fMRI study of the neural correlates of graded visual perception. *NeuroImage, 31*(4), 1711–1725.

Christoff, K., Irving, Z. C., Fox, K. C. R., Spreng, R. N., & Andrews-Hanna, J. R. (2016). Mind-wandering as spontaneous thought: A dynamic framework. *Nature Reviews Neuroscience, 17*, 718–731.

Cui, X., Jeter, C. B., Yang, D., Montague, P. R., & Eagleman, D. M. (2007). Vividness of mental imagery: Individual variability can be measured objectively. *Vision Research, 47*(4), 474–478.

D'Esposito, M., & Postle, B. (2015). The cognitive neuroscience of working memory. *Annual Review of Psychology, 66*, 115–142.

Dehaene, S., Changeux, J., Naccache, L., Sackur, J., & Sergent, C. (2006). Conscious, preconscious, and subliminal processing: A testable taxonomy. *Trends in Cognitive Sciences, 10*(5), 204–211.

Dehaene, S., & Naccache, L. (2001). Towards a cognitive neuroscience of consciousness: Basic evidence and a workspace framework. *Cognition, 79*(1–2), 1–37.

Delamillieure, P., Doucet, G., Mazoyer, B., Turbelin, M.-R., Delcroix, N., Mellet, E., … Joliot, M. (2010). The resting state questionnaire: An introspective questionnaire for evaluation of inner experience during the conscious resting state. *Brain Research Bulletin, 81*(6), 565–573.

Dijkstra, N., Bosch, S. E., & van Gerven, M. A. J. (2017). Vividness of visual imagery depends on the neural overlap with perception in visual areas. *The Journal of Neuroscience, 37*(5), 1367–1373.

Domhoff, G. W. (2011). The neural substrate for dreaming: Is it a subsystem of the default network? *Consciousness and Cognition, 20*(4), 1163–1174.

Domhoff, G. W. (2018). *The Emergence of Dreaming: Mind-Wandering, Embodied Simulation, and the Default Network*. New York: Oxford University Press.

Domhoff, G. W., & Fox, K. C. R. (2015). Dreaming and the default network: A review, synthesis, and counterintuitive research proposal. *Consciousness and Cognition, 33*, 342–353.

Ester, E. F., Anderson, D. E., Serences, J. T., & Awh, E. (2013). A neural measure of precision in visual working memory. *Journal of Cognitive Neuroscience, 25*(5), 754–761.

Fazekas, P. (2009). Reconsidering the role of bridge laws in inter-theoretical reductions. *Erkenntnis, 71*(3), 303–322.

Fazekas, P., & Kertesz, G. (2011). Causation at different levels: tracking the commitments of mechanistic explanations. *Biology & Philosophy, 26*, 365–383.

Fazekas, P., & Nanay, B. (2018). Attention is amplification, not selection. *British Journal for the Philosophy of Science*, in press. https://academic.oup.com/bjps/advance-article/doi/10.1093/bjps/axy065/5112967.

Fazekas, P., & Nemeth, G. (2018). Dream experiences and the neural correlates of perceptual consciousness and cognitive access. *Philosophical Transactions of the Royal Society B: Biological Sciences, 373*, 20170356.

Fazekas, P., Nemeth, G., & Overgaard, M. (2019). White dreams are made of colours: What studying contentless dreams can teach about the neural basis of dreaming and conscious experiences. *Sleep Medicine Reviews, 43*, 84–91.

Fazekas, P., Nemeth, G., & Overgaard, M. (forthcoming). Perceptual representations and the vividness of stimulus-triggered and stimulus-independent experiences. *Perspectives on Psychological Science.*

Fazekas, P., & Overgaard, M. (2016). Multidimensional models of degrees and levels of consciousness. *Trends in Cognitive Sciences, 20*(10), 715–716.

Fazekas, P., & Overgaard, M. (2018a). A multi-factor account of degrees of awareness. *Cognitive Science, 42*(6), 1833–1859.

Fazekas, P., & Overgaard, M. (2018b). Multiple factors and multiple mechanisms determine the quality of conscious experiences: A reply to Anzulewicz and Wierzchoń. *Cognitive Science, 42*(6), 2101–2103.

Fosse, R. (2000). REM mentation in narcoleptics and normals: An empirical test of two neurocognitive theories. *Consciousness and Cognition, 9*(4), 488–509.

Foulkes, D. (1990). Dreaming and consciousness. *European Journal of Cognitive Psychology, 2,* 39–55.

Foulkes, D. (1999). *Children's Dreaming and the Development of Consciousnes.* Cambridge, MA: Harvard University Press.

Foulkes, D., & Domhoff, G. W. (2014). Bottom-up or top-down in dream neuroscience? A top-down critique of two bottom-up studies. *Consciousness and Cognition, 27,* 168–171.

Foulkes, D., & Pope, R. (1973). Primary visual experience and secondary cognitive elaboration: A modest confirmation and an extension. *Perceptual and Motor Skills, 37,* 107–118.

Fox, K. C. R., Nijeboer, S., Solomonova, E., Domhoff, G. W., & Christoff, K. (2013). Dreaming as mind wandering: Evidence from functional neuroimaging and first-person content reports. *Frontiers in Human Neuroscience, 7,* 412.

Fox, K. C. R., Spreng, R. N., Ellamil, M., Andrews-Hanna, J. R., & Christoff, K. (2015). The wandering brain: Meta-analysis of functional neuroimaging studies of mind-wandering and related spontaneous thought processes. *NeuroImage, 111,* 611–621.

Fu, Q., Liu, Y.-J., Dienes, Z., Wu, J., Chen, W., & Fu, X. (2017). Neural correlates of subjective awareness for natural scene categorization of color photographs and line-drawings. *Frontiers in Psychology, 8,* 210.

Fulford, J., Milton, F., Salas, D., Smith, A., Simler, A., Winlove, C., & Zeman, A. (2017). The neural correlates of visual imagery vividness – An fMRI study and literature review. *Cortex 105,* 26–40.

Fuller, S., & Carrasco, M. (2006). Exogenous attention and color perception: Performance and appearance of saturation and hue. *Vision Research, 46*(23), 4032–4047.

Hiscock, M., & Cohen, D. B. (1973). Visual imagery and dream recall. *Journal of Research in Personality, 7,* 179–188.

Hobson, A., Pace-Schott, E. F., & Stickgold, R. (2000). Dreaming and the brain: Toward a cognitive neuroscience of conscious states. *Behavioral and Brain Sciences, 23*(6), 793–842.

James, T. W., Humphrey, G. K., Gati, J. S., Menon, R. S., & Goodale, M. A. (2000). The effects of visual object priming on brain activation before and after recognition. *Current Biology, 10*(17), 1017–1024.

Kahn, D., Pace-Schott, E. F., & Hobson, A. (1997). Consciousness in waking and dreaming: The roles of neuronal oscillation and neuromodulation in determining similarities and differences. *Neuroscience, 78*(1), 13–38.

Kerr, N. (1993). Mental imagery, dreams and perception. In C. Cavallero & D. Foulkes (Eds.), *Dreaming as Cognition* (pp. 18–37). New York, NY: Harvester Wheatsheaf.

Kerr, N., & Foulkes, D. (1981). Right hemispheric mediation of dream visualization: A case study. *Cortex, 17*(4), 603–609.

King, J.-R., Pescetelli, N., & Dehaene, S. (2016). Brain mechanisms underlying the brief maintenance of seen and unseen sensory information. *Neuron, 92*(5), 1122–1134. doi:10.1016/j.neuron.2016.10.051.

Koch, C., Massimini, M., Boly, M., & Tononi, G. (2016). Neural correlates of consciousness: Progress and problems. *Nature Reviews Neuroscience, 17*, 307.

Kosslyn, S. (1994). *Image and Brain*. Cambridge: MIT Press.

Kosslyn, S., Ganis, G., & Thompson, W. L. (2001). Neural foundations of imagery. *Nature Reviews Neuroscience, 2*(9), 635–642.

Lamme, V. A. F. (2006). Towards a true neural stance on consciousness. *Trends in Cognitive Sciences, 10*(11), 494–501.

Lau, H., & Rosenthal, D. (2011). Empirical support for higher-order theories of conscious awareness. *Trends in Cognitive Sciences, 15*(8), 365–373.

Laureys, S. (2005). The neural correlate of (un)awareness: Lessons from the vegetative state. *Trends in Cognitive Sciences, 9*(12), 556–559.

Lavie, N. (2006). The role of perceptual load in visual awareness. *Brain Research, 1080*(1), 91–100.

Lavie, N., Beck, D. M., & Konstantinou, N. (2014). Blinded by the load: Attention, awareness and the role of perceptual load. *Philosophical Transactions of the Royal Society B: Biological Sciences, 369*(1641), 20130205.

Le Van Quyen, M., Staba, R., Bragin, A., Dickson, C., Valderrama, M., Fried, I., & Engel, J. (2010). Large-scale microelectrode recordings of high-frequency gamma oscillations in human cortex during sleep. *The Journal of Neuroscience, 30*(23), 7770.

Marks, D. F. (1973). Visual imagery differences in the recall of pictures. *British Journal of Psychology, 1*, 17–24.

Martinez-Trujillo, J. C., & Treue, S. (2004). Feature-based attention increases the selectivity of population responses in primate visual cortex. *Current Biology, 14*(9), 744–751.

Mason, M. F., Norton, M. I., Van Horn, J. D., Wegner, D. M., Grafton, S. T., & Macrae, C. N. (2007). Wandering minds: The default network and stimulus-independent thought. *Science, 315*, 393–395.

Masuda, N., & Doiron, B. (2007). Gamma oscillations of spiking neural populations enhance signal discrimination. *PLoS Computational Biology, 3*(11), 2348–2355.

Maunsell, J. H. R., & Treue, S. (2006). Feature-based attention in visual cortex. *Trends in Neurosciences, 29*(6), 317–322.

McCauley, R., & Bechtel, W. (2001). Explanatory pluralism and heuristic identity theory. *Theory & Psychology, 11*(6), 736–760.

Molinari, S., & Foulkes, D. (1969). Tonic and phasic events during sleep: Psychological correlates and implications. *Perceptual and Motor Skills, 29*(2), 343–368.

Murri, L., Massetani, R., Siciliano, G., Giovanditti, L., & Arena, R. (1985). Dream recall after sleep interruption in brain-injured patients. *Sleep, 8*(4), 356–362.

Nemeth, G., & Fazekas, P. (2018). Beyond the REM-NREM dichotomy: A multidimensional approach to understanding dreaming. *Journal of Consciousness Studies, 25*(11–12), 13–33.

Nielsen, T. (2017). Microdream neurophenomenology. *Neuroscience of Consciousness, 2017*(1), nix001.

Nir, Y., & Tononi, G. (2010). Dreaming and the brain: From phenomenology to neurophysiology. *Trends in Cognitive Sciences, 14*(2), 88–100.

Odegaard, B., Knight, R., & Lau, H. (2017). Should a few null findings falsify prefrontal theories of conscious perception? *The Journal of Neuroscience, 37*(40), 9593–9602.

Okada, H., Matsuoka, K., & Hatakeyama, T. (2000). Dream-recall frequency and waking imagery. *Perceptual and Motor Skills, 91*(3), 759–766.

Overgaard, M., Fehl, K., Mouridsen, K., Bergholt, B., & Cleeremans, A. (2008). Seeing without seeing? Degraded conscious vision in a blindsight patient. *PLoS ONE, 3*(8), e3028.

Overgaard, M., Feldbæk Nielsen, J., & Fuglsang-Frederiksen, A. (2004). A TMS study of the ventral projections from V1 with implications for the finding of neural correlates of consciousness. *Brain and Cognition, 54*(1), 58–64.

Overgaard, M., Rote, J., Mouridsen, K., & Ramsøy, T. Z. (2006). Is conscious perception gradual or dichotomous? A comparison of report methodologies during a visual task. *Consciousness and Cognition, 15*(4), 700–708.

Panzeri, S., Macke, J. H., Gross, J., & Kayser, C. (2015). Neural population coding: Combining insights from microscopic and mass signals. *Trends in Cognitive Sciences, 19*(3), 162–172.

Pearson, J., & Brascamp, J. (2008). Sensory memory for ambiguous vision. *Trends in Cognitive Sciences, 12*(9), 334–341.

Pearson, J., Clifford, C. W. G., & Tong, F. (2008). The functional impact of mental imagery on conscious perception. *Current Biology, 18*(13), 982–986.

Pearson, J., Rademaker, R. L., & Tong, F. (2011). Evaluating the mind's eye: The metacognition of visual imagery. *Psychological Science, 22*(12), 1535–1542.

Perogamvros, L., Baird, B., Seibold, M., Riedner, B., Boly, M., & Tononi, G. (2017). The phenomenal contents and neural correlates of spontaneous thoughts across wakefulness, NREM sleep, and REM sleep. *Journal of Cognitive Neuroscience, 29*(10), 1766–1777.

Piaget, J., & Bärbel, I. (1966). *Mental Imagery in the Child.* New York, NY: Routledge.

Pivik, R. T. (1991). Tonic states and phasic events in relation to sleep mentation. In S. J. Ellman & J. Antrobus (Eds.), *The Mind in Sleep: Psychology and Physiology* (pp. 214–247). New York: Wiley.

Postle, B. (2015). The cognitive neuroscience of visual short-term memory. *Current Opinion in Behavioral Sciences, 1*, 40–46.

Rademaker, R., & Pearson, J. (2012). Training visual imagery: Improvements of metacognition, but not imagery strength. *Frontiers in Psychology, 3*(224), 1–11.

Raichle, M. E. (2015). The brain's default mode network. *Annual Review of Neuroscience, 38*(1), 433–447.

Raichle, M. E., MacLeod, A. M., Snyder, A. Z., Powers, W. J., Gusnard, D. A., & Shulman, G. L. (2001). A default mode of brain function. *Proceedings of the National Academy of Sciences, 98*(2), 676.

Ramsøy, T., & Overgaard, M. (2004). Introspection and subliminal perception. *Phenomenology and the Cognitive Sciences, 3*(1), 1–23.

Rechtschaffen, A., & Buchignani, C. (1983). Visual dimensions and correlates of dream images. *Sleep Research, 12*, 189.

Rechtschaffen, A., & Buchignani, C. (1992). The visual appearance of dreams. In J. Antrobus & M. Bertini (Eds.), *The Neuropsychology of Sleep and Dreaming* (pp. 143–156). Hillside, NJ: Lawrence Erlbaum.

Sandberg, K., Bibby, B. M., Timmermans, B., Cleeremans, A., & Overgaard, M. (2011). Measuring consciousness: Task accuracy and awareness as sigmoid functions of stimulus duration. *Consciousness and Cognition, 20*(4), 1659–1675.

Sandberg, K., & Overgaard, M. (2015). Using the perceptual awareness scale (PAS). In M. Overgaard (Ed.), *Behavioural Methods in Consciousness Research* (pp. 181–196). Oxford: Oxford University Press.

Sandberg, K., Timmermans, B., Overgaard, M., & Cleeremans, A. (2010). Measuring consciousness: Is one measure better than the other? *Consciousness and Cognition, 19*(4), 1069–1078.

Schooler, J. W., Smallwood, J., Christoff, K., Handy, T. C., Reichle, E. D., & Sayette, M. A. (2011). Meta-awareness, perceptual decoupling and the wandering mind. *Trends in Cognitive Sciences, 15*(7), 319–326.

Seth, A. K. (2009). Explanatory correlates of consciousness: Theoretical and computational challenges. *Cognitive Computation, 1*(1), 50–63.

Seth, A. K. (2010). The grand challenge of consciousness. *Frontiers in Psychology, 1*(5), 1–2.

Siclari, F., Baird, B., Perogamvros, L., Bernardi, G., LaRocque, J. J., Riedner, B., … Tononi, G. (2017). The neural correlates of dreaming. *Nature Neuroscience, 24*(6), 171–878.

Siclari, F., LaRocque, J., Postle, B., & Tononi, G. (2013). Assessing sleep consciousness within subjects using a serial awakening paradigm. *Frontiers in Psychology, 4*(542), 1–9.

Singer, J., & Antrobus, J. (1972). Daydreaming, imaginal processes, and personality: A normative study. In P. Sheehan (Ed.), *The Function and Nature of Imagery* (pp. 175–202). New York: Academic Press.

Solms, M. (2000). Dreaming and REM sleep are controlled by different brain mechanisms. *Behavioral and Brain Sciences, 23*(6), 843–850.

Storm, J., Boly, M., Casali, A. G., Massimini, M., Olcese, U., Pennartz, C., & Wilke, M. (2017). Consciousness regained: Disentangling mechanisms, brain systems, and behavioral responses. *The Journal of Neuroscience, 37*(45), 10882–10893.

Tagliabue, C. F., Mazzi, C., Bagattini, C., & Savazzi, S. (2016). Early local activity in temporal areas reflects graded content of visual perception. *Frontiers in Psychology, 7*, 572.

Tong, F. (2013). Imagery and visual working memory: One and the same? *Trends in Cognitive Sciences, 17*(10), 489–490.

Watson, D. (2003). To dream, perchance to remember: Individual differences in dream recall. *Personality and Individual Differences, 34*(7), 1271–1286.

Watzl, S. (2017). *Structuring Mind: The Nature of Attention and How it Shapes Consciousness.* Oxford: Oxford University Press.

Wiggs, C. L., & Martin, A. (1998). Properties and mechanisms of perceptual priming. *Current Opinion in Neurobiology, 8*(2), 227–233.

Windey, B., Gevers, W., & Cleeremans, A. (2013). Subjective visibility depends on level of processing. *Cognition, 129*(2), 404–409.

4

CAN WE SEE WITHOUT KNOWING THAT WE SEE? CHALLENGES FOR TWO THEORIES OF CONSCIOUSNESS[1]

Victor A.F. Lamme

Introduction

Since the 1990s, behavioral science, neuroscience, biology, computational science, and philosophy have joined forces to unravel one of the greatest mysteries – that of consciousness. How is it possible that with 1.5 kg of mainly fat and protein enclosed in a bony shell we have conscious experiences? Considerable progress has been made since [1], but we are clearly not there yet. Several promising theories and ideas have emerged, which have been backed up with lots of experimental data. This has led to consensus on some aspects of how, when, and where brains do or do not produce consciousness. But strong controversy remains, in particular on what aspects of consciousness are the explanandum. Does the real mystery of consciousness lie in the fact that we experience the world that surrounds us, or in the ability to reflect on it and cognitively manipulate what we perceive; is consciousness about seeing or about knowing what we see? In the first part of this paper, I will review the current state of that debate, starting with a brief overview of what we know about visual processing. Then we delve into the question about where, when, and how the transition from unconscious to conscious visual processing occurs. It appears impossible to ascertain where this transition occurs, unless we resort to metaphysical arguments about the ontology of consciousness, and what exactly about consciousness we want to explain. However, clear conclusions emerge from such arguments, in that we either eliminate consciousness from our scientific taxonomy or adopt the position that consciousness is about seeing and not about knowing.

Note that the paper will focus almost entirely on visual consciousness. That is not because other sensory modalities of more executive faculties have no relevance. It is just a consequence of my ignorance on these other matters.

The intelligent reflex arc

There is little controversy on how visual processing proceeds. With every saccade – and we make about three per second – the eye lands on a new scene and the image is processed by the retina. In about 50 ms, this information has reached primary visual cortex, and from there on is distributed along a large number of other visual areas. Within 100–200 ms (depending on species and brain size), the whole brain is updated about the new image in front of us. During this rapid *feedforward sweep*, many features have been extracted from the image [2]. Neurons have detected shapes, colors, motion, or depth. Higher-level cells have signaled the presence of faces or animals [3] or other complex constellations that we are strongly familiar with (e.g. letters and words in humans [4]). We even have a rough idea about what the image is about: scene gist is extracted within that time frame as well [5]. You might say that almost everything there is to know about the image has been signaled by the powerful machinery of visual cortex and its many low- and high-level feature selective cells (Figure 4.1).

It doesn't end there. The feedforward sweep continues to proceed, now feeding into motor and frontal cortices. Here, visual information is transformed into execution – what can you do with what you see? If a ball is looming towards you, you instinctively dodge or catch it. The feats of such feedforward *sensorimotor transfer* are often quite remarkable. The eyes can saccade towards a visual stimulus within 120 ms [6], manual reaction times can be as short as 180 ms. Tennis players can return a ball serviced at 130 mph (world record is 163 mph), implying a reaction time of 400 ms, which includes deciding between forehand or backhand, doing a backswing and hitting the right way. You may have noticed yourself miraculously catching a glass of red wine that unexpectedly fell from a table directly on its way to cause a horrible stain on the white carpet beneath. Before you knew what happened, the glass was in your hands, saving the day.

The feedforward sweep is the brain at its best. It shows how it can function as a reflex arc, not very different from the simple sensorimotor transfer that occurs in the knee-jerk reflex. Infinitely more complex and intelligent, of course, but a reflex arc nonetheless, where sensory input is as swiftly as possible translated into motor output. Note that this even involves some forms of decision-making: which of the many objects in a natural scene do we react to? How do we respond? In such reflex-like responses, this strongly depends on the saliency or innate value of the external stimuli [6], but also internal variables (e.g. danger [7]) are taken into account. The feedforward sweep therefore is not a rigid process. What pathways are followed and how deep each of these is penetrated depends on temporal and focused attention, task sets, expectation, brain state, and many other factors [8–11].

Where does the magic happen?

From a behavioral or neuroscience point of view, this is all fairly straightforward. Of course some mysteries remain, among which the most prominent are how the

FEEDFORWARD SWEEP: UNCONSCIOUS

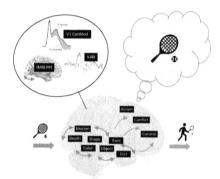

RECURRENT PROCESSING: P-CONSCIOUS

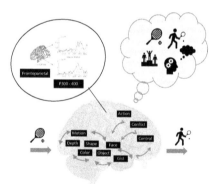

GLOBAL IGNITION: A-CONSCIOUS

FIGURE 4.1   Three successive stages of visual processing after stimulus presentation. *The feedforward sweep proceeds within 150–200 ms, during which low- and high-level features are extracted and translated into a (potential) motor output. This stage is unconscious.*

Recurrent processing starts within 100 ms after stimulus presentation, at first between low-level visual areas, and then more widespread between visual cortex. Neural correlates such as V1 contextual modulation, PPI, and VAN (see text) are shown. These recurrent interactions enable phenomenal (P–) consciousness of the visual stimulus: you SEE.

Eventually, recurrent interactions spread through the whole brain, causing 'global ignition'. At the neural level, this is expressed in P300 responses and the involvement of fronto-parietal areas. The result is access (A–) consciousness, the ability to cognitively manipulate the stimulus, your reaction to it, its consequences, etc.: you KNOW.From Lamme, V.A.F. (2018): Challenges for theories of consciousness: seeing or knowing, the missing ingredient and how to deal with panpsychism. Phil. Trans. R. Soc. B 373: 20170344. doi:10.1098/rstb.2017.0344.

brain detects objects for which there are no dedicated neurons, how it is possible to extract scene gist as fast as we can (the 'seeing the forest before the trees' problem), and how we select among the many motor plans that are activated by the multitude of stimuli in our surroundings. But when we take into consideration how we *experience* our brains doing this, an entirely different matter arises: that of consciousness. We are not mere automatons executing reflexes 'in the dark'. We see the ball that we hit during a tennis match, we feel the urgency when we grasp that glass. Somewhere along the way a conscious experience of what we see arises. Where, when, and how does that 'magic' happen? And why?

The short answer to the when and how is: after the fact. Feedforward processing itself is unconscious. The arguments for that have been laid out in many past reviews [12–15] showing considerable consensus on the matter. In short, when visual processing is artificially restricted to the feedforward sweep, it appears that features are extracted and that potential motor responses are activated, yet that people remain completely unconscious of these events or of the visual stimulus that has set them in motion. The most widely applied method for doing so has been backward masking – i.e. showing a visual stimulus very briefly and then have it followed by another stimulus, the mask. This typically renders the visual stimulus completely invisible [16]. However, information about it travels pretty much throughout the brain, activating visual [17], motor [18], and even prefrontal areas [19, 20]. The feedforward sweep, as intelligent as it may be, apparently does not suffice to give you a conscious sensation of the image that ignited it. So what is generating the conscious sensation that we automatically have when something hits our eyes?

What typically follows feedforward processing is recurrent or re-entrant processing. Via horizontal and feedback connections, neurons that initially responded to very different parts of the scene, or that had extracted different types of lower- or higher-level features, start to influence each other's activity patterns (Figure 4.1) [2, 21]. Neurons in primary visual cortex (V1) typically have small receptive fields that are selective for particular features – say the orientation of line segments within a scene. Because of their small receptive fields, the neurons will respond identically, regardless of these line segments belonging to either a background or a figure. That is, up to about 100 ms. After that, the neurons' responses start to diverge for figure and background, as if they suddenly start to care about the larger perceptual context of the line segments they are responding to [22]. Quite strikingly for neurons in as 'low' a visual area as V1, this 'contextual modulation' of neural responses typically follows the perceptual interpretation that subjects have of the scene [23–25]. That is possible because it is mediated by horizontal connections and feedback connections from higher-level areas [26], as lesions to these areas abolish the modulation [21, 27]. Modeling has shown how neurons first do their independent job of detecting features and objects in a hierarchical cascade of feedforward processing, and then start to influence each other's activity via intricate inhibitory and excitatory interactions mediated by horizontal and feedback connections [28]. What we observe at the single unit level as contextual modulation can be observed in humans using scalp recorded ERP potentials in response to similar stimuli [29, 30]. Latency is typically larger than in monkeys, more in the order of 200 ms, but the characteristics are very much the same.

Recurrent processing doesn't stop in visual cortex. The more activity advances towards frontal and motor regions, larger the network of recurrent interactions. The inclusion of motor-related activity (e.g. task relevance) may cause the visual activity to modulate accordingly [31]. Fronto-parietal activity may induce attention-related modulation of visual responses [32], which can reach back all the way to V1 [33]. Evaluation by medial prefrontal cortex will cause emotional valence to influence sensory activity [34] and so on. Thus, the network of recurrent interactions grows in size and complexity, making responses of neurons in this network more and more interdependent (Figure 4.1). With that, the neural signals also come at longer latencies than those of purely visual recurrent signals. Attentional modulation of V1 neurons may start at 150 ms or more in monkeys [33]. In humans, using EEG, we are dealing with latencies of up to 300–400 ms [15], for example, as expressed in P300 responses [35].

It is important to not let these interactions get out of hand; if everything is functionally connected to everything, all neurons will eventually do the same – which is known in pathology as epilepsy. Several mechanisms are in place for that. Recurrent modulation is selective: only when neurons are activated by the feedforward sweep can their activity be modulated by feedback [36]. This may be mediated by feedback connections primarily targeting NMDA receptors [37], whose ion channels only open when the membrane potential is already depolarized. In addition, feedback connections may specifically target inhibitory interneurons, given that they release excitatory neurotransmitters (glutamate) [38] yet primarily exert inhibitory effects on neural activity in distant regions [39].

Ample evidence emphasizes the importance of these recurrent interactions in conscious experience. They are abolished in anesthesia, while feedforward processing is not [40, 41]. Masking likewise selectively disrupts recurrent processing [17, 42, 43]. Dichoptic masking can render visual stimuli invisible for prolonged periods of time, which does not affect selective processing of faces in fusiform cortex (FFA) yet disrupts recurrent interactions between the FFA and early visual cortex, as shown with psychophysiological interaction (PPI) analysis of fMRI [44]. Transcranial Magnetic Stimulation (TMS) can target visual areas with high temporal precision, which has shown that conscious percepts typically depend on early activity in high-level areas and on *later* activity in lower-level ones, indicating that information has to be sent back along the visual hierarchy to become conscious [45]. Various manipulations of conscious perception consistently show to influence EEG activity in the 200 ms latency range – known as the Visual Awareness Negativity (VAN) – which is the typical latency of recurrent visual processing [46]. In monkeys trained to report conscious perception of texture defined figures, contextual modulation of V1 neurons was selectively absent, while feedforward signals were unaffected [47]. In sum, recurrent interactions between visual neurons, expressed as contextual modulation at the single neuron level or as 200 ms latency EEG signals (VAN) or PPI in humans, are crucial for the emergence of conscious experience.

Also the disruption of longer latency recurrent interactions causes a failure to report conscious percepts. For example, when people fail to attend to stimuli, they will report not having seen them, as is the case in conditions like change blindness, inattentional blindness, or the attentional blink. These manipulations typically leave early recurrent signals relatively intact, while selectively disrupting later recurrent signals (e.g. P300 or N400 EEG responses [48, 49], but see [50]).

While the importance of recurrent processing for visual consciousness is widely accepted, the main controversy lies in the question about what extent of recurrent processing is sufficient for conscious experience to arise. The two main positions and their respective arguments (briefly) are:

1 *Only when recurrent processing includes the fronto-parietal network do we experience the visual input.* At the basis of this line of reasoning is that for sensory information to become conscious it must become available to what is called the 'global (neuronal) workspace' (Global Ignition in Figure 4.1) [15, 51, 52]. This global availability enables the cognitive manipulation of that information (e.g. storage in working memory), conscious access to the information, and eventually also the ability to report about it [53]. Hence, when subjects report not to have seen visual (or other modality) stimuli – as happens in cases like change blindness, attentional blink, neglect, and so on – this is taken at face value: it is then considered unconscious [54]. The neural correlates of such global availability are the involvement of fronto-parietal activation and the later onset (P300) recurrent interactions [15]. Closely linked are theories that consider consciousness a higher order thought (HOT) [55], implying that a higher order representation of the visual experience must be present before it becomes conscious. A specific version of this idea is that consciousness requires (or is somehow linked to) metacognition, which can be briefly summarized as the 'knowing that you see' or 'the knowing that you know' [56, 57].

2 *Recurrent processing between visual areas suffices for conscious visual experience to arise.* The hallmark of conscious vision, it is argued, is the integration of visual features into a coherent single scene. Once this is achieved, all the necessary and sufficient requirements for conscious vision have been fulfilled [14]. Unconscious vision, however, is characterized by unbound visual features, detected by neurons in distributed areas [58]. The boundary between unconscious and conscious vision is therefore put at the transition between feedforward and recurrent processing (middle panel in Figure 4.1) [59]. Adding more widespread recurrent interactions – including fronto-parietal activation – may give you the ability to cognitively manipulate and report the conscious visual percept, but this is not explaining the unconscious/

conscious transition itself [60]. Conditions like change blindness, neglect, etc. are considered failures of attention and report, not of conscious vision [14, 61]. Experimental support comes primarily from findings showing that report, cognitive access, or attention does not change the quality of (neural) visual representations [62]; they just add report, access, and attention [63].

Further arguments in favor of the one or the other have been laid out extensively elsewhere [14, 15, 53, 60]. The discussion is reminiscent of some older philosophical discussions, for example, about the distinction between A (access) and P (phenomenal) consciousness [64–66], or that of easy versus hard problems of consciousness [67]. The controversy between the two ideas seems to be in a stalemate, with support for one or the other swinging back and forth [54, 60, 61, 68]. There is sufficient data for either point of view; it mainly boils down to the two theories having clearly different explananda: are you interested in explaining the seeing or the knowing that we see? Crucial is whether we should consider consciousness as closely intertwined with attention and cognition (as in the first view) or as a function or phenomenon with its own ontological status (as in the second view)[14, 58, 69, 70].

Not that both types of theories wouldn't argue to explain the 'seeing'. HOT, for example, argues that the higher order representation of visual experience renders the experience conscious, hence truly 'seen', even when that higher order representation has nothing to do with knowing or other higher levels of cognition. Similarly, in Global Workspace Theory (GWT), it is argued that local recurrence leads to stimuli being 'pre-conscious', and that only after global ignition the 'seeing' arises.[2] Either way, however, according to these theories something beyond (recurrent) visual processing is necessary to explain the seeing. Similarly, neural correlates of these types of theories (when given) typically go beyond visual cortex and require the involvement of fronto-parietal or other non-visual regions. The second type of theories, however, confines all the necessary ingredients for seeing to the visual processes (or visual pathways) themselves.

An argument from taxonomy

How could the stalemate between the two theories be resolved? It may be fruitful to evaluate the two types of theories with respect to their *explanatory power* [13, 14]. For example, does frontal involvement mechanistically explain something fundamental about the difference between conscious and unconscious vision or rather about the difference between the ability to report or not [63]? Or is it instead the difference between feedforward and recurrent processing that best explains the transition from unconscious to conscious vision?

To do so, one would first need to establish what the key difference between conscious and unconscious vision is. This is essentially an exercise in taxonomy, not unlike the taxonomy of species in biology. Such a taxonomy always starts at the extreme ends. For example, if we consider the difference between the animal classes of fish and mammals, we first look at 'uncontroversial fish' (sea bass, shark, salmon, etc.) and 'uncontroversial mammals' (wolves, lions, buffalos, etc.), and compare their features. We then decide what the *defining features* are of the two different classes, and on the basis of that decide whether problematic cases (like dolphins) are either mammals or fish. This leads to the conclusion that some features are irrelevant (like living in water), while other features are critical (like breathing apparatus and breast feeding). Importantly, this then leads to the firm conclusion (or consensus) that – despite appearances – dolphins are in fact mammals and not fish.

Something similar can be done to resolve the controversy about consciousness discussed here: what are the *defining features* of conscious experience, and which features are irrelevant? As in animal taxonomy, we should start with uncontroversial extremes, hence cases where no one would argue the presence or absence of conscious experience. An unequivocally reported visual percept – as in someone firmly stating that he saw, recognized, and otherwise identified a face that was shown to him – would be an example of the former. A strongly masked visual stimulus, which a subject is unable to report, identify, or even forced choice guess about, even though all attention is on the screen and the only task of the subject is to detect the stimulus, would be an example of the latter. Denying presence and respectively absence of conscious experience in these two extremes would amount to in fact eliminating the whole idea of conscious experience.

On the basis of a large body of evidence [72], I have identified visual functions that mark the transition between conscious and unconscious vision, leading to the conclusion that it is longer range and incremental Gestalt grouping and figure-ground organization that are critically dependent on conscious vision and hence can be considered defining features of conscious vision. Functions like low- and high-level feature detection and categorization (e.g. face selective responses), base groupings (conjunctions of basic features like shape and color), perceptual interference (as in contrast or color constancy illusions), and inference (as in the Kanizsa triangle) proceed unconsciously, and hence should not be used as defining features to distinguish between conscious and unconscious vision (see Figure 4.2).

It is fairly straightforward then to conclude that indeed the difference between feedforward and recurrent processing fully captures and explains these defining features. Feature detection and categorization, base groupings, and interference are readily established during the feedforward sweep. Gestalt grouping and figure-ground organization (or perceptual organization in general) typically require recurrent interactions, as has been shown in numerous experiments [21, 24, 27]. These neural interactions also explain how these functions operate [28]. Prefrontal involvement (or 'global ignition', access or attention) does nothing of the sort, as the defining features of conscious vision (i.e. perceptual organization) are equally present when access, attention, or report are absent [63, 73].

GWT has suggested an alternative taxonomy, in which unattended, unaccessed, or unreportable visual information is *preconscious*, and only becomes

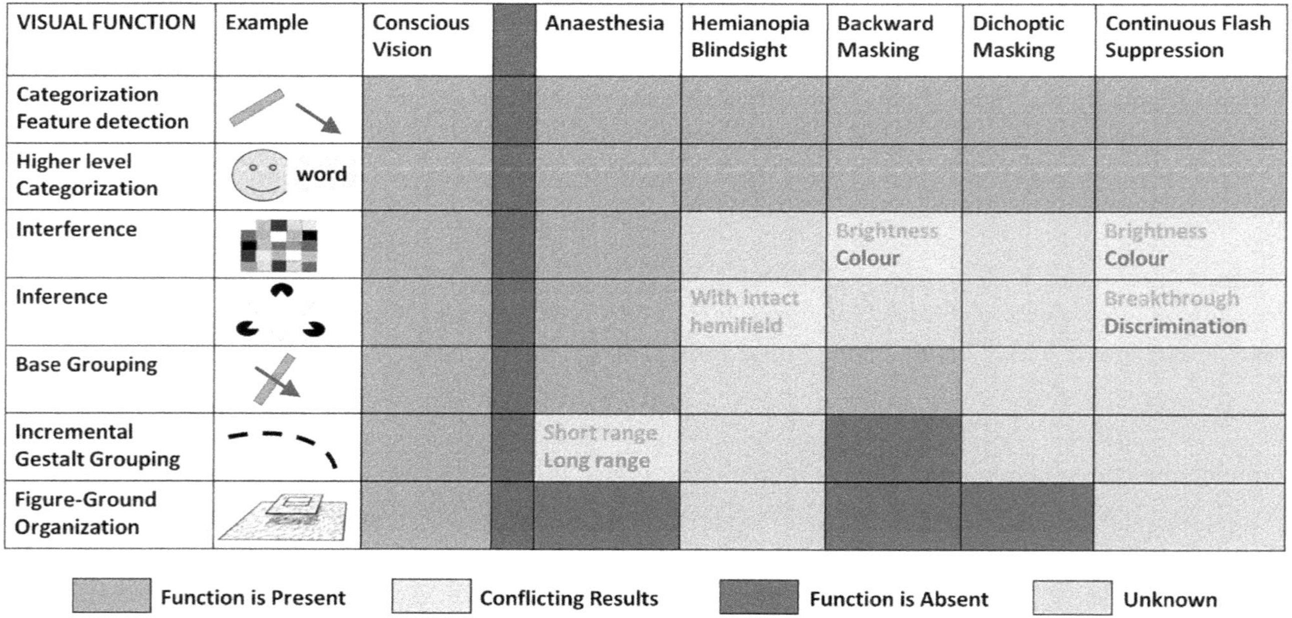

VISUAL FUNCTION	Example	Conscious Vision	Anaesthesia	Hemianopia Blindsight	Backward Masking	Dichoptic Masking	Continuous Flash Suppression
Categorization Feature detection							
Higher level Categorization	word						
Interference					Brightness Colour		Brightness Colour
Inference				With intact hemifield			Breakthrough Discrimination
Base Grouping							
Incremental Gestalt Grouping			Short range / Long range				
Figure-Ground Organization							

Legend: Function is Present | Conflicting Results | Function is Absent | Unknown

FIGURE 4.2   The influence of consciousness manipulations on various visual functions.

Functions (rows) operate under a particular manipulation (columns). All functions are assumed to be present in conscious vision. For each visual function, an icon depicts its most prominent example (see text for explanation).

fully conscious once attended and accessed. Truly unconscious information simply cannot be accessed. For example, a masked stimulus would then be classified as unconscious, an unmasked yet unattended stimulus would be preconscious, to become conscious once attended. The term preconscious is somewhat ambiguous and seems to suggest that GWT refuses to bite the bullet with respect to where exactly the transition from unconscious to conscious occurs. It is either that or GWT is introducing a truly third class of phenomenological experiences, a bit like refusing to classify dolphins as either fish or mammal, yet as 'fimmals'. Needless to say, this would hardly clarify matters. It would completely obscure the search for the neural correlate of consciousness (NCC) – as the distinction between subjects having conscious experiences or not (regardless of whether this distinction is gradual or discrete) would vanish: one would now have to find the NCC of the transition between preconscious and conscious, while not knowing what this transition entails phenomenologically. Finding the NCC is only meaningful if it is about finding the neural correlate of the *contrast* between conscious and unconscious processing. The neural correlate of access consciousness is well established (global workspace 'ignition', fronto-parietal activation, P300, etc. see above), but this is meaningless if it cannot be contrasted with the neural correlate of unconscious representations. Putting a phenomenologically undefined state ('preconscious') between conscious and unconscious processes makes it impossible to evaluate what GWT tries to explain.

However, on closer reading of the literature one cannot but conclude that GWT holds the view that things are only *really* conscious when they enter the global workspace, implying that preconscious is in fact synonymous to unconscious, at least from an introspective point of view – from the point of view of the subject having a conscious experience or not. If we take this GWT stance – preconscious equals unconscious[3] – seriously, some strange conclusions follow. It implies that only cognitive access elevates otherwise unconscious information to conscious experience. But why would this happen? There is a clear lack of explanatory power in this assertion; cognitive access can explain why things get reportable, stored in working memory, or prone to other cognitive manipulations. But how can it ever explain why conscious experiences look the way they do, why we have a unified conscious percept, how conscious perception differs qualitatively from unconscious processing, why we have qualia? It cannot begin to explain the differences between visual functions that occur in conscious versus unconscious vision (Table 3.1). For example, why can we not simply access masked stimuli, given that their neural signals travel all the way up to frontal cortex [74]? How can access explain why there is no perceptual organization in unconscious vision? Access does not seem to capture or explain anything at all about the transition from unconscious to conscious processing. An even more obvious problem is this: we can have access to both the fact that we see and that we *do not* see, implying that access is not generating the experience itself. It is just enabling the cognitive manipulation and report about us seeing or not seeing.

How has one ever come to the conclusion that access has any explanatory power towards the unconscious-conscious contrast?

Another problem with this taxonomy is that it undermines the ontological status of consciousness. By equating consciousness to cognitive processes like attention, access, or reportability, GWT is following an eliminative agenda, where consciousness disappears as a phenomenon on its own. GWT simply states that consciousness equals attention or access, cognitive operations that have their own ontological status, along with fairly well-established neural correlates. GWT is 'giving up' on the problem of consciousness, very much in line with the eliminative agenda of philosophers like Dennett, who – no surprise – is quite strongly endorsing GWT and its related ideas [54].

Escaping panpsychism, or what it is like to be a fly

Both models of consciousness suffer from the same problem: at their core they are fairly simple, too simple maybe. The distinction between feedforward and recurrent processing already exists between two reciprocally connected neurons. Add a third and we can distinguish between 'local' and 'global' recurrent processing. From a functional perspective, processes like integration, feature binding, global access, attention, report, working memory, metacognition, and many others can be modeled with a limited set of mechanisms (or lines of Matlab code). More importantly, it is getting increasingly clear that versions of these functions exist throughout the animal kingdom, and maybe even in plants.

Effects of anesthesia are a good example of the problem we run into. At comparable doses of the volatile anesthetics isoflurane or halothane, animals as different as worms, flies, goldfish, ducks, rats, horses, monkeys, and man stop exhibiting responses to nociceptive or otherwise threatening stimuli [75]. Moreover, in all animals, 'higher'-level cognitive functions are more susceptible to anesthesia than more primitive, reflex-like reactions. In the nematode, a creature with 302 neurons, the order of functions that 'go' under increasing levels of isoflurane anesthesia are male mating, coordinated movement, chemotaxis, and pharyngeal pumping until the worm stops moving at all [75]. Flies have larger brains, and neural activity shows similar spectra of local field potentials as can be found in mammals, with lower frequencies having more power than higher frequencies (roughly $1/f$ spectrum). In man and other mammals, it has been consistently shown that the higher frequencies (gamma band) are indicative of feedforward or local processing, while lower frequencies (alpha and beta bands) are linked to feedback or recurrent processing and top-down influences. Using Granger causality analysis of local field potentials, a similar distinction was found in the fly. Moreover, feedback and recurrent processing are more susceptible to anesthesia than feedforward activation in mammals like man, monkey, rodents, or ferrets. The same was recently found in the fly [76]. So in sum, both from functional and neural perspectives, anesthesia has the same effects in species as different as humans or flies. It may not even stop there. Plants such as the Venus flytrap stop responding to stimulation of their trigger hairs (normally excited by prey insects) when exposed to ether [77], a volatile anesthetic also working in man.[4] The natural counterpart of anesthesia – sleep – is equally ubiquitous in the animal and plant kingdoms. Animals that don't sleep have yet to be found [78], and many plants show clearly different metabolic activity patterns (and appearances) during day and night. We experience the difference between awake and asleep as one of the most fundamental transitions of consciousness, and the fact that conscious sensations are lost during sleep is possibly the number one reason why we believe there *is* consciousness. If this transition between awake and asleep is present in all living beings, does that imply that to these other beings the transition 'feels' equally dramatic? And does it then follow that these beings should therefore be granted consciousness – when awake? We run into similar problems when we assign specific functions as central to consciousness. Cognitive function like attention, access, or metacognition, often linked to consciousness in 'type 1' theories, seems similarly widespread throughout the animal kingdom. Attentional processes such as increased reaction times in the presence of distractors or the suppression of behavioral responses to non-attended stimuli are present in bees and flies [79]. Ants can navigate home in the absence of a sensory stimulus (such as the scent of the nest) guiding their way. They seem to do so via an internally represented 'home vector' that is based on an integration of its own past movements relative to the polarization plane of the sky. This way, the ant, after having found food, can run straight back to the nest, regardless of the often haphazard way it left it. Importantly, however, the ant also can invert its home vector to then run straight back from the nest to the location where the food was found. Similarly, bees have the well-known capacity to convert similar vectors into dances that are signaling other bees where food can be found. Crabs combine several home vectors for other purposes than just homing, for example, to defend their burrow [80]. At the core, such capacities fulfill all requirements for what we call 'cognitive manipulation' or 'access' in higher animals like man, given that access is generally defined as the making flexibly available of sensed or memorized information for different types of behavior. In line with this, bees can abstract at least two different concepts from a set of complex pictures and combine them in a rule for subsequent choices.

Metacognition is generally studied using paradigms where animals can choose to opt-out if they consider the task too difficult. The idea is that in doing so the animal expresses knowledge of its own performance or of the probability that his stimulus-response coupling is the right one [81]. Also, opting out has been used to distinguish blindsight from conscious vision in monkeys [82]. Honey bees were presented with visual targets that either indicated a positive (sucrose) or negative (quinine) reinforcement. The more difficult the visual discrimination became, the more often the bees opted to not respond at all, thereby increasing their overall performance. Moreover, they easily transferred this strategy to another task [79]. Whether it would qualify for metacognition is debatable, but even plants (peas) can adopt different root-growing strategies depending on the variability of nutrients in their soils, showing risk appetite and aversion not unlike animals do [83]. What would follow from such findings? If we take the functional perspective and state that attention, access, or metacognitive faculties are the hallmark of consciousness, we would have to conclude that these simple animals have conscious sensations of their surroundings, home vectors, and stimulus response-couplings. If not willing to accept that, one would have to resort to meta or higher order variants of these functions and deny consciousness to animals that just execute the 'simple versions'. But what higher order variants would that be: 'super-attention', 'super-access', or 'super-metacognition' of some sort? We cannot argue that attention, access, or metacognition are central to consciousness in humans, and then suddenly retreat if animals that we don't 'believe' to have consciousness execute those same functions. It's either that these functions are not constituting consciousness or that the lower animals have consciousness too.

Functional and neural definitions of consciousness as currently formulated thus direct us towards a rather panpsychistic view,[5] where all animals and possibly even plants would be conscious, or at least express the unconscious/conscious dichotomy. One may even start to worry over cultures of neurons in a petri dish, or slices of cortex, or hippocampus as often studied in electrophysiological experiments. Another obvious extension would be consciousness in AI systems. It has been argued that current AI generally lacks mechanisms for global access and availability of information or for metacognition (required for consciousness according to view 1 above), so that fears of conscious machines are premature [84]. Others, however, have opposed this view, arguing that many AI systems in fact do have these properties (either in rudimentary or more advanced forms). Moreover, if conscious experience is better explained by recurrent interactions (view 2 above), we may already have created conscious machines [85].

Do such considerations falsify these theories of consciousness? It seems entirely plausible that other animals than us have conscious sensations, fitting with the propensity of science to remove man from its pedestal, acknowledging that we are just animals too. However, it feels unsatisfactory to equate consciousness as we experience it to whatever happens in the mind of a fly. Recurrent processing theory (RPT) offers some potential solutions to this problem. It would argue that while the conscious/unconscious dichotomy should be present in many animals (or even devices), the 'what it is like' may differ vastly between them. Of the senses, vision and olfaction are most important in the fly, and it has been shown that there is multisensory integration between the two. The visual system of the fly is dominated by neurons and pathways that detect motion (even second order and illusory motion), not surprising given its behavior. Second are pathways related to color vision. Much less prominent are systems that would enable the fly to discriminate between all sorts of objects and shapes [86]. So what 'is it like' to see like a fly? Obviously, conscious content can only be about information that the neural machinery detects. RPT would argue that a fly sees an amalgam of motion and color, quite 'objectless' in fact. Objectless vision is not unlike what patients with damage to visual object areas see, like the famous D.F., studied extensively by Milner and Goodale, who cannot identify objects and shapes, yet is seeing features like color and motion [87]. Apperceptive agnosia patients have similar sensations of unbound basic features [88, 89]. In blindsight, humans report to even have no conscious visual sensations at all (in the affected hemifield), apart from a vague sensation of objectless motion when things move fast enough [90, 91]. So what the fly sees may be similar to the limited experiences of blindsight and other patients, who would qualify their vision as severely impaired or even 'unconscious'. Add to that the obvious other differences between fly and human visual systems (resolution, numbers of neurons and areas, etc.), and it will be quite clear that we would probably qualify what the fly sees as not (or hardly) seeing at all.

This hints towards an important conclusion. What we consider highly impaired vision or even blindness, is what the fly may see consciously. Both we and flies have an unconscious/conscious dichotomy. When a fly escapes from a swat it executes a very intelligent reflex arc, where it positions its middle legs to jump in a direction orthogonal to the approaching danger [92], not unlike what we do when a large object is looming. After the fact, when recurrent processing has kicked in, the fly may experience the fear associated with it (flies show fear conditioning [93]). But the experience will never transcend beyond 'something nasty that moved'. In our minds, however, we will come to recognize that the looming object was a pickup truck, running off the road, steered by a bearded man. We heard the engine roaring, felt the gush of wind when the car almost hit us. And in doing so, we exclude millions of other possible percepts. So although our reflex may be similar to that of the fly, the sensory experience that follows is infinitely richer. In fact, what the fly experiences may be very similar to what we experience in a masking experiment,[6] or when we choose 'not seen' on a perceptual awareness scale. What we call unconscious may be the richest experience a fly or worm ever experiences.

Should we then conclude that flies do not have consciousness after all? That is missing the point. The notion of conscious versus unconscious is still useful – or even necessary – to grasp what goes on in the mind of a fly. The unconscious to conscious transition occurs in flies just like it does in humans, in the sense that it is a radical – and probably non-linear – phase transition, supported by the transition between feedforward to recurrent processing. This is accompanied by a sudden transition from processing 'in the dark' to conscious phenomenology. Therefore, to the fly being awake will 'feel' clearly different from being anesthetized. So there should be a clear and rather dichotomous distinction between the two states from the perspective of the fly, just as there is this distinction in our phenomenology when we go from awake to asleep. But conscious experience in the fly is just not comparable in richness, quality, and extent to ours.

Such considerations call for another distinction: that between unconscious and non-conscious or death. No matter how deep the sleep or anesthesia, there remain clear differences between brains that live and those that don't, both in

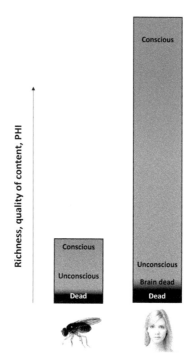

FIGURE 4.3   Phenomenal content is conscious in the fly, yet comparable to unconscious content in humans.

The figure depicts the richness or quality of phenomenal content (calculated as PHI in IIT) on the vertical axis. In both fly and man, there is a non-linear transition in this richness, marking the transition between unconscious to conscious processing, corresponding to the transition from feedforward to recurrent processing at the neural level. At the lower end, there is a second non-linear transition: that between dead or alive. In both species, it therefore makes sense to talk about 'conscious' versus 'unconscious'. However, the content of conscious processing in the fly is comparable to unconscious processing (e.g. deep sleep) in humans. From Ref. [111].

terms of remaining functionality and neural processing. Anesthetized brains process information in a feedforward fashion, and potentially also exhibit limited recurrent information exchange. Clinically, we know there are differences between brain death, coma, vegetative state, or minimally conscious state. In sleep, we recognize different depths. In other words, there are *gradations* of unconscious. These gradations are all accompanied by differences in the extent of neural processing, for example, expressed in the spread of neural signals evoked by TMS of localized regions of cortex [95, 96]. But when dead, all that stops; clearly another non-linear transition in the level of consciousness. Does that imply that being asleep or anesthetized 'feels' different from being dead? Nobody knows, of course, but it is an interesting speculation. It is getting increasingly clear that sleep is not always as unconscious as we may think it is. Sensory processing continues, allowing a child sobbing in the distance waking up a worried mother or outside events to get integrated into dreams. People with neurophysiological signs of sleep may feel awake [97]. This idea of 'multiple gradations' of unconsciousness is also suggested by studies in awake subjects, where masked and inattended items may feel equally 'unconscious' (as in 'not accessible by the self'), yet for entirely different reasons, and supporting taxonomically different types of unconsciousness (in that case unconscious and preconscious) [98].

Together, we arrive at a view where we can objectively define strong and non-linear transitions in states of consciousness that most likely occur in many animals. Because of differences in cognitive machinery that these animals are endowed with (different sensory modalities and capabilities, emotion, social cognition, language, self, etc.), these different states of consciousness support highly different phenomenal experiences. These will feel so entirely different: that what we 'experience' during deep sleep is similar in richness to what a fly experiences during wakefulness (Figure 4.3). It would be human chauvinist to deny the fly its state transitions, however, and claim that it would not feel different to the fly to be awake, anesthetized, or dead. More importantly, however, it would deny consciousness its own ontological status, separate from the cognitive machinery it supports [14].

The missing ingredient

Another and highly related problem is equally present in theories of consciousness: that of the missing ingredient. Recurrent processing will not grind to a complete halt in anesthesia. Although monkey experiments have shown the abolishment of interareal (e.g. between V1 and extrastriate areas) or maybe even local (horizontal) interactions [40], it is inconceivable that at more local levels (between nearby neurons), recurrent interactions remain. In brain death, recurrent processing is probably completely absent, as even feedforward signals such as the N20 SSEP are absent. In coma, however, some recurrent signals may be present, expressed in burst suppression EEG, where complete absence of coherent activity alternates with bursts of synchronous cortical activity. In vegetative state,[7] connectivity is similar to that of deep sleep or anesthesia, all showing coherent EEG signals [95]. If some levels of recurrent processing are compatible with unconsciousness, 'something else' beyond mere recurrency apparently is needed for consciousness.

A potential 'missing ingredient' may be that some types of recurrency are more likely to induce changes to the connectivity of the neural network, and do so at different time scales and using different molecular mechanisms. A longstanding idea is that recurrent interactions between neurons, particularly if they involve burst firing of neurons, are likely to induce synaptic plasticity involving NMDA receptor activation and subsequent CA^{2+} influx, which induces a cascade of molecular and genetic events, changing the efficacy of the synapses involved [99]. Indeed, NMDA receptor activation has been tightly linked to cortico-cortical feedback [37], and NMDA receptor blockers impair feature integration [100]. Some have proposed that the final common pathway of many anesthetics is NMDA receptor inactivation [101]. Synaptic plasticity typically occurs at time scales too slow for a direct involvement in generating conscious experience, yet NMDA receptor activation may be one of the required preconditions for effective large-scale recurrent interactions to occur [102]. Also, more rapid changes in synaptic efficacy occur, such as paired pulse facilitation or suppression, each having various potential underlying mechanisms [103]. Another important role may be played by GABA, as it is actively involved in the dynamics of the neuronal competition underlying binocular rivalry [104]. In sum, it may be that recurrent interactions are just the first step in a more complex cascade of molecular events that induce changes to the network at various time scales. These changes to the network – and not the recurrency per se – may then be the ingredient that generates the conscious experience, and these changes may only happen when recurrency fulfils certain temporal or spatial conditions (Figure 4.4).

Also theories that propose higher cognitive functioning as the key ingredient for consciousness suffer from the 'missing ingredient' problem, as many high-level cognitive functions occur unconsciously. For example, masked No-Go stimuli activate prefrontal inhibition networks in such a way that they induce a slowing of reactions [20], indicating that cognitive control can be executed unconsciously. Also task switching, attention shifting, conflict monitoring, error detection, and evidence accumulation can occur unconsciously [74, 105]. Do such results suggest the existence of unconscious access or metacognition? Using unconscious cues to adapt or control behavior, to change or make decisions, or to switch strategies certainly qualifies for unconscious access, as these are often ways in which conscious access is operationalized. The case for unconscious metacognition is more difficult.[8] However, post-error slowing is very similar to opting out, in that the system seems to know something about its own performance and adapts its behavior accordingly. Post-error slowing does occur for unconscious errors [106], yet is typically weaker than after conscious errors. When comparing conscious to unconscious cognition, it is often found that the former is more flexibly deployed and has stronger effects on behavior as well as stronger associated brain signals. This doesn't solve the 'missing ingredient' issue, however, unless that ingredient is 'more' or 'stronger'. Some have therefore proposed that not cognitive functioning per se is the key ingredient of consciousness, but learning to continuously redescribe the cause-effect relations of these functions, whether simple or complex and internal or external. Once these relations are well established, they leave the conscious domain (as in well-learned skills) [107]. Naccache proposes that a multitude of functions (or ingredients) may be simultaneously required to produce consciousness [108]. In his dialectic approach, the starting point would be the set of cognitive functions that in a healthy awake adult support self-reportability (in its widest sense, so also non-verbal), as this is the aspect of consciousness that is central to the phenomenon, at least according to longstanding philosophical and introspective

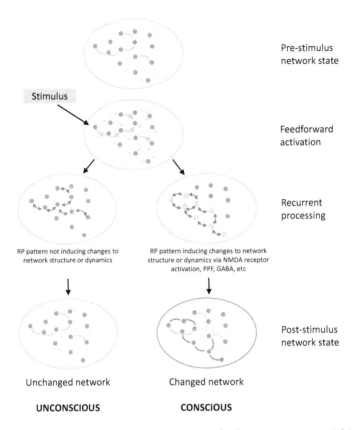

Pre-stimulus
network state

Stimulus

Feedforward
activation

Recurrent
processing

RP pattern not inducing changes to
network structure or dynamics

RP pattern inducing changes to network
structure or dynamics via NMDA receptor
activation, PPF, GABA, etc

Post-stimulus
network state

Unchanged network   Changed network

UNCONSCIOUS   **CONSCIOUS**

FIGURE 4.4 Recurrent processing induced network plasticity as a potential 'missing ingredient'.

A pre-stimulus network state is depicted, with varying strengths of connections. A stimulus evokes a feedforward sweep, followed by recurrent processing. Recurrent processing may then either induce changes to the strengths of connections (f.i. via long or short term, or pre- or postsynaptic plasticity; right) or not (left). Only in the case of network changes will conscious experience arise.
From Ref. [111].

intuitions. The next step would be to find the neural mechanisms that support such self-reportability, which in the healthy human seems to be recurrent interactions between highly educated and sophisticated cortical regions [52]. Only when all the necessary ingredients coincide, that is, when both sufficiently educated cortical areas are active and engage in recurrent interactions, does consciousness as experienced by a normal adult emerges. It should be possible to infer the psychological states going along with recurrent interactions between less sophisticated cognitive modules (say in animals, babies, etc.), such that at some point one would have to conclude that 'consciousness as we experience it' is no longer present. The same logic could be applied to difficult to categorize patients suffering from disorders of consciousness [109].

Concluding remarks

I have tried to highlight some pregnant issues in our current knowledge about consciousness and how it may relate to what happens in brains. Focus was on two theories in particular: RPT and (neuronal) GWT. I noticed the stalemate between RPT and GWT, primarily caused by them having different explananda. I also provided arguments for why GWT does not seem to have any explanation to offer for the most prominent changes that occurs at the transition from unconscious to conscious vision, a contrast that is well captured by RPT. I discussed how both theories endorse panpsychism and how this could potentially be solved, and that each of them still miss 'key ingredients' to satisfactorily distinguish unconscious from conscious processing. Many other theories [110] exist, of course. Readers are encouraged to comment on how some of these other theories may solve the issues raised, because the science of consciousness will clearly benefit from an open exchange of ideas, based on the wealth of experimental data that exists and is produced every day. I hope I have inspired such an exchange.

Acknowledgements

Considerable parts of this chapter have been published in [111].

Notes

1 Parts of this chapter have been published in Lamme, V.A.F. (2018): Challenges for theories of consciousness: seeing or knowing, the missing ingredient, and how to deal with panpsychism. *Phil. Trans. R. Soc. B* 373: 20170344. doi:10.1098/rstb.2017.0344.

2 Although often GWS is rather ambiguous about whether it explains seeing or access to seeing. For example, the somewhat cryptical phrase 'access *to* consciousness' is often used to describe what the GWS is providing [71].

3 With 'preconscious' being short for all situations where attention, access, reportability, etc. is compromised, such as in the attentional blink, change blindness, inattentional blindness, neglect, extinction, or split brain.

4 The effect is caused by a suppression of action potentials generated by touch sensitive ion channels, which is feedforward as far as we know, so vegetarians need not worry yet…

5 Real panpsychism goes somewhat further, in that it would also grant consciousness to any item that processes information (such as thermostats) or even those that do not (such as stones).

6 There is some recent discussion as to whether masking indeed takes away all visual experience or just renders the experience highly degraded. In other words, a masked visual stimulus is never the same as no visual stimulus at all. Peters and Lau, for example, had subjects discriminate oriented Gabor patches and bet on their performance to gauge metacognitive awareness. They found above chance betting only for stimuli that also can be discriminated, and that subjects behave as ideal observers with different levels of noise for the two tasks. They assert that masking may in fact never completely remove awareness when other functions remain, implying that previous experiments showing unconscious cognition in fact study cognition under limited rather than eliminated awareness [94].

7 This refers to VS patients in which conscious sensations seem absent. In some (20%) of VS patients, clear signs of conscious experience are present, as indicated by fMRI

experiments that even showed some patients being able to communicate using their brain signals.

8 Also because in the 'knowing that you know', the first 'knowing' to some researchers or philosophers only qualifies when it is 'conscious knowing'. In that case, unconscious metacognition cannot exist by definition.

References

Alkire MT, Hudetz AG, Tononi G. 2008 Consciousness and anesthesia. *Science* **322**, 876–880. (doi:10.1126/science.1149213)

Baars BJ. 2005 Global workspace theory of consciousness: Toward a cognitive neuroscience of human experience. *Progress in Brain Research* **150**, 45–53. (doi:10.1016/S0079-6123(05)50004-9)

Bi G, Poo M. 2001 Synaptic modification by correlated activity: Hebb's postulate revisited. *Annual Review of Neuroscience* **24**, 139–166. (doi:10.1146/annurev.neuro.24.1.139)

Block N. 1996 How can we find the neural correlate of consciousness? *Trends in Neurosciences* **19**, 456–459. (doi:10.1016/S0166-2236(96)20049-9)

Block N. 2005 Two neural correlates of consciousness. *Trends in Cognitive Sciences* **9**, 46–52. (doi:10.1016/j.tics.2004.12.006)

Block N. 2007 Consciousness, accessibility, and the mesh between psychology and neuroscience. *Behavioral and Brain Sciences* **30**, 481–499. (doi:10.1017/S0140525X07002786)

Boly M, Massimini M, Tsuchiya N, Postle BR, Koch C, Tononi G. 2017 Are the neural correlates of consciousness in the front or in the back of the cerebral cortex? Clinical and neuroimaging evidence. *Journal of Neuroscience* **37**, 9603–9613. (doi:10.1523/JNEUROSCI.3218-16.2017)

Breitmeyer BG, Ogmen H. 2000 Recent models and findings in visual backward masking: A comparison, review, and update. *Perception & Psychophysics* **62**, 1572–1595. (doi:10.3758/BF03212157)

Buetti S, Juan E, Rinck M, Kerzel D. 2012 Affective states leak into movement execution: Automatic avoidance of threatening stimuli in fear of spider is visible in reach trajectories. *Cognition and Emotion* **26**, 1176–1188. (doi:10.1080/02699931.2011.640662)

Caputo G, Casco C. 1999 A visual evoked potential correlate of global figure-ground segmentation. *Vision Research* **39**, 1597–1610.

Card G, Dickinson MH. 2008 Visually mediated motor planning in the escape response of Drosophila. *Current Biology* **18**, 1300–1307. (doi:10.1016/j.cub.2008.07.094)

Carter O, Hohwy J, van Boxtel J, Lamme V, Block N, Koch C, Tsuchiya N. 2018 Conscious machines: Defining questions. *Science* **359**, 400. (doi:10.1126/science.aar4163)

Chalmers, David, J. 1995 Facing up to the problem of consciousness, *Journal of Consciousness Studies* **2**(3), 200–219.

Cirelli C, Tononi G. 2017 The Sleeping Brain. *Cerebrum* **2017**. https://www.ncbi.nlm.nih.gov/pmc/articles/PMC5501041/.

Cleeremans A, Timmermans B, Pasquali A. 2007 Consciousness and metarepresentation: A computational sketch. *Neural Networks* **20**, 1032–1039. (doi:10.1016/j.neunet.2007.09.011)

Cleeremans A. 2011 The radical plasticity thesis: How the brain learns to be conscious. *Frontiers in Psychology* **2**. (doi:10.3389/fpsyg.2011.00086)

Cohen D, van Swinderen B, Tsuchiya N. 2018 Isoflurane impairs low frequency feedback but leaves high frequency feedforward connectivity intact in the fly brain. *eNeuro* (doi:10.1523/eneuro.0329-17.2018)

Cohen MA, Dennett DC. 2011 Consciousness cannot be separated from function. *Trends in Cognitive Sciences (Regular Edition)* **15**, 358–364. (doi:10.1016/j.tics.2011.06.008)

Cohen MX, van Gaal S, Ridderinkhof KR, Lamme VAF. 2009 Unconscious errors enhance prefrontal-occipital oscillatory synchrony. *Frontiers in Human Neuroscience* **3**. (doi:54 10.3389/neuro.09.054.2009)

Dehaene S, Changeux J-P. 2005 Ongoing spontaneous activity controls access to consciousness: A neuronal model for inattentional blindness. *PLoS Biology* **3**, e141. (doi:10.1371/journal.pbio.0030141)

Dehaene S, Changeux JP, Naccache L, Sackur J, Sergent C. 2006 Conscious, preconscious, and subliminal processing: A testable taxonomy. *Trends in Cognitive Sciences* **10**, 204–211. (doi:10.1016/j.tics.2006.03.007)

Dehaene S, Lau H, Kouider S. 2017 What is consciousness, and could machines have it? *Science* **358**, 486–492. (doi:10.1126/science.aan8871)

Dehaene S, Naccache L, Le Clec'H G, Koechlin E, Mueller M, Dehaene-Lambertz G, van de Moortele PF, Le Bihan D. 1998 Imaging unconscious semantic priming. *Nature* **395**, 597–600. (doi:10.1038/26967)

Dehaene S, Naccache L. 2001 Towards a cognitive neuroscience of consciousness: Basic evidence and a workspace framework. *Cognition* **79**, 1–37.

de Lange FP, van Gaal S, Lamme VA, Dehaene S. 2011 How awareness changes the relative weights of evidence during human decision-making. *PLOS Biology* **9**, e1001203. (doi:10.1371/journal.pbio.1001203)

Dener E, Kacelnik A, Shemesh H. 2016 Pea plants show risk sensitivity. *Current Biology* **26**, 1763–1767. (doi:10.1016/j.cub.2016.05.008)

Ekstrom LB, Roelfsema PR, Arsenault JT, Bonmassar G, Vanduffel W. 2008 Bottom-up dependent gating of frontal signals in early visual cortex. *Science* **321**, 414–417. (doi:10.1126/science.1153276)

Fahrenfort JJ, Lamme VA. 2012 A true science of consciousness explains phenomenology: Comment on Cohen and Dennett. *Trends in Cognitive Sciences* **16**, 138–139; author reply 139–140. (doi:10.1016/j.tics.2012.01.004)

Fahrenfort JJ, Scholte HS, Lamme VA. 2007 Masking disrupts reentrant processing in human visual cortex. *Journal of Cognitive Neuroscience* **19**, 1488–1497. (doi:10.1162/jocn.2007.19.9.1488)

Fahrenfort JJ, Snijders TM, Heinen K, van Gaal S, Scholte HS, Lamme VA. 2012 Neuronal integration in visual cortex elevates face category tuning to conscious face perception. *Proceedings of the National Academy of Sciences of the United States of America* **109**, 21504–21509. (doi:10.1073/pnas.1207414110)

Fleming SM, Lau HC. 2014 How to measure metacognition. *Frontiers in Human Neuroscience* **8**. (doi:10.3389/fnhum.2014.00443)

Flohr H, Glade U, Motzko D. 1998 The role of the NMDA synapse in general anesthesia. *Toxicology Letters* **100–101**, 23–29.

Flohr H. 2006 Unconsciousness. *Best Practice & Research Clinical Anaesthesiology* **20**, 11–22. (doi:10.1016/j.bpa.2005.08.009)

Giurfa M. 2015 Learning and cognition in insects. *Wiley Interdisciplinary Reviews: Cognitive Science* **6**, 383–395. (doi:10.1002/wcs.1348)

Goodale MA, Milner AD. 1992 Separate visual pathways for perception and action. *Trends in Neurosciences* **15**, 20–25.

Gosseries O, Di H, Laureys S, Boly M. 2014 Measuring consciousness in severely damaged brains. *Annual Review of Neuroscience* **37**, 457–478. (doi:10.1146/annurev-neuro-062012-170339)

Grainger J, Rey A, Dufau S. 2008 Letter perception: From pixels to pandemonium. *Trends in Cognitive Sciences* **12**, 381–387. (doi:10.1016/j.tics.2008.06.006)

Grossman M, Galetta S, D'Esposito M. 1997 Object recognition difficulty in visual apperceptive agnosia. *Brain and Cognition* **33**, 306–342. (doi:10.1006/brcg.1997.0876)

Hsiao F-C et al. In press. The neurophysiological basis of the discrepancy between objective and subjective sleep during the sleep onset period: An EEG-fMRI study. *Sleep.* (doi:10.1093/sleep/zsy056)

Huang W-J, Chen W-W, Zhang X. 2015 The neurophysiology of P 300—An integrated review. *European Review for Medical and Pharmacological Sciences* **19**, 1480–1488.

Hupé JM, James AC, Payne BR, Lomber SG, Girard P, Bullier J. 1998 Cortical feedback improves discrimination between figure and background by V1, V2 and V3 neurons. *Nature* **394**, 784–787. (doi:10.1038/29537)

Kirchner H, Thorpe SJ. 2006 Ultra-rapid object detection with saccadic eye movements: Visual processing speed revisited. *Vision Research* **46**, 1762–1776. (doi:10.1016/j.visres.2005.10.002)

Koch C, Massimini M, Boly M, Tononi G. 2016 Neural correlates of consciousness: Progress and problems. *Nature Reviews Neuroscience* **17**, 307–321. (doi:10.1038/nrn.2016.22)

Koivisto M, Revonsuo A. 2003 An ERP study of change detection, change blindness, and visual awareness. *Psychophysiology* **40**, 423–429. (doi:10.1111/1469-8986.00044)

Koivisto M, Revonsuo A. 2010 Event-related brain potential correlates of visual awareness. *Neuroscience & Biobehavioral Reviews* **34**, 922–934. (doi:10.1016/j.neubiorev.2009.12.002)

Kottler B, van Swinderen B. 2014 Taking a new look at how flies learn. *eLife* **3**. (doi:10.7554/eLife.03978)

Kouider S, de Gardelle V, Sackur J, Dupoux E. 2010 How rich is consciousness? The partial awareness hypothesis. *Trends in Cognitive Sciences (Regular Edition)* **14**, 301–307. (doi:10.1016/j.tics.2010.04.006)

Kouider S, Dehaene S. 2007 Levels of processing during non-conscious perception: A critical review of visual masking. *Philosophical Transactions of the Royal Society B: Biological Sciences* **362**, 857–875. (doi:10.1098/rstb.2007.2093)

Kunde W, Kiesel A, Hoffmann J. 2003 Conscious control over the content of unconscious cognition. *Cognition* **88**, 223–242. (doi:10.1016/S0010-0277(03)00023-4)

Lamme V. 2015 The crack of dawn: Perceptual functions and neural mechanisms that mark the transition from unconscious processing to conscious vision. In *Open MIND* (eds TK Metzinger, JM Windt). Frankfurt am Main: MIND Group. (doi:10.15502/9783958570092)

Lamme VA, Rodriguez-Rodriguez V, Spekreijse H. 1999 Separate processing dynamics for texture elements, boundaries and surfaces in primary visual cortex of the macaque monkey. *Cerebral Cortex* **9**, 406–413.

Lamme VA, Roelfsema PR. 2000 The distinct modes of vision offered by feedforward and recurrent processing. *Trends in Neurosciences* **23**, 571–579.

Lamme VA, Super H, Spekreijse H. 1998 Feedforward, horizontal, and feedback processing in the visual cortex. *Current Opinion in Neurobiology* **8**, 529–535.

Lamme VA, Van Dijk BW, Spekreijse H. 1993 Contour from motion processing occurs in primary visual cortex. *Nature* **363**, 541–543.

Lamme VA, Zipser K, Spekreijse H. 1998 Figure-ground activity in primary visual cortex is suppressed by anesthesia. *Proceedings of the National Academy of Sciences of the United States of America* **95**, 3263–3268.

Lamme VA. 1995 The neurophysiology of figure-ground segregation in primary visual cortex. *Journal of Neuroscience* **15**, 1605–1615.

Lamme VA. 2000 Neural mechanisms of visual awareness: A linking proposition. *Brain and Mind* **1**, 385–406.

Lamme VA. 2003 Why visual attention and awareness are different. *Trends in Cognitive Sciences* **7**, 12–18.

Lamme VA. 2005 Independent neural definitions of visual awareness and attention. In *Cognitive Penetrability of Perception: Attention, Action, Strategies, and Bottom-Up Constraints* (ed A Raftopoulos), pp. 171–191. New York: Nova Science Publishers.

Lamme VA. 2006 Towards a true neural stance on consciousness. *Trends in Cognitive Sciences* **10**, 494–501. (doi:10.1016/j.tics.2006.09.001)

Lamme VA. 2010 How neuroscience will change our view on consciousness. *Journal of Cognitive Neuroscience* **1**, 204–220. (doi:10.1080/17588921003731586)

Lamme VAF, Zipser K, Spekreijse H. 2001 Masking interrupts figure-ground signals in V1. *Journal of Vision* **1**, 32–32.

Lamme VAF. 2010 What introspection has to offer, and where its limits lie reply to commentaries. *Cognitive Neuroscience* **1**, 232–235. (doi:10.1080/17588928.2010.502224)

Lamme VAF. 2015 *The Crack of Dawn. Perceptual Functions and Neural Mechanisms that Mark the Transition from Unconscious Processing to Conscious Vision.* Open MIND. Frankfurt am Main: MIND Group, DE..

Lamme VAF. 2018 Challenges for theories of consciousness: Seeing or knowing, the missing ingredient and how to deal with panpsychism. *Philosophical Transactions of the Royal Society B: Biological Sciences* **373**, 20170344. (doi:10.1098/rstb.2017.0344)

Lee TS, Yang CF, Romero RD, Mumford D. 2002 Neural activity in early visual cortex reflects behavioral experience and higher-order perceptual saliency. *Nature Neuroscience* **5**, 589–597. (doi:10.1038/nn860)

Li FF, VanRullen R, Koch C, Perona P. 2002 Rapid natural scene categorization in the near absence of attention. *Proceedings of the National Academy of Sciences of the United States of America* **99**, 9596–9601. (doi:10.1073/pnas.092277599)

Meuwese JD, van Loon AM, Scholte HS, Lirk PB, Vulink NC, Hollmann MW, Lamme VA. 2013 NMDA receptor antagonist ketamine impairs feature integration in visual perception. *PLoS One* **8**, e79326. (doi:10.1371/journal.pone.0079326)

Moore T, Rodman HR, Repp AB, Gross CG. 1995 Localization of visual stimuli after striate cortex damage in monkeys: Parallels with human blindsight. *Proceedings of the National Academy of Sciences of the United States of America* **92**, 8215–8218.

Naccache L, Blandin E, Dehaene S. 2002 Unconscious masked priming depends on temporal attention. *Psychological Science* **13**, 416–424. (doi:10.1111/1467-9280.00474)

Naccache L. 2008 Conscious influences on subliminal cognition exist and are asymmetrical: Validation of a double prediction. *Consciousness and Cognition* **17**, 1359–1360. (doi:10.1016/j.concog.2008.01.002)

Naccache L. 2018 Minimally conscious state or cortically mediated state? *Brain* **141**, 949–960. (doi:10.1093/brain/awx324)

Naccache L. 2018 Reply: Response to 'minimally conscious state or cortically mediated state?' *Brain* **141**, e27. (doi:10.1093/brain/awy026)

Odegaard B, Knight RT, Lau H. 2017 Should a few null findings falsify prefrontal theories of conscious perception? *Journal of Neuroscience* **37**, 9593–9602. (doi:10.1523/JNEUROSCI.3217-16.2017)

Oppermann F, Hassler U, Jescheniak JD, Gruber T. 2011 The rapid extraction of gist— Early neural correlates of high-level visual processing. *Journal of Cognitive Neuroscience* **24**, 521–529. (doi:10.1162/jocn_a_00100)

Peters MAK, Lau H. 2015 Human observers have optimal introspective access to perceptual processes even for visually masked stimuli. *eLife Sciences* **4**, e09651. (doi:10.7554/eLife.09651)

Roelfsema PR, Lamme VA, Spekreijse H, Bosch H. 2002 Figure-ground segregation in a recurrent network architecture. *Journal of Cognitive Neuroscience* **14**, 525–537. (doi:10.1162/08989290260045756)

Roelfsema PR, Lamme VA, Spekreijse H. 1998 Object-based attention in the primary visual cortex of the macaque monkey. *Nature* **395**, 376–381.

Ro T, Breitmeyer B, Burton P, Singhal NS, Lane D. 2003 Feedback contributions to visual awareness in human occipital cortex. *Current Biology* **13**, 1038–1041. (doi:10.1016/S0960-9822(03)00337-3)

Ro T. 2010 What can TMS tell us about visual awareness? *Cortex* **46**, 110–113. (doi:10.1016/j.cortex.2009.03.005)

Schmitz TW, De Rosa E, Anderson AK. 2009 Opposing influences of affective state valence on visual cortical encoding. *Journal of Neuroscience* **29**, 7199–7207. (doi:10.1523/JNEUROSCI.5387-08.2009)

Scholte HS, Spekreijse H, Lamme VAF. 2001 Neural correlates of global scene segmentation are present during inattentional blindness. *Journal of Vision* **1**, 346–346.

Scholte HS, Witteveen SC, Spekreijse H, Lamme VA. 2006 The influence of inattention on the neural correlates of scene segmentation. *Brain Research* **1076**, 106–115. (doi:10.1016/j.brainres.2005.10.051)

Self MW, Kooijmans RN, Supèr H, Lamme VA, Roelfsema PR. 2012 Different glutamate receptors convey feedforward and recurrent processing in macaque V1. *Proceedings of the National Academy of Sciences of the United States of America* **109**, 11031–11036. (doi:10.1073/pnas.1119527109)

Sergent C, Baillet S, Dehaene S. 2005 Timing of the brain events underlying access to consciousness during the attentional blink. *Nature Neuroscience* **8**, 1391–1400. (doi:10.1038/nn1549)

Seth AK. 2010 The grand challenge of consciousness. *Frontiers in Psychology* **1**, 5. (doi:10.3389/fpsyg.2010.00005)

Shafto JP, Pitts MA. 2015 Neural signatures of conscious face perception in an inattentional blindness paradigm. *Journal of Neuroscience* **35**, 10940–10948. (doi:10.1523/JNEUROSCI.0145-15.2015)

Shao Z, Burkhalter A. 1996 Different balance of excitation and inhibition in forward and feedback circuits of rat visual cortex. *Journal of Neuroscience* **16**, 7353–7365.

Shelton PA, Bowers D, Duara R, Heilman KM. 1994 Apperceptive visual agnosia: A case study. *Brain and Cognition* **25**, 1–23. (doi:10.1006/brcg.1994.1019)

Sillito AM, Cudeiro J, Jones HE. 2006 Always returning: Feedback and sensory processing in visual cortex and thalamus. *Trends in Neurosciences* **29**, 307–316. (doi:10.1016/j.tins.2006.05.001)

Squire RF, Noudoost B, Schafer RJ, Moore T. 2013 Prefrontal contributions to visual selective attention. *Annual Review of Neuroscience* **36**, 451–466. (doi:10.1146/annurev-neuro-062111-150439)

Super H, van der Togt C, Spekreijse H, Lamme VA. 2003 Internal state of monkey primary visual cortex (V1) predicts figure–ground perception. *The Journal of Neuroscience* **23**, 3407–3414.

Supèr H, Lamme VAF. 2007 Altered figure-ground perception in monkeys with an extra-striate lesion. *Neuropsychologia* **45**, 3329–3334. (doi:10.1016/j.neuropsychologia.2007.07.001)

Supèr H, Spekreijse H, Lamme VAF. 2001 Two distinct modes of sensory processing observed in monkey primary visual cortex (V1). *Nature Neuroscience* **4**, 304–310. (doi:10.1038/85170)

Terrace HS, Son LK. 2009 Comparative metacognition. *Current Opinion in Neurobiology* **19**, 67–74. (doi:10.1016/j.conb.2009.06.004)

Tononi G, Massimini M. 2008 Why does consciousness fade in early sleep? *Annals of the New York Academy of Sciences* **1129**, 330–334. (doi:10.1196/annals.1417.024)

Tononi G. 2008 Consciousness as integrated information: A provisional manifesto. *The Biological Bulletin* **215**, 216–242.

Tsuchiya N, Wilke M, Frässle S, Lamme VA. 2015 No-report paradigms: Extracting the true neural correlates of consciousness. *Trends in Cognitive Sciences* **19**, 757–770. (doi:10.1016/j.tics.2015.10.002)

Vandenbroucke AR, Fahrenfort JJ, Sligte IG, Lamme VA. 2014 Seeing without knowing: Neural signatures of perceptual inference in the absence of report. *Journal of Cognitive Neuroscience* **26**, 955–969. (doi:10.1162/jocn_a_00530)

van Gaal S, Lamme VA. 2012 Unconscious high-level information processing: Implication for neurobiological theories of consciousness. *Neuroscientist* **18**, 287–301. (doi:10.1177/1073858411404079)

van Gaal S, Ridderinkhof KR, Fahrenfort JJ, Lamme VAF. 2008 Electrophysiological correlates of unconsciously triggered inhibitory control. *Perception* **37**, 139–139.

van Gaal S, Ridderinkhof KR, Fahrenfort JJ, Scholte HS, Lamme VAF. 2008 Frontal cortex mediates unconsciously triggered inhibitory control. *Journal of Neuroscience* **28**, 8053–8062. (doi:10.1523/jneurosci.1278-08.2008)

van Loon AM, Knapen T, Scholte HS, St John-Saaltink E, Donner TH, Lamme VA. 2013 GABA shapes the dynamics of bistable perception. *Current Biology* **23**, 823–827. (doi:10.1016/j.cub.2013.03.067)

Webb B. 2012 Cognition in insects. *Philosophical Transactions of the Royal Society B: Biological Sciences* **367**, 2715–2722. (doi:10.1098/rstb.2012.0218)

Weiskrantz L. 1996 Blindsight revisited. *Current Opinion in Neurobiology* **6**, 215–220.

Yokawa K, Kagenishi T, Pavlovič A, Gall S, Weiland M, Mancuso S, Baluška F. In press. Anaesthetics stop diverse plant organ movements, affect endocytic vesicle recycling and ROS homeostasis, and block action potentials in Venus flytraps. *Annals of Botany* (doi:10.1093/aob/mcx155)

Zalucki O, van Swinderen B. 2016 What is unconsciousness in a fly or a worm? A review of general anesthesia in different animal models. *Consciousness and Cognition* **44**, 72–88. (doi: 10.1016/j.concog.2016.06.017)

Zeki S, Ffytche DH. 1998 The Riddoch syndrome: Insights into the neurobiology of conscious vision. *Brain* **121**(Pt 1), 25–45.

Zhu Y. 2013 The Drosophila visual system. *Cell Adhesion & Migration* **7**, 333–344. (doi:10.4161/cam.25521)

Zipser K, Lamme VA, Schiller PH. 1996 Contextual modulation in primary visual cortex. *Journal of Neuroscience* **16**, 7376–7389.

Zucker RS, Regehr WG. 2002 Short-term synaptic plasticity. *Annual Review of Physiology* **64**, 355–405. (doi:10.1146/annurev.physiol.64.092501.114547)

5

INTEGRATED INFORMATION THEORY

Larissa Albantakis

Introduction

Consciousness is subjective experience. Everything that we perceive, feel, study, or deliberate exists first and foremost as part of our experience. That our experiences are based on a world that exists outside our experiences, at least when we are awake and not dreaming, cannot be proven or falsified experimentally. It is merely an inference, albeit a very useful one, with immense explanatory power, as it is the basis for science. When consciousness fades for the experiencing subject, the world vanishes. While we ultimately cannot be sure that an outside world exists, the existence of our own conscious experience is immediately given to us.

The subjectivity of our experiences has impeded the scientific study of consciousness for a long time. Recent advances in identifying the neural correlates of consciousness (NCC) take advantage of the fact that experiences are empirically accessible to the experiencing subject. This means that in many situations, people can reliably report on (aspects of) their experiences. These behavioral correlates of consciousness can then be related to their underlying neural mechanisms.

A sufficiently detailed map of the NCC would ideally allow us to predict both the state of consciousness of a healthy adult human subject and also the content of their experience in every accessible case. However, prediction does not equal explanation: knowing *that* certain physical phenomena in the healthy adult human brain correlate with certain experiences does not mean that we understand *why* they are accompanied by subjective experience. Moreover, the NCC will not tell us which properties a physical system, more generally, has to fulfill for it to "feel like something" to be that system. How could we decide, for instance, whether a biological basis is necessary for consciousness? Without a proper theory of what consciousness is, how it emerges from physical systems, and what determines its quantity and quality, we cannot confidently attribute consciousness or a lack thereof to other physical systems, including infants, patients with brain lesions, animals, or machines.

Integrated information theory (IIT) aims to provide such a theory of consciousness with explanatory, predictive, and inferential power. Originally conceived by Giulio Tononi (Tononi, 2004), IIT and its theoretical framework have been developed and expanded by Tononi and colleagues over the past few years (Tononi, 2008, 2012; Oizumi et al., 2014; Tononi et al., 2016). In contrast to current approaches that start from the NCC with the hope of identifying generalized principles about the nature of consciousness, IIT instead starts from phenomenology itself, while the NCC serve as a substrate for evaluation. IIT takes advantage of the fact that experiences are empirically accessible to the experiencing subject not by correlating reportable aspects of consciousness to neural mechanisms, but by identifying the essential properties of the experiences that are immediately available (the "axioms" of phenomenology). Positing a physical basis for these phenomenal properties, IIT then proposes a corresponding set of required physical properties (the "postulates") that a system must fulfill to account for the identified phenomenal properties. According to IIT, where an experience exists for the experiencing subject in phenomenal terms, its underlying physical substrate must exist for itself in physical terms. This notion is formalized into a rigorous theoretical framework that, in principle, could predict which (neural) elements form the physical substrate of consciousness (PSC) in the brain and could thus be evaluated against the empirically determined NCC. In the following, I will highlight IIT's particular approach, including relevant specifics of its theoretical framework, before discussing resulting predictions and implications regarding the NCC.

Starting from phenomenology: from axioms to postulates

IIT's first aim is to identify the essential properties of every experience from phenomenology itself. In other words, IIT tries to characterize what consciousness *is*, based on a set of defining phenomenological features, which are termed 'axioms'. The first IIT axiom is *intrinsicality*—the fact that experience exists for the experiencing subject from its intrinsic perspective. The other four IIT axioms taken to be true for any experience are: *composition*—that experience has structure, being composed of several phenomenal distinctions and relations between them; *information*—that every experience has specific components that make it what it is and thus different from other experiences; *integration*—that all aspects of an experience are unified within it and cannot be subdivided into independent subsets; and *exclusion*: that the experience is definite in its content, i.e., not more or less than it is, with definite borders (Oizumi et al., 2014; Tononi, 2015; Tononi et al., 2016).

Based on these five axioms, IIT then derives a corresponding set of postulates that a physical system has to comply with in order to be a PSC. The argument here is that any physical system that can account for *all* essential properties of experience has all it takes to be a substrate of consciousness. Specifically, a PSC has to exist intrinsically for itself. In physical terms, to 'exist' means to have cause-effect power, to be manipulable and observable (Alexander, 1920). In the most basic sense, this means that a physical mechanism[1] must be a difference (i.e., it must be able to change its state) that can make a difference to other physical mechanisms. As a simple example, take a neuron in the brain that changes its state (e.g., inactive to active) based on the inputs it receives from other neurons (causes), which makes a difference to the neurons it outputs to (effects).

Hence, a PSC is a physical system that is constituted of physical elements that constrain each other (*intrinsicality*), alone or in combination (*composition*), in specific ways depending on their states (*information*), such that they cannot be subdivided into independent subsets (*integration*), and moreover has self-defined, definite borders (*exclusion*). Because its mechanisms constrain each other in a unified manner, such a system has cause-effect power onto itself, and thus exists for itself in physical terms.

According to IIT, such a system also exists for itself in phenomenological terms. The specific way in which the elements within the PSC causally constrain each other and relate to each other at any given moment is structurally identical to the system's phenomenal experience. This set of mutual constraints is called the PSC's *cause-effect structure* and corresponds to the quality of the experience. The level or quantity of consciousness corresponds to how much a PSC exists from its intrinsic perspective, i.e., how much cause-effect power it has onto itself. This is captured by its value of *integrated information* Φ, which measures how integrated a system's cause-effect structure is across the partition that affects it the least (see below). The PSC defines its borders by including those physical elements that would increase its intrinsic existence if included and excluding those that would decrease it. This means that the set of elements that constitutes a PSC is a maximum of integrated information Φ and thus excludes all overlapping sets of elements with less Φ from being PSCs themselves.

A distinctive feature of IIT is that, instead of relying on current evidence about the NCC, IIT's postulates about the PSC are derived directly from phenomenology. For this reason, IIT does not presuppose that the elements of the PSC are neurons, instead of, e.g., atoms, or molecules, or whole brain areas. Nevertheless, according to IIT's exclusion postulate, also the spatio-temporal grain at which the elements constituting the PSC and their interactions are defined have to be definite. The spatio-temporal scale of the PSC should again correspond to the one that maximizes its intrinsic existence, i.e., the one at which the system has maximal Φ; all others are excluded from being PSCs themselves.

Current experimental evidence suggests that (groups of) neurons located in certain parts of the cortico-thalamic system contribute directly to human experience (Koch et al., 2016), meaning that they specify a particular phenomenal content when they are in a particular state (activity pattern). Activity in the fusiform gyrus, for example, is associated with the conscious perception of faces (Koch, 2004; Rangarajan et al., 2014). In the light of IIT, the NCC should be understood as the set of neuronal elements that constitute the PSC of consciousness within the brain. At any given moment, the NCC that specify phenomenological content should thus be part of a set of elements that forms a maximum of intrinsic cause-effect power (Φ). This general principle is IIT's most basic testable prediction.

A rigorous evaluation of IIT's predictions will require more detailed knowledge about the NCC and the anatomical and functional structure of the brain than is currently available. In addition, it also necessitates a quantitative formalism to assess which part of the brain complies with IIT's postulates. To this end, IIT provides a theoretical framework for assessing the amount of integrated information (Φ) and the cause-effect structure of physical systems, such as neural networks (Oizumi et al., 2014), with specific mathematical formulations for discrete dynamical systems that can be expressed as causal Bayesian networks (Pearl, 2000).

Theoretical framework

Ultimately, IIT's theoretical framework aims to identify whether a physical system in a specific state complies with the IIT postulates and thus forms a PSC, to quantify the level of consciousness (Φ) of such a system and to provide a full account of its phenomenological sucture in causal terms.

The starting point is the insight that existence in physical terms requires cause-effect power, which underlies the translation of the phenomenal axioms into postulates about the physical substrate.

Given a system of interacting physical elements that have at least two states and can be manipulated and observed, IIT proposes an algorithm to evaluate the system's cause-effect structure and to quantify the cause-effect power that the system has onto itself (Φ).[2] (For a detailed account, the reader is referred to Oizumi et al., 2014; Tononi, 2015; Mayner et al., 2017.) Here I will briefly outline some key features which motivate IIT's predictions and implications discussed below.

The cause-effect structure: First, let us assume a simple binary mechanism within a system, with inputs that can influence it and outputs that are influenced by it, such as a neuron that can be in state "on" (firing) or state "off" (silent), which fires whenever it receives sufficient synaptic inputs from other neurons. By being in state "on", for example, the neuron specifies information about the past state of its inputs (sufficient input neurons must have fired) and about the future state of its outputs (those neurons are now more likely to fire as well). The neuron thus has cause-effect power, since it constrains its possible causes and effects.

How much the neuron in state "on" constrains the system's past and future can be quantified precisely if a full account of the system's state-to-state transition probabilities is available, which includes states the system would never enter without intervention.[3] Given these transition probabilities, the neuron's constraints can be expressed as conditional[4] probability distributions over all possible past and future states of the system, called a *cause-effect repertoire*. The neuron's cause-effect power can then be measured in informational terms, as the distance between the cause-effect repertoire, given the constraint that the neuron is "on", and the unconstrained probability distributions of possible past and future system states when the neuron's current state is unknown.

Crucial for IIT's causal analysis is that not only single elements, such as individual neurons, can have cause-effect power within the system. Multiple neurons with overlapping inputs and outputs can jointly constrain their causes and effects in ways that are not captured by the constraints of the individual neurons taken separately. Sets of elements that have such *irreducible* constraints also form mechanisms with cause-effect power within the system.

The cause-effect structure of a physical system, such as a network of neurons, is then composed of the set of cause-effect repertoires of all mechanisms within the system and their relations (overlapping constraints).

Intrinsicality: The cause-effect structure of a system specifies how the elements within the system causally constrain *each other* alone and in combination. Yet, cortical neurons, for example, receive many inputs from other brain areas, and their activity is to a large part determined by sensory inputs from the environment (but see Muckli and Petro, 2013). Such external influences from elements outside the system are treated as background conditions and are fixed in their state during the causal analysis. They may influence the system by setting it to its current state or modulating the system's mechanisms, but do not contribute directly to the system's cause-effect structure.

Composition: Standard approaches for studying the causal or informational properties of a system typically assume either a reductionist or holist perspective. Yet, analyzing only constraints of individual system elements or the system as a whole would disregard the compositional causal structure of the system, and would be inconsistent with the principle that physical existence translates into having cause-effect power (Alexander, 1920). The irreducible constraints of a set of elements in their current state are just as "real" (i.e., it exists, having specific causes and effects) as the constraints of individual elements. That two neurons receive inputs from the same source and have common outputs is a difference that makes a difference to the system. Nevertheless, not all possible combinations of elements automatically form mechanisms with irreducible constraints and typically not all mechanisms are related (have overlapping constraints).

Information: The specific shape of the cause-effect structure of a system in a state corresponds to the information the system specifies about itself at any given moment. By contrast to the notion of Shannon information introduced within the framework of communication theory (Shannon and Weaver, 1949), this type of information is physical (i.e., causal), intrinsic, and state-dependent (Oizumi et al., 2014; Tononi et al., 2016). For the system itself, only those properties of its past state matter that also have effects on its future. An external observer of the system may thus infer (extrinsic) information about a system that does not actually play a causal role within the system. The shape of the cause-effect structure, moreover, changes with the state of the system. A neuron in state "off" specifies the opposite constraints compared to when it is "on", and its cause-effect power, i.e., how much it constraints its inputs and outputs, may be different in the two cases.

Integration: A system in its current state forms an integrated whole, if there is no part of the system that is not constrained by the rest. This can be tested in a principled manner by partitioning the system, which means eliminating any potential constraints from one part of the system to the rest. The impact of the partition can be evaluated by comparing the cause-effect structure of the intact system against the cause-effect structure of the partitioned system. The integrated information Φ of a system quantifies this difference for the partition that makes the least difference to the system's cause-effect structure. This means that a system is only as integrated as its weakest link. It also means that unidirectionally ("feedforward") connected sets of elements cannot form an integrated whole, and thus cannot be a PSC since the upstream elements are not constrained by the more downstream elements.

Exclusion: Specifying an integrated cause-effect structure with $\Phi > 0$ is a necessary, but not a sufficient, requirement for a set of elements to be a PSC. The set of elements that forms the PSC within our brain at a given moment is likely not the only one with positive Φ. Other overlapping sets of elements, such as the PSC plus or minus a couple of neurons, will also form integrated cause-effect structures.[5] What distinguishes the PSC and specifies its borders is that its cause-effect structure is a maximum of cause-effect power Φ. Identifying the PSC with IIT's causal analysis thus requires testing all relevant sets of elements in order to find the one with maximal Φ. Since the cause-effect structure of a set of elements and its Φ value are state-dependent, the PSC's borders may also vary from state to state. Whether a system gives rise to a stable PSC thus depends on its physical properties (Marshall et al., 2017).

Spatio-temporal scales: The IIT formalism includes methods for evaluating the cause-effect structure of a system at various spatio-temporal grains (Hoel et al., 2013, 2016; Marshall et al., 2018). While the state-to-state transitions of a system at a macro level of description always supervene upon those of its micro constituents,[6] the cause-effect structure of a system may include more intrinsic mechanisms and may be more integrated with higher Φ at a macro level of description than at the micro level. According to IIT, the PSC corresponds to the particular set of elements at the particular spatio-temporal grain at which Φ is maximized. Identifying the correct grains again requires evaluating Φ across all relevant micro and macro levels of description.

Applicability: Identifying the set of elements with maximal Φ rigorously, according to the exact mathematical algorithm, is only possible for very small networks constituted of only a few interacting elements, chiefly because the number of mechanisms, partitions, and sets of elements to be evaluated grows exponentially with the size of the system. Applying IIT's causal analysis to biological systems, moreover, requires extensive perturbational data, or an already established causal model of the basic system elements and their interactions.

While a full evaluation of all IIT postulates in the brain is currently unfeasible, IIT already inspired a series of experiments which established that consciousness requires both causal integration and differentiation of cortical areas (Massimini et al., 2005; Ferrarelli et al., 2010; Pigorini et al., 2015). These experiments have motivated an empirical measure of consciousness, the perturbational complexity index (PCI) (Casali et al., 2013), which can be used to assess the level of consciousness for individual subjects. Following a perturbation of the cerebral cortex using transcranial magnetic stimulation (TMS), the resulting response is recorded using electroencephalography. The more incompressible and thus complex the response, the higher the PCI. Since complex responses to TMS require both cortical integration and differentiation, the PCI may serve as a practical proxy of Φ.

The growing evidence that information integration is at least a necessary condition for consciousness has also led to the development of alternative empirical measures applicable to time-series data from spontaneous neural recordings based on mutual information (Barrett and Seth, 2011; Oizumi et al., 2016; Tegmark, 2016) and multivariate prediction (Sasai et al., 2016). These approaches capture important aspects of Φ. How well they correlate with the actual quantity, however, still has to be determined. To this end, efforts are underway to develop efficient algorithms (Mayner et al., 2017; Toker and Sommer, 2019; Kitazono et al., 2018) and approximations (Marshall et al., 2016; Mayner et al., 2017) for the explicit algorithm.

While stringent practical measures to determine the PSC in the brain and other biological systems are still being developed, several interesting predictions and inferences already follow from the basic, rigorous formalism. These will be discussed below.

Explanations, predictions, and implications

IIT's specific explanations and predictions regarding the PSC within the brain follow from three, more general principles. First, IIT specifies that a PSC must correspond to a maximum of intrinsic cause-effect power Φ. With respect to the NCC, this principle should address why certain cortical regions contribute directly to experience and others do not, why phenomenology seems to correlate with the state of (groups of) neurons while the specific state of their constituting atoms or molecules does not seem to matter, and why our experiences have the specific timescale they have. The anticipated explanation in all cases is that this particular set of cortical elements at that particular spatial and temporal scale maximizes its intrinsic cause-effect power Φ.

Second, the quantity or level of consciousness corresponds to the amount of integrated information Φ specified by its physical substrate, i.e., how much cause-effect power it has onto itself. This IIT principle may explain why the cerebral cortex with its functional specialization and integration is an ideal substrate for consciousness while, for example, the cerebellum with its modular organization is not. Moreover, it should be possible to explain changes in the level of consciousness through changes in the Φ value of its PSC. When consciousness fades during dreamless sleep, general anesthesia, or epileptic seizures, the integrated information Φ of relevant regions in the cerebral cortex should dramatically decrease. This has recently been demonstrated for the PCI, a proxy of Φ, at the level of single subjects (Casali et al., 2013), which opened up the possibility of assessing the level of consciousness in the clinic, independent of a patient's ability to report (Casarotto et al., 2016).

Third, IIT postulates that the quality or content of an experience is structurally identical to the cause-effect structure specified by its physical substrate. Every aspect of the experience should correspond to a feature of the PSC's cause-effect structure and similar experiences should correspond to similar cause-effect structures. The cause-effect structures corresponding to our phenomenology should, for example, reflect its organization into distinct modalities and submodalities. The relations between components in the cause-effect structure should also capture the binding of features within the experience (Treisman, 1996), such as seeing a green car and a red light without also seeing a green light. Finally, changes in the cause-effect structure due to changes in the efficacy of the connections among elements of the PSC should be accompanied by corresponding changes in the experience, even if the level of activity remains unchanged.

Overall, testing IIT's predictions experimentally remains challenging. Nevertheless, initial proposals for feasible experiments that test some of the predictions outlined above can be found in Tononi et al., 2016. Continued validation of IIT's predictions in increasingly detailed experimental tests should result in increased confidence in its explanations and implications.

How to comprehend the PSC within the brain

While there is broad consensus that the NCC are located in certain parts of the cortico-thalamic system (Koch et al., 2016), it is still under debate which specific areas directly contribute to phenomenology (e.g.: Boly et al., 2017; Odegaard et al., 2017). Recent developments, including no-report paradigms (Frässle et al., 2014) and within-state paradigms (Siclari et al., 2017), aim to dissociate the true NCC from neural processes that merely precede or follow the experience itself (Aru et al., 2012; Pitts et al., 2014; Tsuchiya et al., 2015), or act as enabling or modulating factors, but do not contribute to the experience directly (Koch et al., 2016; Boly et al., 2017).

IIT clearly distinguishes between elements that are part of the PSC and thus contribute directly to phenomenology and external influences, the so-called "background conditions". Elements included in the PSC form a maximum of intrinsic cause-effect power Φ and their cause-effect structure corresponds to the experience. Elements that act as background conditions are excluded from the PSC, because including them would decrease its Φ. Nevertheless, certain background conditions may be necessary to enable functional interactions between the elements of the PSC. An example may be the presence of sufficient excitatory inputs originating from the brainstem to maintain adequate cortical excitability (Parvizi and Damasio, 2001), but also sufficient oxygen in the blood to keep cortical neurons alive. Other external influences such as sensory inputs may influence the state of the elements within the PSC.

Purely afferent or efferent connections to and from other brain regions, such as neural connections from the retina, cannot be part of the PSC even in principle, since they are connected in a feedforward manner and thus cannot be integrated with the rest (see the *Integration* section above). Some cortical areas may be included in the PSC under certain circumstances and act as background conditions in others.

To what extent the PSC in the brain is static or dynamic is an interesting open question. It is possible that the PSC may shrink, expand, or move due to attentional modulation of neural excitability and functional connectivity, depending on specific task conditions (Sasai et al., 2016). Initial evidence, moreover, suggests that during rapid eye movement (REM) sleep, the PSC might become restricted to more posterior or anterior cortical regions, as high-frequency activity in the respective areas correlated with more perceptual or thought-like dream experiences (Siclari et al., 2017). During slow-wave sleep, local bistability (oscillations between up- and down-states) may causally disconnect different regions from the PSC at different times (Nir et al., 2011; Pigorini et al., 2015).

Neural elements that are permanently or temporarily inactivated, for instance, due to a lesion, or a TMS pulse, or by being hyperpolarized during a slow-wave down-state, cannot be part of the PSC, as they cannot influence or be influenced by the rest of the system and thus lack cause-effect power. In that case, whatever phenomenal distinctions they usually contribute will be lost to the experiencing subject. In most cases, the cause-effect structure of such a reduced experience will differ from the cause-effect structure when these neural elements are inactive, but functional. Inactive neurons still constrain their causes and effects and may thus be part of the PSC and contribute to the experience (see *Information* section above). In this picture, the neural correlates of experiencing color when inactive may still contribute negative color concepts ("no color", "no blue", "no red", etc.) to the experience, for example, while watching a black and white movie. By contrast, a recent case study suggests that patients with complete lesions to cortical areas responding to color seem to lack such concepts of "no color" and, in fact, any understanding about what they are lacking (von Arx et al., 2010).

In principle, which elements constitute the PSC may also be dependent on the state, i.e., activity pattern, of the system. Whether and to what extent the PSC in the brain encompasses the same neural elements in different states of activation remains to be investigated in more detail. Nevertheless, IIT allows for the possibility that the cerebral cortex may support experience even if it is almost silent, which contrasts with the assumption that neurons only contribute to consciousness if their activity is sufficiently amplified to "ignite" a large cortical network (Dehaene and Changeux, 2011). Here, the neural correlates of special, meditative experiential states of "contentless consciousness" (Sullivan, 1995) may shed some light on the phenomenal contribution of inactive cortical areas.

While inactive neural elements can still, in principle, form a maximum of integrated information Φ and thus a PSC, high Φ is generally associated with high functional differentiation and integration. Whether high-level cognitive tasks, including certain metacognitive processes, can be performed unconsciously is still an area of active research (Charles et al., 2017; Kouider and Faivre, 2017). From the perspective of the PSC that corresponds to our daily experiences, any cognitive tasks performed by neural elements outside the PSC will appear to be carried out unconsciously. Some of these functions may be mediated by feed-forward circuits which lack any integration and thus are strictly unconscious according to IIT, or they may be supported by neural elements that are (weakly) integrated but still excluded from the PSC. In principle, IIT even allows for the possibility that multiple substrates of consciousness may coexist within a single brain as long as their (neural) elements do not overlap. This may be the case in certain pathological conditions, for example, after a split-brain operation where the neural elements that typically constitute the PSC are anatomically split in two, but could also happen temporarily due to functional disconnection, for example, in subjects that were over-trained in dual-task conditions (Sasai et al., 2016).

In sum, which neural elements constitute the PSC is determined both by their functional connectivity as well as their activation pattern.

Phenomenal content and the PSC's cause-effect structure

IIT postulates an identity between the phenomenal structure of the experience and the PSC's cause-effect structure, and not between the former and its constituting elements or their activation pattern. An intriguing prediction of IIT is that in certain cases, small changes in the activation pattern or the efficacy of certain neural connections of elements within the PSC, or even its background conditions, may drastically change the cause-effect structure and thus the subject's experience. One reason for this is the compositional nature of the cause-effect structure which allows an element to contribute not just once, but in all possible combinations with other elements of the PSC, as long as their joint constraints on the PSC are irreducible. All such sets of elements correspond to phenomenal distinctions or "concepts" within the experience.

As is apparent from IIT's algorithm for causal analysis, the number of possible phenomenal distinctions grows exponentially with the number of elements in the PSC. Already a small system comprised of 5 interacting neurons may specify as many as 31 intrinsic mechanisms that could contribute to the cause-effect structure (Oizumi et al., 2014). Since the PSC within the human brain is likely constituted of many neural elements at any given time, human phenomenology according to IIT is extremely rich in content. This contrasts with the supposedly very small number of reportable, consciously perceived items estimated from psychological experiments that aim to assess the information capacity of human consciousness (Miller, 1956). Experimental tests of conscious contents typically probe specific features, such as the identity of particular letters in a display (Sperling, 1960), and thus omit many other concepts that would, in principle, be reportable, such as the color, size, spacing, and background of the display, and also the vast number of negative concepts, such as "no face", "no animal", etc., which also distinguish the particular experience from other possible experiences. Still, the number of phenomenal distinctions that can be accessed by downstream regions, such as Broca's area, at any given time will necessarily be limited, as it would be impossible to transfer the vast amount of information specified by the cause-effect structure all at once. Nevertheless, per IIT, access or reportability is not a requisite for a physical mechanism to contribute a concept to experience, as postulated by functionalist approaches to consciousness (Cohen and Dennett, 2011), which might lead us to underestimate the richness of experience (see Cohen et al., 2016 and response by Haun et al., 2017).

On a similar note, IIT recognizes dreams as phenomenal experiences, even though the experiencing subject is functionally disconnected from its environment. As long as during sleep cortical neural elements form a PSC with a maximally integrated cause-effect structure, the subject will be conscious irrespective of their capacity to report or remember their experiences. Their dream experiences will match experiences during wakefulness to the extent that their cause-effect structures are similar. Indeed, recent evidence suggests that the same content specific NCC are present during dreams as in wakefulness (Siclari et al., 2017) and that REMs in sleep are associated with visual-like activity (Andrillon et al., 2015). Finally, evaluating the level of consciousness of dreaming subjects using the PCI, a proxy for Φ, revealed similar PCI levels in REM sleep with subsequent dream reports as during wakefulness (Casali et al., 2013).

IIT grants experiences an immense richness in phenomenal distinctions, based on the compositional nature of its corresponding cause-effect structure, which specifies the informational content of the experience. That every element within the PSC contributes to the cause-effect structure alone or in combination, however, does not mean that every piece of information that could be extracted from the PSC will be part of the experience. Machine-learning approaches, such as classifiers trained to decode specific stimulus features, are now frequently applied to neuroimaging data (Quian Quiroga and Panzeri, 2009; King and Dehaene, 2014). These tools alone, however, cannot capture whether the identified representations actually make a difference to the conscious subject. Being able to extract information about specific stimuli from the brain does not mean that the brain itself is "using" this information (Haynes, 2009). In order to contribute to the cause-effect structure, a set of elements must have specific causes and effects within the PSC. While testing the predicted one-to-one correspondence between the PSC's cause-effect structure and a subject's experience in detail in every case is unfeasible, certain experiences may be more accessible than others. For example, it may already be possible to demonstrate that the experience of visual space with all its possible locations and their relations could be captured by the highly compositional cause-effect structures of relatively simple, grid-like neural networks that are organized similar to neurons in visual cortical areas.

Beyond the human PSC

Our own experiences are the only example of consciousness that is directly accessible to each of us. We typically grant consciousness to other human beings, since they are very much like us in anatomy and functional capability. Many assume that mammals and other "intelligent" animals are conscious, though maybe less so than we are, depending on how similar their behavior and their brains are to ours, in evolutionary and neural terms (Edelman and Seth, 2009). What is the relation between consciousness, intelligence, and evolution? Does consciousness come with specific functional capabilities that can explain why and when it evolved? And should we consider engineered systems, such as computers, as conscious beings once they become sufficiently intelligent, even though they lack a biological basis?

IIT does not presuppose any specific set of functions to be associated with consciousness. Nevertheless, IIT still offers an explanation for why consciousness evolved, based on adaptive advantages of having the type of brain structures that are suitable for high integrated information Φ (Edlund et al., 2011; Albantakis et al., 2014). Integrated neural networks are more efficient in terms of the amount of functions that can be specified by a given number of neurons and connections and provide a more adaptive substrate for selection (Albantakis et al., 2014). Evolution should also ensure that the intrinsic cause-effect structure of an organism "matches" the causal structure of its environment (Tononi, 2012, 2015). In short, according to IIT, evolution connects consciousness with intelligence.

In general, however, IIT dissociates between consciousness and intelligence, which is especially relevant with respect to recent advances in artificial intelligence. Deep neural networks, for example, have already surpassed human-level capacity in a number of complex tasks using a purely feedforward network structure (Gregor et al., 2013). Such systems lack intrinsic cause-effect power ($\Phi = 0$) and would thus be unconscious per IIT, no matter how intelligent they could become. In general, current computers based on a "von Neumann" architecture do not qualify as physical substrates of consciousness according to IIT, as they are intentionally modular in their design. While the computer as a whole specifies at most very little integrated information, also the cause-effect structures of its parts would hardly be more integrated than those of other inanimate objects comprised of atoms and molecules. Again, this holds regardless of the software that is executed by the computer. Even computers that simulate our behavior or neural activity in extraordinary detail would thus remain unconscious.

Nevertheless, IIT does not presuppose a biological basis for consciousness. If the set of axioms identified by IIT is consistent and complete, and all accompanying postulates have been correctly inferred, then any physical system that fulfills

IIT's postulates will meet all necessary and sufficient conditions to be a PSC. If, for example, an artificial, silicon-based brain complies with all IIT postulates, it would be conscious in the same sense as we are. In this case, there would be no room to argue for a biological basis as an additional requirement for consciousness, since it could not explain any additional facts about our phenomenology.

At the other end of the intelligence spectrum, IIT allows for very simple systems to be conscious (Tononi and Koch, 2015) and does not require, for example, the ability to report or self-monitor one's internal states (Dehaene et al., 2017). Higher-order, metacognitive capabilities are necessary to introspect on one's conscious experiences. Being conscious in the first place, however, only requires intrinsic existence, i.e., a PSC that is a maximum of intrinsic cause-effect power Φ. Even very small systems of only a couple of interacting elements can, in principle, give rise to a cause-effect structure that fulfills all IIT postulates (Oizumi et al., 2014; Tononi and Koch, 2015). Since all matter interacts with each other physically, IIT has been related to panpsychism, the philosophical proposal that consciousness is fundamental and universal (Chalmers, 2015). While IIT treats consciousness as a fundamental property of reality, and also implies that consciousness is graded, and most likely widespread in nature, it also clearly implies that not everything is conscious (Tononi and Koch, 2015). While single cell bacteria, for example, might form maxima of intrinsic cause-effect power, by the exclusion postulate, the neurons that constitute our PSC are excluded from being consciousnesses of their own. For the same reason, groups of people are excluded from being conscious even if they are performing a complex, collaborative task, as long as their interconnectedness does not surpass that of the cerebral cortices of the individuals. Finally, invoking panpsychism to resolve the nature of consciousness still leaves the essential properties of experience, its composition, information, irreducibility, and definiteness unaccounted for while they are central to IIT's framework.

Conclusion

To conclude, IIT provides a theory of consciousness that aims to account for the quantity and quality of consciousness in terms of the intrinsic cause-effect power (Φ) and structure of its physical substrate. Instead of circumventing the problem of subjectivity by correlating reportable aspects of consciousness to neural mechanisms, IIT derives most of its explanatory, predictive, and inferential power from the fact that consciousness exists intrinsically for the experiencing subject. Following the principle that existence in physical terms corresponds to having cause-effect power, IIT translates the essential properties of experience into requirements for the causal structure of its physical substrate. The accompanying theoretical formalism, in principle, makes it possible to evaluate whether a physical system complies with the IIT postulates and should therefore be regarded as a PSC, to quantify the level of consciousness of such a system and to provide a full account of its phenomenological structure in causal terms. Whether the exclusive and detailed predictions following from this formalism can be validated remains to be determined. Experiments that could test not only IIT's general approach, but also its specific theoretical framework, still require neuroscientific, mathematical, and computational advances. To the extent that such future experiments corroborate IIT's predictions, its principled approach offers many intriguing implications and makes it possible to extrapolate from our experiences to the phenomenology of other physical entities.

Acknowledgements

I thank Giulio Tononi for his continuing support and helpful comments on this chapter. L.A. receives funding from the Templeton World Charities Foundation (Grant #TWCF0196).

Notes

1 A physical mechanism here is a set of physical elements with cause-effect power.
2 The python toolbox "Pyphi" (Mayner et al., 2017) allows evaluating all IIT quantities for small systems of binary elements and is available here: https://github.com/wmayner/pyphi.
3 IIT's approach for determining causal relations is related to Judea Pearl's calculus of interventions (Pearl, 2000) and measures of information flow (Ay and Polani, 2008), as it is based on interventional, not observed, conditional probabilities and probability distributions.
4 "Conditional" here means the probability distributions over possible past and future states of the system *given* the current state of the neuron is known.
5 Note that this boundary problem likely arises for any physical, computational, or informational property of an open system (Fekete et al., 2016).
6 This means that the macro-level dynamics are completely determined by its underlying micro constituents.

References

Albantakis L, Hintze A, Koch C, Adami C, Tononi G (2014) Evolution of integrated causal structures in animats exposed to environments of increasing complexity. *PLoS Comput Biol* 10:e1003966.
Alexander S (1920) *Space, Time, and Deity: The Gifford Lectures at Glasgow, 1916–1918.* London: Macmillan.
Andrillon T, Nir Y, Cirelli C, Tononi G, Fried I (2015) Single-neuron activity and eye movements during human REM sleep and awake vision. *Nat Commun* 6:7884.
Aru J, Bachmann T, Singer W, Melloni L (2012) Distilling the neural correlates of consciousness. *Neurosci Biobehav Rev* 36:737–746.
Ay N, Polani D (2008) Information flows in causal networks. *Adv Complex Syst* 11:17–41.
Barrett AB, Seth AK (2011) Practical measures of integrated information for time-series data. *PLoS Comput Biol* 7:e1001052.
Boly M, Massimini M, Tsuchiya N, Postle BR, Koch C, Tononi G (2017) Are the neural correlates of consciousness in the front or in the back of the cerebral cortex? Clinical and neuroimaging evidence. *J Neurosci* 37:9603–9613.

Casali AG, Gosseries O, Rosanova M, Boly M, Sarasso S, Casali KR, Casarotto S, Bruno M-A, Laureys S, Tononi G, Massimini M (2013) A theoretically based index of consciousness independent of sensory processing and behavior. *Sci Transl Med* 5:198ra105.

Casarotto S, Comanducci A, Rosanova M, Sarasso S, Fecchio M, Napolitani M, Pigorini A, G. Casali A, Trimarchi PD, Boly M, Gosseries O, Bodart O, Curto F, Landi C, Mariotti M, Devalle G, Laureys S, Tononi G, Massimini M (2016) Stratification of unresponsive patients by an independently validated index of brain complexity. *Ann Neurol* 80:718–729.

Chalmers D (2015) Panpsychism and panprotopsychism. In: *Consciousness in the Physical World: Perspectives on Russellian Monism* (Alter T, Nagasawa Y, eds), pp. 246–276. Oxford: Oxford University Press.

Charles L, Gaillard R, Amado I, Krebs MO, Bendjemaa N, Dehaene S (2017) Conscious and unconscious performance monitoring: evidence from patients with schizophrenia. *Neuroimage* 144:153–163.

Cohen MA, Dennett DC (2011) Consciousness cannot be separated from function. *Trends Cogn Sci* 15:358–364.

Cohen MA, Dennett DC, Kanwisher N (2016) What is the bandwidth of perceptual experience? *Trends Cogn Sci* 20:324–335.

Dehaene S, Changeux J-P (2011) Experimental and theoretical approaches to conscious processing. *Neuron* 70:200–227.

Dehaene S, Lau H, Kouider S (2017) What is consciousness, and could machines have it? *Science* (80-) 358:486–492.

Edelman DB, Seth AK (2009) Animal consciousness: a synthetic approach. *Trends Neurosci* 32:476–484.

Edlund JA, Chaumont N, Hintze A, Koch C, Tononi G, Adami C (2011) Integrated information increases with fitness in the evolution of animats. *PLoS Comput Biol* 7:e1002236.

Fekete T, van Leeuwen C, Edelman S (2016) System, subsystem, hive: boundary problems in computational theories of consciousness. *Front Psychol* 7:1041.

Ferrarelli F, Massimini M, Sarasso S, Casali A, Riedner BA, Angelini G, Tononi G, Pearce RA (2010) Breakdown in cortical effective connectivity during midazolam-induced loss of consciousness. *Proc Natl Acad Sci U S A* 107:2681–2686.

Frässle S, Sommer J, Jansen A, Naber M, Einhäuser W (2014) Binocular rivalry: frontal activity relates to introspection and action but not to perception. *J Neurosci* 34(5):1738–1747.

Gregor K, Danihelka I, Mnih A, Blundell C, Wierstra D (2013) Deep autoregressive networks. arXiv 1310.8499.

Haun AM, Tononi G, Koch C, Tsuchiya N (2017) Are we underestimating the richness of visual experience? *Neurosci Conscious* 2017: 1–4.

Haynes J-D (2009) Decoding visual consciousness from human brain signals. *Trends Cogn Sci* 13:194–202.

Hoel EP, Albantakis L, Marshall W, Tononi G (2016) Can the macro beat the micro? Integrated information across spatiotemporal scales. *Neurosci Conscious* 2016:1–13.

Hoel EP, Albantakis L, Tononi G (2013) Quantifying causal emergence shows that macro can beat micro. *PNAS* 110:19790–19795.

King J-R, Dehaene S (2014) Characterizing the dynamics of mental representations: the temporal generalization method. *Trends Cogn Sci* 18:203–210.

Kitazono J, Kanai R, Oizumi M (2018) Efficient algorithms for searching the minimum information partition in integrated information theory. *Entropy* 20:173.

Koch C (2004) *The Quest for Consciousness: A Neurobiological Approach.* Greenwood Village, CO: Roberts and Co.

Koch C, Massimini M, Boly M, Tononi G (2016) Neural correlates of consciousness: progress and problems. *Nat Rev Neurosci* 17:307–321.

Kouider S, Faivre N (2017) Conscious and unconscious perception. In: Schneider, S., & Velmans, M. (Eds.) *The Blackwell Companion to Consciousness*, pp. 551–561. Chichester: John Wiley & Sons, Ltd.

Marshall W, Albantakis L, Tononi G (2018) Black-boxing and cause-effect power. *PLOS Comput Biol* 14:e1006114.

Marshall W, Gomez-Ramirez J, Tononi G (2016) Integrated information and state differentiation. *Front Psychol* 7:926.

Marshall W, Kim H, Walker SI, Tononi G, Albantakis L (2017) How causal analysis can reveal autonomy in models of biological systems. *Philos Trans A Math Phys Eng Sci* 375:20160358.

Massimini M, Ferrarelli F, Huber R, Esser SK, Singh H, Tononi G (2005) Breakdown of cortical effective connectivity during sleep. *Science* 309:2228–2232.

Mayner WGP, Marshall W, Albantakis L, Findlay G, Marchman R, Tononi G (2017) PyPhi: A toolbox for integrated information theory. arXiv 1712.09644.

Miller GA (1956) The magical number seven, plus or minus two: some limits on our capacity for processing information. *Psychol Rev* 63:81–97.

Muckli L, Petro LS (2013) Network interactions: non-geniculate input to V1. *Curr Opin Neurobiol* 23:195–201.

Nir Y, Staba RJ, Andrillon T, Vyazovskiy VV, Cirelli C, Fried I, Tononi G (2011) Regional slow waves and spindles in human sleep. *Neuron* 70:153–169.

Odegaard B, Knight RT, Lau H (2017) Should a few null findings falsify prefrontal theories of conscious perception? *J Neurosci* 37:9593–9602.

Oizumi M, Albantakis L, Tononi G (2014) From the phenomenology to the mechanisms of consciousness: integrated information theory 3.0. *PLoS Comput Biol* 10:e1003588.

Oizumi M, Amari S, Yanagawa T, Fujii N, Tsuchiya N (2016) Measuring Integrated Information from the decoding perspective. *PLOS Comput Biol* 12:e1004654.

Parvizi J, Damasio A (2001) Consciousness and the brainstem. *Cognition* 79:135–160.

Pearl J (2000) *Causality: Models, Reasoning and Inference.* Cambridge, UK: Cambridge University Press.

Pigorini A, Sarasso S, Proserpio P, Szymanski C, Arnulfo G, Casarotto S, Fecchio M, Rosanova M, Mariotti M, Russo G Lo, Palva MJ, Nobili L, Massimini M (2015) Bistability breaks-off deterministic responses to intracortical stimulation during non-REM sleep. *Neuroimage* 112:105–113.

Pitts MA, Metzler S, Hillyard SA (2014) Isolating neural correlates of conscious perception from neural correlates of reporting one's perception. *Front Psychol* 5:1078.

Quian Quiroga R, Panzeri S (2009) Extracting information from neuronal populations: information theory and decoding approaches. *Nat Rev Neurosci* 10:173–185.

Rangarajan V, Hermes D, Foster BL, Weiner KS, Jacques C, Grill-Spector K, Parvizi J (2014) Electrical stimulation of the left and right human fusiform gyrus causes different effects in conscious face perception. *J Neurosci* 34:12828–12836.

Sasai S, Boly M, Mensen A, Tononi G (2016) Functional split brain in a driving/listening paradigm. *Proc Natl Acad Sci* 113:14444–14449.

Shannon CE, Weaver W (1949) *A Mathematical Theory of Communication* Urbana, IL: University of Illinois press.

Siclari F, Baird B, Perogamvros L, Bernardi G, LaRocque JJ, Riedner B, Boly M, Postle BR, Tononi G (2017) The neural correlates of dreaming. *Nat Neurosci* 20:872–878.

Sperling G (1960) The information available in brief visual presentations. *Psychol Monogr Gen Appl* 74:1–29.

Sullivan PR (1995) Contentless consciousness and information-processing theories of mind. *Philos Psychiatry Psychol* 2:51–59.

Tegmark M (2016) Improved measures of integrated information. *PLoS Comput Biol* 12:e1005123.

Toker D, Sommer FT (2019) Information Integration In Large Brain Networks, *PLoS Comput Biol* 15(2): 1–26.

Tononi G (2004) An information integration theory of consciousness. *BMC Neurosci* 5:42.

Tononi G (2008) Consciousness as integrated information: a provisional manifesto. *Biol Bull* 215:216–242.

Tononi G (2012) Integrated information theory of consciousness: an updated account. *Arch Ital Biol* 150:56–90.

Tononi G (2015) Integrated information theory. *Scholarpedia* 10:4164.

Tononi G, Boly M, Massimini M, Koch C (2016) Integrated information theory: from consciousness to its physical substrate. *Nat Rev Neurosci* 17:450–461.

Tononi G, Koch C (2015) Consciousness: here, there and everywhere? *Philos Trans R Soc Lond B Biol Sci* 370: 1–18. DOI: 10.1098/rstb.2014.0167

Treisman A (1996) The binding problem. *Curr Opin Neurobiol* 6:171–178.

Tsuchiya N, Wilke M, Frässle S, Lamme VAF (2015) No-report paradigms: extracting the true neural correlates of consciousness. *Trends Cogn Sci* 19:757–770.

von Arx SW, Müri RM, Heinemann D, Hess CW, Nyffeler T (2010) Anosognosia for cerebral achromatopsia—a longitudinal case study. *Neuropsychologia* 48:970–977.

6

GLOBAL WORKSPACE MODELS OF CONSCIOUSNESS IN A BROADER PERSPECTIVE

Antonino Raffone & Henk P. Barendregt

Introduction

Models of consciousness based on the notion of *global workspace* (GW), as the core processor of the brain for conscious access and processing of information for higher-level cognitive functions, have been influential in consciousness studies and related neuroscientific investigations over about three decades (Baars, 1988, 1997, 1998; Baars et al., 2003; Dehaene & Naccache, 2001; Dehaene et al., 1998, 2006, 2011; Raffone et al., 2014; Simione et al., 2012).

In this chapter, we address GW models of consciousness and their implications in a broader perspective, by approaching a range of consciousness domains with reference to GW principles, beyond the generally addressed domains of visual cognition phenomena and executive control processes (e.g., Dehaene & Changeux, 2005; Dehaene et al., 1998, 2003, 2006; Raffone et al., 2014; Simione et al., 2012).

We present, in the next sections, the Global Workspace Theory and the Global Neuronal Workspace Model with related developments and approaches. We then proceed to sequentially address GW model principles and implications as related to the influential distinction between phenomenal and access consciousness, mental programs and adaptive brain responses in higher-level cognition, discrete processing and multiple time scales for conscious representation in the brain, perspectives and theories about the self, the phenomenology and neuroscience of dreaming, meditation and mindfulness, and hypnosis. We conclude with a summary of the chapter.

Global workspace theory

Global Workspace Theory (GWT) of Bernard Baars (Baars, 1988, 1997, 1998; Baars et al., 2003) is currently one of the most influential theories of human consciousness. It has fundamental implications for addressing the neurocognitive correlates of consciousness. In this theory, the GW system of neurocognitive information processing enables conscious access to and processing of contents represented in different perceptual/cognitive modules associated to widespread brain areas. By contrast, in unconscious processing these modules represent and process information in a substantially segregated fashion. Thus, the GW system enables a gateway to a large set of active representations in the brain, making them accessible for conscious representation and processing.

GWT has been related to a theater metaphor (Baars, 1997); convergence zones in the brain (i.e. the *theater stage*) are needed for the emergence of integrated conscious perceptual information (e.g., in the visual domain). It is as if signals from sensory projection cortical areas are "lit up" by attentional activation, and provide consciousness contents by converging at the level of more anterior areas. Conscious states can involve a large set of cortical and subcortical brain regions (the *audience*) that can be recruited on an intentional basis for conscious access operations. One may also compare the GW with a cockpit with many displays of sensors and many actuators that are able to influence the position of the plane and thereby the values of the display. In GWT, a key role is played by *broadcasting* of selected contents, i.e. "speaking to the audience"; in this way, conscious information can be widely disseminated in the brain. In a GW, broadcasting process perceptual inputs can be intentionally enhanced, new memories and motor responses can be selected.

In his GWT, Baars (1998, 2002) remarked that conscious events are likely to imply self-systems in the brain, and in particular a "narrative interpreter". Metaphorically, this interpreter would operate as a *stage director* in a theater or pilot in a cockpit. Baars particularly refers to Gazzaniga's (1985) findings with split-brain patients, and argues that the two hemispheres might each have an "observer" (or executive interpreter) of the respective conscious flow of visual information. To address the issue that conscious perception may entail a dialog between specific self-related prefrontal regions (stage director or executive interpreter) and sensory cortex (Baars et al., 2003), brain activity patterns produced by a demanding sensory categorization task were compared to those engaged during self-reflective introspection using similar sensory stimuli (Goldberg et al., 2006). The results showed a complete segregation between the two brain activity patterns. This challenges Baars' hypothesis of an involvement of self-related, observer-like prefrontal regions in perceptual awareness. Moreover, areas characterized by enhanced activity during introspection exhibited a robust inhibition during the demanding perceptual task. In terms of the comparison with a cockpit: there is not necessarily a pilot, an automatic pilot suffices. In line with this evidence, a compelling view of the phenomenal self as an ongoing integrated process and not as a separate overarching thing has been proposed by Metzinger (2004, 2013), also in resonance with ancient Buddhist teachings (Harvey, 1995).

In Baars' GWT, unconscious or "contextual" brain systems play an essential role in shaping conscious events by acting as the *backstage* of the theater.

Contextual systems for conscious representation in the brain include the "where" or dorsal pathway for visual processing, with a key role in representing the spatial location of objects (Milner & Goodale, 2008). Regions of the prefrontal cortex (e.g., medial prefrontal cortex) appear to play the same role in other aspects of experience, including emotional, goal-related, and self-representational processes (Baars et al., 2003). To the point, Baars noticed that unilateral neglect, a syndrome characterized by an altered spatial framework for vision which is often associated to damage within parietal, temporal superior, and insular cortices, is frequently accompanied by anosognosia, i.e. a massive loss of awareness of an individual's body space (Pia et al., 2004). Thus, contextual spatial and body representations appear to act as a crucial backstage for conscious experiences.

Contextual systems or the backstage in GW processing for conscious access can be linked with the notion of *penumbra* suggested by Crick and Koch (2003) in their framework for consciousness with reference to the dynamics of the Neural Correlate of Consciousness (NCC). In their framework, the NCC stands for the transiently dominant neuronal coalition (assembly) for a given conscious representation, as in the GW:

> The NCC at any one time will only directly involve a fraction of all pyramidal cells, but this firing will influence many neurons that are not part of the NCC. These we call the 'penumbra'. The penumbra consists of both synaptic effects and also firing rates. The penumbra is not the result of just the sum of the effects of each essential node separately, but the effects of that NCC as a whole. This penumbra includes past associations of NCC neurons, the expected consequences of the NCC, movements (or at least possible plans for movement) associated with NCC neurons, and so on. For example, a hammer represented in the NCC is likely to influence plans for hammering. The penumbra, by definition, is not itself conscious, although part of it may become part of the NCC as the NCC shifts. Some of the penumbra neurons may project back to parts of the NCC, or its support, and thus help to support the NCC. The penumbra neurons may be the site of unconscious priming.
>
> *(Crick & Koch, 2003, p. 124)*

Interestingly, the backstage of the GW or the penumbra of consciousness can support the sequential temporal binding of conscious contents. As observed in the 19th century by Francis Galton and William James, conscious contents seem to jump from one to the next, although they also seem to be linked by associative themes that emerge many times across the moments of consciousness.

In the contextual systems of the GW, emotions may exert a deep influence on both unconscious and conscious processing. As remarked by LeDoux (2000), by its projections to cortical areas, the amygdala can influence perceptual and short-term memory processes as well as processing in higher-order areas, including likely GW areas, such as the anterior cingulate cortex. The amygdala also projects to nonspecific systems involved in the regulation of arousal and bodily responses (behavioral, autonomic, endocrine), and can thus influence cortical processing indirectly. Thus, after a fast unconscious response which is effective at an unconscious level on the mind and body state, an emotional stimulus can access consciousness with a GW representation.

Maia and Cleeremans (2005) proposed a connectionist framework in which conscious representations linked to the GW for conscious processing involve a distributed neural network arriving at an "interpretation" of a given input by settling into a stable state, as in classic connectionist networks. Thus, according to Maia and Cleeremans, conscious experiences reflect stable states corresponding to interpretations that the brain makes of its current inputs. We furthermore argue that contextual systems such as self-related goal contexts, biases, and categories as well as mental programs (see below), can crucially contribute to select such stable conscious states as well as in setting "themes" across multiple selected states (see also Barendregt & Raffone, 2013; Crick & Koch, 2003).

GWT has been interestingly revised over the last few years to emphasize dynamic aspects and processing flexibility (Baars et al., 2013). In this more recent version of the approach, the GW is considered a functional capacity for dynamically coordinating and propagating neural signals over different task-related networks.

The global neuronal workspace model

The notion of GW is also central in the influential Global Neuronal Workspace (GNW) model proposed by Stanislas Dehaene and collaborators, with a higher focus on the brain processes, regions and mechanisms linked to the GW (Dehaene & Naccache, 2001; Dehaene et al., 1998, 2006, 2011; Gaillard et al., 2009). In a first proposal of this model, Dehaene et al. (1998) suggested that the GW for consciousness can access five major information categories involving perceptual systems, long-term memory, evaluation, motor systems, and attention focusing (see Figure 6.1). In such neurocognitive processing architecture, the GW thus accesses perceptual and memory representations, performs conscious decision-making and the choice of motor responses, controls (top-down) attentional selection, and is involved in conscious evaluation processes. In the GNW model, a key role for conscious access is attributed to executive areas such as the dorsolateral prefrontal, posterior parietal, and anterior cingulate cortices, which can interact with virtually all brain areas to support the large-scale functional processes for conscious access and processing (e.g., Dehaene et al., 1998, 2006, 2011; Gaillard et al., 2009).

As suggested by Dehaene et al. (2006), a stimulus can be selected for conscious access in the GW only if the *bottom-up* representation of the stimulus is sufficiently strong *and* if there is a concurrent *top-down* (endogenous) attention allocated to it. Also, in a related neurodynamical framework, Varela et al. (2001) emphasized the concurrency of bottom-up (incoming) and endogenous (top-down) neural activity for perception and awareness, with endogenous activity being provided by the states of expectation, motivation, emotion, and attention (among others), which

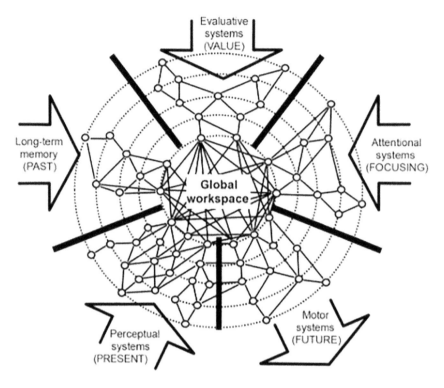

FIGURE 6.1 Illustration of the global neuronal workspace. Global workspace neurons in the brain receive inputs from multiple sources for conscious access, including perceptual systems in different modalities, (explicit) memory systems, evaluative systems, and attentional focusing maps, and send signals to select motor actions based on conscious decisions. From Dehaene et al. (1998).

are necessarily active at the same time as the sensory input, with psychophysical and physiological evidence for their active participation even at early stages of sensory perception (e.g., von Stein et al., 2000). Endogenous states influencing perception and conscious processing can be related to the notion of *mental state* (Barendregt & Raffone, 2013; Salzman & Fusi, 2010).

The GNW model is characterized by a winner-take-all dynamics at higher stages of neural processing (involving prefrontal cortex), a sort of "neural bottleneck", such that only one large-scale reverberating neural assembly is active in the neuronal GW at a given moment. These winner-take-all processes have been highlighted in experimental and related computational settings using the *attentional blink* paradigm, in which the subjects have to report the identity of two target stimuli (e.g., digits) in a series of rapidly presented visual stimuli, most of which are distracters (e.g., letters). If the second (T2) of the two target stimuli is presented within 500 ms of the first one (T1) in a rapid sequence of distracters, it is often not detected, thus resulting in an AB.

In the GNW model, subsets of GW neurons interact cooperatively for coherent encoding of mental objects, such as visual or memory items, and cause inhibition of neurons coding for competing ones (Dehaene & Changeux, 2005; Dehaene et al., 2003). This process is likely to be reflected in brain activity by states (modes) of enhanced and highly correlated (coherent or synchronous) neural activity within assemblies of distributed neurons coding for a given object. Entering such a state is characterized by amplification of local activity and subsequent ignition, i.e. a sudden rise in activation and coherence involving multiple, even distant areas in the thalamo-cortical system. Simulation studies have shown that these states can be entered rapidly (Dehaene & Changeux, 2005).

On the basis of the GNW model, Dehaene and Naccache (2001; see also Dehaene et al., 2006), proposed an useful taxonomy, in which some information encoded in the nervous system is inaccessible to the conscious level (set I1), other information is potentially accessible in the GW, since it can be consciously amplified if it is attended to (set I2), with only one selected content (object) of the latter being at any one time accessed in the workspace (set I3). Set I1 has been related to *unconscious* representation, set I2 to *preconscious* representation, and set I3, given by an assembly of widely distributed, activated, and interacting neurons, to *conscious* representation (Dehaene et al., 2006). The penumbra discussed above can be related in particular to set I2, although it can also be related to set I1 in cases in which activated preconscious information cannot be accessed even if attention is directed at it, such as in the well-known "tip of the tongue" phenomenon, which is the phenomenon of failing to retrieve a word or term from semantic long-term memory, combined with partial recall and the feeling that retrieval is imminent (Schwartz, 1999).

We suggest that a fourth set, I4, can be added to the taxonomy, as related to *meta-awareness*. The term *meta-awareness* has been introduced to describe a metacognitive function of being reflectively aware of the contents and processes of consciousness, including the contents and processes of thinking (Dahl et al., 2015; Smallwood & Schooler, 2006), and can be related to the notion of *mindfulness* and trained by *meditation* (Barendregt & Raffone, 2013; Raffone & Srinivasan, 2009), which will be further addressed below.

In an interesting intracranial electroencephalographic (EEG) investigation, Gaillard et al. (2009) provided an important contribution to characterize GNW processes and their time course, by comparing conscious and non-conscious processing of briefly flashed words. Non-conscious processing of masked words was observed in multiple cortical areas, mostly within an early time window (300 ms), accompanied by induced gamma band activity, but in the absence of coherent long-distance neural activity. In contrast, conscious processing of unmasked words was characterized by the convergence of four distinct neurophysiological markers: sustained voltage changes, particularly in prefrontal cortex, large increases in spectral power in the gamma oscillatory range, increases in long-distance phase synchrony in the beta range, and increases in long-range Granger causality. The analyses of Gaillard et al. (2009) suggested that only late sustained long-distance synchrony and late amplification (after 300 ms) may be causally related to conscious-level processing.

By developing the GNW principles, Simione et al. (2012) proposed the ViSA (*Vi*sual *S*election and *A*wareness) model, whose simulation accounted for a range of effects in visual conscious cognition, including key attentional blink and visuo-spatial working memory effects, with the additional capacity to maintain more than one object (up to four) in the GW, as also related to the limited capacity of visual working memory (Luck & Vogel, 1997; Raffone & Wolters, 2001). This model showed the flexibility of a GW account of a range of AB phenomena via the involvement of temporal gating dynamics and parallel representations in the GW, thus contrasting the earlier claim that key AB effects cannot be explained in terms of GW principles (Bowman & Wyble, 2007).

Following the lead of computational modeling investigations based on GW principles (Raffone & Pantani, 2010; Simione et al., 2012), a *Theory of Attention and Consciousness* (TAC) (Raffone et al., 2014) was further developed to provide a neurocognitive characterization of processing from early stages of sensory processing to encoding in working memory. This theory provides a novel taxonomy of attentional functions, including attentional filtering, attentional selection, and top-down attentional modulation, as also related to conscious access in the GW. TAC endorses the notion of GW from the earlier theories and models reviewed above; however, it originally postulates higher-order representations of executive operations besides object (target) representations in the GW. These include conscious access for motor response selection, access for consolidation in (visual) WM, top-down attentional modulation and amplification, and top-down executive inhibition. Each of these operations is represented and activated (ignited) by a control (or executive) router in the GW, i.e. an assembly of neurons which codes coherently for a given executive operation and inhibits neurons encoding competing operations in a higher-order winner-takes-all GW dynamics. The theory thus posits that a winner-takes-all competition between executive operations in the GW is critical to enable coherent top-down amplification in the thalamo-cortical system, together with coherent amplification and ignition processes occurring at the level of (target) object representation, as in GWT and the GNW model. Finally, TAC can also be regarded as a synthesis of all-or-none (such as in the GNW model) and graded (Overgaard et al., 2006) views of conscious representation. Indeed, through the stages of representations and processing in TAC, both all-or-none ignition processes and gradual evidence accumulation, amplification, and consolidation processes take place.

Global workspace, phenomenal and access consciousness

The philosopher Ned Block (1995, 2005) incorporated the notion of GW in his influential distinction between phenomenal and access consciousness. Phenomenal consciousness refers to qualia, i.e. first-person experiences (see also Huxley, 1874; Nagel, 1974). Thus, *phenomenally* conscious content refers to subjective experience, such as in the perceptual experiences of red and green. *Access* conscious content is information which is *broadcast* in the GW and made functionally available to the brain's "consuming" systems, including systems for the higher-level cognitive functions of reasoning, planning, evaluation of alternatives, decision-making, and voluntary direction of attention.

Set I2, i.e. the intermediate level of representation according to the taxonomy of Dehaene and Naccache (2001) described above, was linked by Block (2007) to a "broad cognitive accessibility" and related to the notion of phenomenal consciousness (Block, 2007). According to Block (2007), I3 representations in the workspace are actively connected with and potentially accessible to the consuming systems, which in turn are able to employ them. Block (2007) further emphasizes the difference between I3 representations that are cognitively accessible in the narrow sense, i.e. the consuming mechanisms using available content and those that are accessible in a broad sense, i.e. representations active in both I3 and I2 (Block, 2007), and thus beyond the GW. Block further interprets Dehaene and colleagues' (e.g., Dehaene & Naccache, 2001) position as equating the narrow sense with phenomenology. It is however Block's position "that the capacity of phenomenology is greater than that of the workspace – so it is narrow accessibility that is at issue" (Block, 2007, p. 492).

The GNW model suggests that conscious access is an "all-or-nothing" process involving *recurrent* interactions between multiple brain modules and key GW areas for conscious access, i.e., dorsolateral prefrontal and parietal posterior cortices (linked to set I3 in the taxonomy of Dehaene and Naccache). Within a related but substantially different approach, Lamme (2003, 2007, 2010) also suggested that phenomenally conscious experiences critically depend on recurrent signaling and processing, which can however take place in a more localized manner in posterior cortical areas without a necessary involvement of GW areas for conscious access (to set I2).

A salient characterization of set I2 in visual perception has been put forth by Lamme (2007): "Since there is little disagreement about the absence of conscious experience in I1, or about its presence in I3, the question becomes whether I2 is more like I1 (i.e., unconscious) or like I3 (conscious)" (p. 512). According to Lamme (2007), neuroscientific evidence suggests that I2 is more closely linked with I3 than I1, due to recurrent processing in both I2 and I3 versus non-recurrent ("feedforward") processing in I1. Thus, set I2 can be associated to phenomenal consciousness (Block, 2007; Lamme, 2003), characterized by a graded rather than an all-or-none activation. This view was supported by a neurocomputational modeling study (Raffone & Pantani, 2010) showing plausible neural mechanisms for recurrent interactions not only for access consciousness, but also for phenomenal consciousness.

Global workspace and mental programs

Zylberberg et al. (2011) outlined a theory of how individual neural processing steps might be combined into serial mental programs which are so essential for conscious human thought, as in decision, planning, or reasoning. They endorsed a hybrid approach combining the serial and discrete conscious processing, as in a Turing machine, with parallel distributed computations within each processing step (see also Barendregt & Raffone, 2013, for a similar approach, but with a stronger emphasis on the notion of "state"). Zylberberg et al. explicitly link their brain Turing machine framework with GWT, with emphasis on sequences of GW content activations. They endorse the notion of *production*, as in other cognitive architectures (Anderson & Lebiere, 1998; Laird et al., 1987; Meyer & Kieras, 1997), to factorize complex cognitive tasks into a discrete sequence of operations based on conscious access in the GW (see also Kamienkowski et al., 2018).

According to Zylberberg et al., the selection of productions or of their actions is determined by the contents of working memory, which crucially is, in turn, modified by the productions themselves in a recursive (circular) manner. Also attentional focusing can be redirected by the selected productions, in turn influencing the following conscious access or action selection. The selection process of productions or their actions takes place in parallel. This process is based on the converging influence of broadly distributed sensory and memory states. Remarkably, as in the GW, only one production can be selected at a time in a winner-take-all competition. Zylberberg et al. (2011) also remarked the relevance of spontaneous brain activity for the selection of conscious productions, in line with a previous neurocomputational study by Dehaene and Changeux (2005). In this view, conscious access and productions are far from being reactive, i.e. being only dependent on the input, but rather based on intrinsic brain or mental states (see also Barendregt & Raffone, 2013).

It has been observed that the activity of virtually all neurons, even those in primary sensory areas, can be influenced by the current task context (Gilbert & Sigman, 2007; Roelfsema et al., 1998; Zylberberg et al., 2011). Such evidence sheds light on the adaptivity of brain responses at different levels of representation, which can potentially support *cognitive flexibility*. In particular, a common or multiple-demand pattern of frontal and parietal activity is associated with diverse cognitive demands and with structured *mental programs*. In such mental programs, goals are achieved by assembling a series of sub-tasks (Duncan, 2010). For example, in cooking a meal or finding the roots of a cubic equation, goals are achieved by assembling a series of sub-tasks, which are separately defined and solved. This resembles the serial and recursive processing steps in conventional computer algorithms to achieve a final goal. Multiple-demand areas also include parts of dorsolateral prefrontal cortex, anterior cingulated cortex, and anterior insula, to which we pay particular attention in this article. Interestingly, Duncan (2010) remarked that dorsolateral prefrontal and anterior cingulate cortices can flexibly exhibit either sustained or transient activities depending on the task demand.

Duncan's (2010) multiple-demand framework can be related to a previous model of the same author (Duncan, 2001), emphasizing adaptive neuronal coding in prefrontal cortex. In this model, prefrontal cortex acts as a GW or working memory onto which can be written those data that are needed in a current mental program. And thus, in a particular task context, many neurons become adaptively tuned to code information that is specifically relevant to that task. Inspired by Duncan's (2001) perspective, Raffone and Srinivasan (2009) proposed a neurocognitive framework for awareness, meta-awareness, and circular interactions with top-down attention, also with reference to meditation states.

As emphasized by Dehaene and collaborators in their GNW approach (e.g., Dehaene et al., 2006), conscious access takes place only with concurrent strong sensory input for a given stimulus and top-down attention being allocated to that stimulus. However, it appears crucial to determine what directs attention in the first place. Recursive or circular determinations in mental programs (Zylberberg et al., 2011) might bridge such crucial gap: the focus of attention determines conscious access, and such conscious access within active mental programs determines the next focus of attention. Such mental programs and recursive operations do suggest the *selfless* nature of the GW for conscious access: one does not need a stage director for central executive control and for a terminal stage of conscious access. Such selfless view of the GW appears more plausible than the view previously suggested by Baars (1998; Baars et al., 2003) in terms of the key role of a superordinate 'executive self' in ruling the GW. Also this perspective resonates with ancient Buddhist teachings regarding consciousness as an integrated selfless process in the mind (Harvey, 1995).

Global workspace and discrete temporal dynamics of consciousness

The GNW model proposed by Dehaene and collaborators posits two main perceptual processing durations: the first one is the duration sufficient for a stimulus to elicit significant changes of activation to be registered at the level of automatic or unconscious sensory processors, and the second one is the duration needed for the represented stimulus to access the GW at a conscious level (Dehaene & Naccache, 2001). It crucially involves thalamo-cortical networks and re-entrant processes for conscious access, with a closed-loop system between bottom-up signal processors and top-down or recurrent signals. An implication of the closed-loop system is that it imposes a temporal resolution or granularity on the stream of consciousness, suggesting that a perceptual awareness moment may have a specific duration, with at least 100 ms required for this process to take place (Dehaene & Naccache, 2001).

Neural integrative processes for consciousness are also central to Varela's approach (Varela, 1995; Varela et al., 2001). In Varela's encompassing view, *for every cognitive act, there is a singular and specific large cell assembly that underlies its emergence and operation.* Such assemblies are integrated in a time frame of 100–300 ms, by re-entrant (recurrent) signaling in the thalamo-cortical system (see also Tononi & Edelman, 1998). Large-scale neural assemblies are thus conceived as transient and dynamical, with a duration (a fraction of a second) that spans the time required to accomplish an elementary cognitive act. Their existence is however long enough for neural activity to propagate at a global brain level through the assembly, involving cycles of re-entrant spike exchanges with transmission cycles lasting tens of milliseconds.

The estimated time periods for consciousness in the models above are consistent with the phenomenon of the psychological refractory period, according to which discriminations occur one at a time (Welford, 1952). The time for such decisions is about 150 ms, remarkably close to the lower limit of the period for conscious integration. Efron (1970) suggested that conscious cognition is temporally discrete and parsed into sensory sampling intervals or "perceptual frames", estimated to be about 70–100 ms in average duration. More recently, a time range of 70–100 ms has been interpreted as an attentional object-based sampling rate for visual motion. This sampling could potentially be related to the rate at which information from the automatic processing level reaches the GW for perceptual awareness. It may provide an estimate of the rate at which temporal representations at an unconscious or automatic processing level can be accessed.

Besides the 100–300 ms lower bound for the integration of GW assemblies for conscious access, chronometric studies have also demonstrated robust periodicities in reaction times (with an average of 25 ms), which are task-dependent and attention-independent (Dehaene, 1993; VanRullen & Koch, 2003). These data strongly suggest that the automatic temporal processes underlying perception and action are also discrete, but with shorter intervals than the periods for attention-based conscious integration. These fast and slow forms of temporal discreteness in mental activity might co-exist, with shorter intervals for temporally structured firing exchanges in a currently dominant large-scale thalamo-cortical assembly for conscious access nested within the longer integration period linked to the short-term stability of the assembly itself (see also VanRullen & Koch, 2003).

According to TAC (Raffone et al., 2014), two different time scales may relate to two different bottlenecks in visual information processing. In fact, based on visual search findings, processing steps of attentional shifting can be estimated in the order of tenths of milliseconds, generally in the 30–60 ms range (see Buschman & Miller, 2010; Wolfe, 2007), whereas GW processing steps can be gauged to be in the order of a few hundred milliseconds, plausibly about 200–400 ms (see Baars & Franklin, 2003; Dehaene & Changeux, 2005; Gaillard et al., 2009; Zylberberg et al., 2011). The theory thus provides a unitary framework or these two different bottlenecks and time scales of discrete processing in the brain.

Interestingly, the temporally discrete view of consciousness processes stemming from psychophysical investigations and neural models of consciousness can be related to Buddhist texts, in which it is asserted that the continuum of awareness is characterized by successive *moments* or *pulses* of cognition (von Rospatt, 1995; Wallace, 1999).

To reconcile conscious framing with the apparent continuity of perceptual experience, John (1990) suggested a mechanism with cortical convergence of a cascade of momentary perceptual frames to establish a steady-state perturbation (spatio-temporal signature) from baseline brain activity. This mechanism has received substantial support from EEG studies, showing that the dynamics of the (EEG) field is represented by intervals of quasi-stability or "microstates" with sudden transitions between them (Strik & Lehmann, 1993). Such EEG microstates have been associated with spontaneous thought and visual imagery as well as abstract thought (Koenig & Lehmann, 1996; Lehmann et al., 1998). And, as argued by Churchland and Sejnowski (1992), sequences of stable activation patterns at the neural level may be consistent with the seamless nature of our ongoing phenomenal experience, as these stabilizations can take place very rapidly (see also Fingelkurts & Fingelkurts, 2006).

Global workspace and self

We now focus on the relationships between the GW of consciousness and the self. A fundamental aspect of conscious experiences is indeed given by the experience of the self. William James (1892) characterized the self as "partly known and partly knower, partly object and partly subject" (p. 159) as the phenomenological correlate of unified mental life. James (1892) suggested that reflections on the self-need to address the fundamental distinction between an *I* and a *Me*. For James, the "I" is "that which at any given moment is conscious, whereas the Me is only one of the things which it is conscious of" (ibid., p. 175, italics in the original). The "I" or "knower" thus entails being the subject of experience in contrast to the "Me" as the object of experience or the "empirical aggregate of things objectively known" (ibid., p. 191). Authors from different theoretical perspectives have concurred with James on the distinction between an "I" corresponding to a subjective sense of the self as a thinker, causal agent, and knower, and the "Me", i.e. as the objective or explicit sense of the self with the unique and identifiable features constituting one's self-image or self-concept (see Tagini & Raffone, 2010, for a review). The ongoing "I experience" in the penumbra of consciousness can thus support the continuity of phenomenal experience, while the "Me cognition" in access consciousness through GW processing can support the coherence of narratives and objective self-reference in conscious cognition (see also Tagini & Raffone, 2010).

   In line with the "I" versus "Me" distinction, Gallagher (2000) defined the "minimal self" as a pre-reflective aspect of the self, corresponding to the personal pronoun "I". The minimal self refers to a sense of being the immediate subject of experience in the present and to taking on a first-person perspective (FPP). In contrast to the minimal self, Gallagher (2000) also defined a reflective "narrative self" or autobiographical self (Damasio, 1999), which can function by taking on a third-person perspective (TPP). This is extended in time and creates a subjective feeling or introspectively available sense of identity, continuity, and coherence across time. According to Gallagher (2000), the narrative self is impaired when subjective linking to past episodes is disrupted, such as in the case of amnesia. The FPP and TPP distinction was summarized by Legrand (2003), who argued that there is a fundamental difference between experiencing something from one's own perspective and being reflectively aware of having a perspective. The latter is in fact often conceived as a higher-order abstraction process involving the allocation of attentional and cognitive resources (Metzinger, 2004), and thus plausibly linked with the GW for conscious access.

As discussed before, it is likely that the cognitive access and control operations of the GW in perception and other domains of conscious cognition are performed without the superordinate involvement of an "executive self". However, conscious self-experiences may involve specific GW systems. In particular, the *Default Mode Network* (DMN) is a set of human brain areas plausibly acting as a workspace for self-related processing within the GW for consciousness in the brain, with particular reference to the Me aspect of the self, as recently discovered in neuroimaging. Activity in the DMN is generally reduced during nonself-referential goal-directed tasks. This might be related to the folk psychological view of "losing one's self in one's work". Several studies indicate that the DMN is involved in GW functions that are self-referential in nature: self-projection in remembering the past and planning the future as well as perspective taking of desires, beliefs, and intentions of others (Buckner et al., 2008; Raichle et al., 2001). Social cognition and cultural development on a more general level have been hypothesized to be anchored in these self-referential functions (Metzinger, 2004), and may thus be linked to the DMN as a workspace for self-representation, with particular reference to the narrative aspects of self-reference, within the GW for consciousness.

According to the "Pattern Theory of Self" by Gallagher (2013), which incorporates the pluralist view that includes most of the aspects or processes that have been traditionally defined as involved in self, a self-pattern integrates a very heterogeneous set of processes: bodily, experiential, affective, behavioral, cognitive, narratival, social, worldly, and normative processes. The self-pattern is constituted by several jointly sufficient conditions from which a particular self will be realized. Some token instances of self-pattern may lack some aspects, and psychopathologies may be understood as involving disruptions of or the elimination of one or more aspects (Gallagher & Daly, 2018). We argue that the self-pattern may be linked to GW dynamics involving the DMN and its widespread recurrent interactions with other brain networks, with each component (sub-network) of the workspace performing the binding of features for a particular self, and thus the GW for the self-pattern performing the global integration of such lower-level self-related binding operations.

Global workspace and dreaming

Dreaming represents one of the most prominent aspects of human experience. According to Metzinger (2013), dreaming can be viewed as a global phenomenally conscious state, waking consciousness as "a kind of on-line dream" (Windt & Metzinger, 2007, p. 198), and perception as dream-like state modulated by the senses (Llinas & Ribary, 1994). In this view, although dreaming and waking consciousness differ with respect to the causal paths of their production, they are ontologically equivalent, as argued by Revonsuo (2006). In fact, this author suggests that since consciousness itself can be regarded as a process of simulation, "not only are dreams experiences but, in a way, all experiences are dreams" (p. 55). Indeed, a number of theories on brain functioning were fundamentally based on the assumption that brain processing is driven by sensory input. This view goes back to the reflexological perspective on brain functioning. It has been contrasted since the beginning of the 19th century by an approach that emphasized intrinsic brain activity (Brown, 1911; see also Krüger, 1991; Llinas, 2013; Llinas et al., 1998).

This perspective on consciousness across waking and dreaming may appear in contrast with approaches to consciousness that emphasize reportability and matching of conscious experiences with external stimuli, such as the GNW model. From this latter point of view, perceptual contents are conscious only if they can be reported and correctly matched to presented stimuli. However, following Pantani and collaborators (2018), we argue that these apparently contrasting approaches can be reconciled by integrating processes, structures, and mechanisms across waking and dreaming, with different causal paths of production for conscious experiences in awake perception and dreams, within a unitary phenomenological and neurocognitive framework.

The implausibility of many dream elements (Hobson et al., 1987; States, 2000), the fact that the dreamer is usually unaware of being in a dream and therefore experiences the dream as a real life experience in waking, with a blunted distinction between FPP and TPP, can be linked to the relative hypoactivation (deactivation) of lateral and inferior prefrontal regions with a key role in GW functions associated with access consciousness in dreaming during REM sleep (Maquet et al., 1996, 2005). However, as reviewed by Hobson (2009), it appears that GW processes related to access consciousness may be regained in *lucid dreaming*, a state of consciousness in which many aspects of waking states seem to be preserved, such as the activation of dorsolateral prefrontal cortex and long-range oscillatory coherence between prefrontal and parietal posterior cortices (Hobson, 2009; LaBerge, 1990; Voss & Hobson, 2015). The lucid dreamer often seems aware of dreaming, with cognitive insight and access to memory, plausibly associated to access consciousness and GW processes. Moreover, to some extent, lucid dreamers can be capable of modifying the content of an ongoing dream, plausibly via GW broadcasting processes. In relation to this perspective, Voss and collaborators (2014) found that current stimulation in the lower gamma band during REM sleep influences ongoing brain activity, with the induction of a reflective awareness during dreams, as during lucid dreaming, which can be related to the reinstatement of conscious access through the GW.

As argued by Pantani and collaborators (2018), some aspects of workspace dynamics related to phenomenal consciousness seem implicated in dreams. Indeed, dream experiences involve images, emotions, and thoughts in complex and integrated scenes with a narrative structure within which the dreamer is immersed; these scenes can include intense interactions with animate and inanimate objects as well as complex storylines (Limosani et al., 2011; Revonsuo & Tarkko, 2002). It is therefore plausible that dreams involve large-scale workspace-like interactions in the brain for their phenomenology rather than functionally segregated modular processing. Neuropsychological and neuroimaging studies indeed suggest that the perceptual aspects of dreams are associated with the activation of areas in the occipital and temporal lobes. In particular, the strong activation of associative occipito-temporal visual cortex could explain the vivid visual imagery during dreams (see De Gennaro et al., 2012, for a review). In fact, a bilateral medial occipito-temporal lesion gives rise to the syndrome termed "visual anoneira" (or nonvisual dreaming), characterized by a full or partial loss of visual imagery in dreaming (Solms, 1997). Further, lesions in or near the right (or in a few cases, bilateral) temporo-parieto-occipital junction are associated to a complete loss of dreaming. This evidence suggests that this area is essential for dreaming itself (Solms, 2000). Thus, cortical areas in the temporo-parieto-occipital region appear to play important roles in dream generation, plausibly with those in the left hemisphere, involved in the narrative organization of dream experiences, and those in the right hemisphere, implicated in the visuo-spatial elements of dreams. Indeed, evidence with neurological patients suggests that the left hemisphere is involved in generating the narrative-like structure of dreaming (McCormick et al., 1997). Finally, the absence of dreams has also been associated with bilateral lesions of white matter surrounding the frontal horns of the cerebral ventricles (Solms, 1997).

Thus, although some key GW hubs (such as dorsolateral prefrontal and parietal posterior cortex) related to conscious access and meta-awareness are deactivated in dreams, some other cortical hubs potentially involved in GW dynamics seem to play a crucial role in dreaming, with particular reference to the integration of perceptual experiences in different modalities, emotion, motivation, memory fragments, and the sequence of episodes in the phenomenal consciousness of dreams (Pantani et al., 2018). Moreover, we argue that a key process in driving GW-like dynamics for phenomenal consciousness in dreaming is given by the ignitions and transitions of mental (emotional and motivational) states rather than by rule- and content-driven transitions such as in mental programs during waking conscious states, thus by what is in the penumbra of consciousness in wakefulness.

Global workspace and meditation

Meditation can be conceptualized as a family of practices regulating awareness and emotions in which mental and related somatic events are affected by engaging a specific attentional set. The training of attention is a central feature of different meditation methods (Davidson & Goleman, 1977). Indeed, several studies have reported the development of more efficient attentional processes with meditation practice, including increased attentional control and sustained attention (e.g., Slagter et al., 2007; van den Hurk et al., 2010; for reviews see Lutz et al., 2008; Malinowski, 2013; Raffone et al., 2019; Tang et al., 2015). More generally, a number of behavioral, EEG, and neuroimaging studies have revealed the importance of investigating states and traits related to meditation to achieve an increased understanding of cognitive and affective neuroplasticity, attention, and awareness (Cahn & Polich, 2006; Lutz et al., 2008; Raffone & Srinivasan, 2010, 2017). Also clinical applications are increasingly recognized (Cahn & Polich, 2006; Hofmann et al., 2010; van Aalderen et al., 2011).

Meta-awareness or the "witnessing observer" function plays a key role in meditation. Such function is also related to the notion of *mindfulness*, which may be characterized as intentionally focusing one's attention in a nonjudgmental or accepting way on the experience occurring in the present moment (e.g., Brown et al., 2007; Kabat-Zinn, 1990). Raffone and Srinivasan (2009) proposed a neurocognitive framework, in terms of the *adaptive workspace hypothesis*, for consciousness, meta-consciousness, and circular interactions with top-down attention, also with reference to meditation states. In such framework, consciousness may refer to an external or internal object per se (*first order consciousness*) or to the subjective or phenomenal experience of such an object (*second order consciousness*). There is then a *non-referential* or "pure" consciousness, associated to a fundamental going beyond the cognitive subject-object duality, as the "awareness of being aware" (see also Arenander & Travis, 2004; Zeki, 2003). According to Raffone and Srinivasan (2009), this transcendent awareness can only be developed through meditation-based intuition, and can thus also be characterized as an *intuitive awareness* (Sumedho, 2004) or as the *reflexive awareness* facet of mindfulness (Siegel, 2007).

In line with GW models of consciousness, Lutz and collaborators (2008) hypothesized that:

> some meditation states might not be best understood as top-down influences in a classical neuroanatomical sense but rather as dynamical global states that, in virtue of their dynamical equilibrium, can influence the processing of the brain from moment to moment.
>
> *(Lutz et al., 2008, p. 5)*

The same authors also argue that:

> In this view, the brain goes through a succession of large-scale brain states, with each state becoming the source of top-down influences for the subsequent state. We predict that these large-scale integrative mechanisms participate in the regulatory influence of these meditation states.
>
> *(Lutz et al., 2008, p. 5)*

Several studies have found changes in the brain workspace for self-reference in mindfulness meditation (e.g., Brewer et al., 2011; Dor-Ziderman et al., 2013;

Farb et al., 2007; Pagnoni et al., 2008). Farb and collaborators' (2007) functional Magnetic Resonance Imaging (fMRI) study characterized the neural bases of two forms of self-awareness: *extended* self-reference linking experiences across time and *momentary* self-awareness centered on the present moment. Specifically, they investigated monitoring of enduring traits ("narrative" focus) or momentary experience ("experiential" focus) in both novice participants and those having attended an eight-week mindfulness-based course. In novices, the experiential focus resulted in focal activity reductions in medial prefrontal cortex associated with the narrative focus and the underlying DMN activity. In trained participants, the experiential focus yielded more pronounced and pervasive activity reductions in medial prefrontal cortex and an increased engagement of a right lateralized network, including the lateral prefrontal cortex, the insula, and the inferior parietal lobule. This brain activity pattern appears substantially overlapping with Duncan's (2010) multiple demand brain activity for mental programs. Following mindfulness training, the experiential focus resulted in a shift away from areas involved in affective reactions, such as the amygdala, toward more lateral prefrontal regions. This finding appears to support a more objective and self-detached analysis of interoceptive (insula) and exteroceptive (somatosensory cortex) sensory events rather than their subjective or affective self-referential evaluation. It can be interpreted in terms of a functional reorganization of the GW for the self-pattern with mindfulness meditation, resulting in an increased cognitive flexibility and a reduced emotional reactivity, both plausibly related to a change in perspective about the self (see also Hölzel et al., 2011). A magnetoencephalographic study (Dor-Ziderman et al., 2013) has also interestingly shown that narrative self-awareness is attenuated in long-term mindfulness meditators as related to extensive decreases of beta and gamma band oscillatory activities in prefrontal and parietal cortices (GW), thus potentially allowing an increased flexibility of the conscious mental programs linked to the self and its involvement in cognition and emotion.

Finally, it is interesting to note that with a deep intensive practice insight, meditators may experience the so-called "insight knowledge of dissolution", a stage of meditative insight in which the apparent continuity of the stream of consciousness is broken together with the underlying backstage experience of a continuous self (Mahasi, 2016). A functional reorganization of consciousness may thus take place via intensified concentration and mindfulness in the ongoing meditation practice after such dissolution stage (see also Barendregt, 1988). Another possibility after accessing the insight knowledge of dissolution may be to reinstate the continuity of the stream of consciousness and of its self-context (the experienced I) via an intensified emotional and motivational backstage of consciousness, in which the intensified emotions and motives act as a "glue" for the continuity of the phenomenal stream of consciousness, described as a "cover up" strategy for meta-awareness, which is however discouraged to enable a deeper progress in meditative insight and a wholesome reorganization of consciousness (Barendregt, 1988).

Global workspace and hypnosis

The American Psychological Association defines *hypnosis* as "a procedure, in which a therapist or researcher suggests a client or subject experience changes in sensations, perceptions, thoughts or behaviors". This procedure is called hypnotic induction. After this phase, a posthypnotic suggestion may be given that often will be obeyed after the subject has come out of the induction. About 10–15% of healthy individuals in an alert state can show marked alterations in many facets of their conscious experience during hypnosis, including a lack of control over their own actions, amnesia for recent events, absence of pain and other sensations, or the apparent reality of illusory events (Hilgard, 1965). The rapid and reversible changes in awareness and cognitive processing in hypnosis can provide remarkable insights in cognitive neuroscience (e.g., Raz & Shapiro, 2002).

Altered conscious experience during hypnosis such as lack of control over own actions, amnesia for recent events, absence of pain and other sensations, or the apparent reality of illusory events are all compatible with a GW account of hypnosis, and in particular with the GNW architecture proposed by Dehaene and collaborators. Thus, an altered function of the GW with reference to perceptual processing (e.g., of body sensations), episodic memory, and action control might arise with hypnosis. The apparent reality of illusory events might be linked to an altered activation of the anterior cingulate cortex, a key GW area, as also shown by patients confusing reality and dreaming (Solms, 1997).

It has been suggested that (pre)frontal cortex plays a key role in hypnosis (Bowers, 1992; Crawford & Gruzelier, 1992; Fingelkurts & Fingelkurts (2006); Gruzelier, 1998, 2000; Woody & Bowers, 1994). Gruzelier and Warren (1993) proposed that in highly hypnotizable individuals (pre)frontal lobe functions become engaged through instructions to focus attention during the hypnotic induction procedure, followed by the inhibition of other (pre)frontal functions such as monitoring and self-awareness. The importance of attentional processes in hypnosis has been highlighted by several authors (see also Crawford et al., 1993; Fingelkurts et al., 2007a; Kallio et al., 1999).

In an EEG case study with a hypnotic virtuoso, Fingelkurts and collaborators (2007b) found an altered functional connectivity in hypnosis. They suggested that such alteration may be regarded as a neural correlate of hypnosis, in which cognitive or brain modules may be temporarily incapable to communicate with each other normally. Note that such characterization implies an altered GW function for conscious access, which is plausibly based on the integration of distributed brain processors with large-scale recurrent signaling (see also Tononi & Edelman, 1998). Also Terhune and collaborators' (2011) study suggests that highly suggestible individuals exhibit a disruption of the frontal-parietal network (GW) that is only observable following a hypnotic induction.

It has been found that during hypnosis, the DMN shows a different pattern of activity compared to the non-hypnosis condition (Oakley & Halligan, 2009). It has also been found that the induction of hypnosis can reduce anterior DMN activity without a concomitant increase of activity in other cortical regions (McGeown et al., 2009). Another fMRI study with a hypnotic "virtuoso" subject has shown that hypnosis is associated with significant modulation of connectivity and activity involving the DMN (Lipari et al., 2011). In the same vein, an fMRI study by Demertzi and collaborators (2011) found a reduced connectivity of self-related DMN areas during hypnosis. Such findings suggest that hypnosis may reduce the constraints on conscious or GW processing stemming from self-related contexts related to the DMN, or goal contexts in Baars and Franklin's (2003) terms. As related to this perspective, based on their fMRI findings, Rainville and collaborators (2002) earlier suggested that "The modulation of activity observed…is consistent with the interpretation that hypnosis produces changes in self-representation construed as an essential element for conscious experience" (p. 898).

Finally, a key GW region, anterior cingulate cortex, seems involved in the regulation of pain in both hypnosis and mindfulness meditation. An fMRI study (Schulz-Stubner et al., 2004) investigated the effects of hypnosis on pain experience and related brain activity patterns, and found an increased activation in the anterior basal ganglia and the (left) anterior cingulate cortex in hypnosis. An increased activation of the anterior cingulate cortex (with the anterior insula) was also found in an fMRI study as related to modulation of pain by mindfulness meditation (Zeidan et al., 2011). Interestingly, Barendregt (1996) hypothesized that the dissolution experience in insight meditation described above is a state of consciousness similar to being in hypnotic induction. In such hypothesis, the posthypnotic order acts as a "glue" to reinstate the continuity of conscious experience and of its self (the I) backstage after hypnotic induction.

Summary

This chapter demonstrates the broad relevance and implications of the GW notion and functional principles for a range of consciousness domains and phenomena, also in terms of their neural correlates. The fundamental GW principles presented in GWT have further been specified and developed in terms of implicated brain regions and neurocognitive processes and mechanisms in the GNW model. Other models and theories based on GNW principles have shown the flexibility of the model to account for a range of visual cognition phenomena, with some additional assumptions. Further theoretical developments have related some core GW processes, such as recurrent interactions within and between brain regions, to phenomenal consciousness, besides their involvement in access consciousness. The extension of conscious GW processing to mental programs and sequential operations has further demonstrated the relevance of GW principles (as particularly related to the GNW model) for a range of higher-level cognitive functions, also with the plausible involvement of adaptive or multiple demand regions of the brain. We have then discussed the discrete temporal dynamics of consciousness and their multiple time scales, including those for access consciousness involving the GW, together with faster discrete processing steps and the related brain oscillations. Then, although neuroscientific studies have found evidence against the superordinate involvement of an executive self in conscious processing posited by GWT, with control operations of conscious access and selective attention plausibly performed by selfless mental programs, GW subsystems related to first- and third-person self-experiences have been characterized over the last two decades in neuroscience, with particular reference to the DMN, and the integration of multiple features of the self-pattern. GW processes related to phenomenal consciousness are also relevant for the occurrence and phenomenology of dreaming, besides their more extended involvement in access consciousness in lucid dreaming. GW dynamics are then extended to characterize meta-awareness or mindfulness in meditation experiences as well as hypnotic states, including the modulation of self-referential states and the regulation of pain in meditation and hypnosis.

Acknowledgments

This work has been supported by the grant from BIAL Foundation (Portugal) on the project "Aware Mind-Brain: bridging insights on the mechanisms and neural substrates of human awareness and meditation". Antonino Raffone has also been supported by the grant from Sapienza University of Rome on the project "Neuro-cognitive and molecular effects of mind-body practices: an integrated approach".

References

Anderson, J.R., & Lebiere, C. (1998). *The Atomic Components of Thought.* , Mahwah, NJ: Lawrence Erlbaum Associates.

Arenander, A., & Travis, F.T. (2004). Brain patterns of self-awareness. In B. Beitman & J. Nair (Eds.) *Self-Awareness Deficits*, 1–12. New York: W.W. Norton.

Baars, B. (1988). *A Cognitive Theory of Consciousness.* New York: Cambridge University Press.

Baars, B. (1997). *In the Theater of Consciousness: The Workspace of the Mind.* New York: Oxford University Press.

Baars, B. (1998). Metaphors of consciousness and attention in the brain. *Trends in Neurosciences, 21*, 58–62.

Baars, B.J. (2002). The conscious access hypothesis: Origins and recent evidence. *Trends in Cognitive Science, 6*, 47–52.

Baars, B.J., & Franklin, S. (2003). How conscious experience and working memory interact. *Trends in Cognitive Science, 7*, 166–172.

Baars, B.J., Ramsoy, T.Z., & Laureys, S. (2003). Brain, conscious experience and the observing self. *Trends in Neuroscience, 26*, 671–675.

Baars, B.J., Franklin, S., & Ramsoy, T.Z. (2013). Global workspace dynamics: Cortical "binding and propagation" enables conscious contents. *Frontiers in Psychology, 4*, 200.

Barendregt, H.P. (1988). Buddhist phenomenology, part I. *Proceedings of the Conference on Topics and Perspectives of Contemporary Logic and Philosophy of Science*, Cesena, Italy, January 7–10, 1987, (Ed. M. dalla Chiara), Clueb, Bologna, 1988, 37–55.

Barendregt, H.P. (1996). Mysticism and beyond, Buddhist phenomenology, part II. *The Eastern Buddhist*, New Series, *29*(2), 262–287.

Barendregt, H.P., & Raffone, A. (2013). Conscious cognition as a discrete, deterministic, and universal Turing Machine process. In B. Cooper & J. van Leeuwen (Eds.) *Alan Turing: His Work and Impact*. Amsterdam: Elsevier.

Block, N. (1995). On a confusion about a function of consciousness. *Behavioral and Brain Sciences, 18*, 227–287.

Block, N. (2005). Two neural correlates of consciousness. *Trends in Cognitive Sciences, 9*, 46–52.

Block, N. (2007). Consciousness, accessibility, and the mesh between psychology and neuroscience. *Behavioural and Brains Sciences, 30*, 481–548.

Bowman, H., & Wyble, B. (2007). The simultaneous type, serial token model of temporal attention and working memory. *Psychological Review, 114*, 38–70.

Brewer, J.A., Worhunsky, P.D., Gray, J.R., Tang, Y.-Y., Weber, J., & Kober, H. (2011). Meditation experience is associated with differences in default mode network activity and connectivity. *Proceedings of the National Academy of Sciences, 108*, 20254–20259.

Brown, T. (1911). The intrinsic factor in the act of progression in the mammal. *Proceedings of the Royal Society B, 84*, 308–319.

Brown, K.W., Ryan, R.M., & Creswell, J.D. (2007). Mindfulness: Theoretical foundations and evidence for its salutary effects. *Psychological Inquiry, 18*, 211–237.

Buckner, R.L., Andrews-Hanna, J.R., & Schacter, D.L. (2008). The brain's default network: Anatomy, function, and relevance to disease. *Annals of the New York Academy of Sciences, 1124*, 1–38.

Buschman, T.J., & Miller, E.K. (2010). Shifting the spotlight of attention: Evidence for discrete computations in cognition. *Frontiers in Human Neuroscience, 4*, 194.

Cahn, B.R., & Polich, J. (2006). Meditation states and traits: EEG, ERP, and neuroimaging studies. *Psychological Bulletin, 132*, 180–211.

Churchland, P.S., & Sejnowski, T. (1992). *The Computational Brain*. Cambridge, MA: MIT Press.

Crawford, H.J., & Gruzelier, J.H. (1992). A midstream view of the neuropsychophysiology of hypnosis: Recent research and future directions. In W. Fromm & M. Nash, (Eds.) *Hypnosis, Research Developments and Pespectives*, 3rd edn. New York: Guildford Press, 227–66.

Crawford, H.J., Brown, A.M., & Moon, C.E. (1993). Sustained attentional and disattentional abilities: Differences between low and highly hypnotizable persons. *Journal of Abnormal Psychology, 102*, 534–543.

Crick, F., & Koch, C. (2003). A framework for consciousness. *Nature Neuroscience, 6*, 119–126.

Dahl, C.J., Lutz, A., & Davidson, R.J. (2015). Reconstructing and deconstructing the self: Cognitive mechanisms in meditation practice. *Trends in Cognitive Sciences, 19*, 515–523.

Davidson, R.J., & Goleman, D.J. (1977). The role of attention in meditation and hypnosis: A psychobiological perspective on transformations of consciousness. *International Journal of Clinical and Experimental Hypnosis, 25*, 291–308.

Damasio, A.R. (1999). *The Feeling of What Happens: Body and Emotion in the Making of Consciousness*. New York: Harcourt.

De Gennaro, L., Marzano, C., Cipolli C., & Ferrara M. (2012). How we remember the stuff that dreams are made of: Neurobiological approaches to the brain mechanisms of dream recall. *Behavioral Brain Research, 226*, 592–596.

Dehaene, S. (1993). Temporal oscillations in human perception. *Psychological Science, 4,* 264–270.

Dehaene, S., & Changeux, J.P. (2005). Ongoing spontaneous activity controls access to consciousness: A neuronal model for inattentional blindness. *PLoS Biology, 3* (5), e141.

Dehaene, S., & Naccache, L. (2001). Towards a cognitive neuroscience of consciousness: Basic evidence and a workspace framework. *Cognition, 79,* 1–37.

Dehaene, S., Kerszberg, M., & Changeux, J.P. (1998). A neuronal model of a global workspace in effortful cognitive tasks. *Proceedings of the National Academy of Sciences USA, 95,* 14529–14534.

Dehaene, S., Sergent, C., & Changeux, J.-P. (2003). A neuronal network model linking subjective reports and objective physiological data during conscious perception. *Proceedings of the National Academy of Science (USA), 100,* 8520–8525.

Dehaene, S., Changeux, J.P., Naccache, L., Sackur, J., & Sergent, C. (2006). Conscious, preconscious, and subliminal processing: A testable taxonomy. *Trends in Cognitive Sciences, 10,* 204–211.

Dehaene, S., Changeux, J.P., & Naccache, L. (2011). The global neuronal workspace model of conscious access: From neuronal architectures to clinical applications. In Dehaene, S., & Christen, Y. (Eds.) *Characterizing Consciousness: From Cognition to the Clinic?,* 55–84 Berlin: Springer-Verlag.

Demertzi, A., Soddu, A., Faymonville, M.E., Bahri, M.A., Gosseries, O., Vanhaudenhuyse, A., Phillips, C., Maquet, P., Noirhomme, Q., Luxen, A., & Laureys, S. (2011). Hypnotic modulation of resting state fMRI default mode and extrinsic network connectivity. *Progress in Brain Research, 19,* 309–322.

Dor-Ziderman Y., Berkovich-Ohana A., Glicksohn J., & Goldstein A. (2013). Mindfulness-induced selflessness: A MEG neurophenomenological study. *Frontiers in Human Neuroscience, 7,* 582.

Duncan, J. (2001). An adaptive coding model of neural function in prefrontal cortex. *Nature Reviews Neuroscience, 2,* 820–829.

Duncan, J. (2010). The multiple-demand (MD) system of the primate brain: Mental programs for intelligent behaviour. *Trends in Cognitive Science, 14,* 172–179.

Efron, E. (1970). The minimum duration of a perception. *Neuropsychologia, 8,* 57–63.

Farb, N.A.S., Segal, Z.V., Mayberg, H., Bean, J., McKeon, D., Fatima, Z., & Anderson, A.K. (2007). Attending to the present: Meditation reveals distinct neural modes of self-reference. *Social Cognitive and Affective Neuroscience, 2,* 313–322.

Fingelkurts, A.A., & Fingelkurts, A.A. (2006). Timing in cognition and EEG brain dynamics: Discreteness versus continuity. *Cognitive Processing, 7,* 135–162.

Fingelkurts, A.A., Fingelkurts, A.A., Kallio, S., & Revonsuo, A. (2007a). Hypnosis induces a changed composition of brain oscillations in EEG: A case study. *Contemporary Hypnosis, 24,* 3–18.

Fingelkurts, A.A., Fingelkurts, A.A., Kallio, S., & Revonsuo, A. (2007b). Cortex functional connectivity as a neurophysiological correlate of hypnosis: An EEG case study. *Neuropsychologia, 45,* 1452–1462.

Gaillard, R., Dehaene, S., Adam, C., Clémenceau, S., Hasboun, D., Baulac, M., Cohen, L., & Naccache, L. (2009). Converging intracranial markers of conscious access. *PLoS Biology, 7*(3), e1000061.

Gallagher, S. (2000). Philosophical conceptions of the self: Implications for cognitive science. *Trends in Cognitive Science, 4,* 14–21.

Gallagher, S. (2013). A pattern theory of self. *Frontiers in Human Neuroscience, 7,* 443.

Gallagher, S., & Daly, A. (2018). Dynamical relations in the self-pattern. *Frontiers in Psychology, 9*, 664.

Gazzaniga, M.S. (1985). *The Social Brain*. New York: Basic Books.

Gilbert, C.D., & Sigman, M. (2007) Brain states: Top-down influences in sensory processing. *Neuron, 54*, 677–696.

Goldberg, I.I., Harel, M., & Malach, R. (2006). When the brain loses its self: Prefrontal inactivation during sensorimotor processing. *Neuron, 50*, 329–339.

Gruzelier, J.H. (1998). A working model of the neurophysiology of hypnosis: A review of the evidence. *Contemporary Hypnosis, 15*, 3–21.

Gruzelier, J.H. (2000). Redefining hypnosis: Theory, methods and integration. *Contemporary Hypnosis, 17*, 51–70.

Gruzelier, J., & Warren, K. (1993). Neuropsychological evidence of reductions on left frontal tests with hypnosis. *Psychological medicine, 23*(1), 93–101.

Harvey, P. (1995). *The Selfless Mind*. New York, NY: Curzon Press.

Hilgard, E.R. (1965). *Hypnotic Susceptibility*. New York: Harcourt, Brace, and World.

Hobson, J.A. (2009). REM sleep and dreaming: Towards a theory of protoconsciousness. *Nature Reviews Neuroscience, 10*, 803–813.

Hobson, J.A., Hoffmann, S.A., Helfand, R., & Kostner, D. (1987). Dream bizarreness and the activation synthesis hypothesis. *Human Neurobiology, 6*, 157–164.

Hofmann, S.G., Sawyer, A.T., Witt, A.A., & Oh, D. (2010). The effect of mindfulness-based therapy on anxiety and depression: A meta-analytic review. *Journal of Consulting and Clinical Psychology, 78*, 169–183.

Hölzel, B.K., Lazar, S.W., Gard, T., Schuman-Olivier, Z., Vago, D.R., & Ott, U. (2011). How does mindfulness meditation work? Proposing mechanisms of action from a conceptual and neural perspective. *Perspectives in Psychological Science, 6*, 537–559.

Huxley, T.J. (1874). On the hypothesis that animals are automata, and its history. *Nature, 10*, 362–66; *Science and Culture, and Other Essays*; CE 1: 199–250.

James, W. (1892). *Psychology*. New York: Henry Holt and Company.

John, E. R. (1990). Representation of information in the brain. In John, E. R., Harmony, T., Prichep, L. S., Valdés-Sosa, M., & Valdés-Sosa, P. A. (Eds.) *Machinery of the Mind* (pp. 27–56). Boston, MA: Birkhäuser.

Kabat-Zinn, J. (1990). *Full Catastrophe Living: Using the Wisdom of Your Body and Mind to Face Stress, Pain and Illness*. New York: Delacourt.

Kallio, S., Revonsuo, A., Lauerma, H., Hämäläinen, H., & Lang, H. (1999). The MMN amplitude increases in hypnosis: A case study. *NeuroReport, 10*, 3579–3582.

Kamienkowski, J.E., Varatharajah, A., Sigman, M., & Ison, M.J. (2018). Parsing a mental program: Fixation-related brain signatures of unitary operations and routines in natural visual search. *NeuroImage, 183*, 73–86.

Koenig, T., & Lehmann, D. (1996). Microstates in language-related brain potentials show noun-verb differences. *Brain and Language, 53*, 169–182.

Krüger, J. (Ed.) (1991). *Neuronal Cooperativity*. Berlin: Springer.

LaBerge, D. (1990). Thalamic and cortical mechanisms of attention suggested by recent positron emission tomographic experiments. *Journal of Cognitive Neuroscience, 2*, 358–372.

Laird, J.E., Newell, A., & Rosenbloom, P.S. (1987). Soar: An architecture for general intelligence. *Artificial Intelligence, 33*, 1–64.

Lamme, V. (2003). Why attention and awareness are different. *Trends in Cognitive Sciences, 7*, 12–18.

Lamme, V. (2007). Sue Ned Block!: Making a better case for P-consciousness. *Behavioural and Brains Sciences, 30*, 481–548.

Lamme, V. (2010). How neuroscience will change our view on consciousness. *Cognitive Neuroscience, 1*, 204–220.

LeDoux, J.E. (2000). Emotion circuits in the brain. *Annual Review of Neuroscience, 23*, 155–184.

Lehmann, D., Strik, W.K., Henggeler, B., Koenig, T., & Koukkou, M. (1998) Brain electric microstates and momentary conscious mind states as building blocks of spontaneous thinking: I. Visual imagery and abstract thoughts. *International Journal of Psychophysiology, 29*, 1–11.

Legrand, D. (2003). How not to find the neural signature of self-consciousness. *Consciousness and Cognition, 12*, 544–546.

Lipari, S., Baglio, F., Griffanti, L., Mendozzi, L., Garegnani, M., Motta, A., Cecconi, P., & Pugnetti, L. (2011). Altered and asymmetric default mode network activity in a "hypnotic virtuoso": An fMRI and EEG study. *Consciousness and Cognition, 21*, 393–400.

Llinas, R. (2013). The olivo-cerebellar system: A key to understanding the functional significance of intrinsic oscillatory brain properties. *Frontiers in Neural Circuits, 7*, 96.

Llinas, R., & Ribary, U. (1994). Coherent 40-Hz oscillation characterizes dream state in humans. *Proceedings of the National Academy of Sciences of the United States of America, 90*, 2078–2081.

Llinas, R., Ribary, U., Contreras, U., & Pedroarena, C. (1998). The neural basis for consciousness. *Philosophical Transactions of the Royal Society of London. Series B: Biological Sciences, 353*, 1841–1849.

Limosani, I., D'Agostino, A., Manzone, M.L., & Scarone, S. (2011). The dreaming brain/mind, consciousness and psychosis. *Conscious Cogniton, 20*, 987–992.

Luck, S.J., & Vogel, E.K. (1997). The capacity of visual working memory for features and conjunctions. *Nature, 390*, 279–281.

Lutz, A., Slagter, H.A., Dunne, J.D., & Davidson, R.J. (2008). Attention regulation and monitoring in meditation. *Trends in Cognitive Sciences, 12*, 163–169.

Sayadaw, M. (2016). *Manual of Insight*. Somerville, MA: Wisdom Publications.

Maia, T.V., & Cleeremans, A. (2005). Consciousness: Converging insights from connectionist modeling and neuroscience. *Trends in Cognitive Sciences, 9*, 397–404.

Malinowski, P. (2013). Neural mechanisms of attentional control in mindfulness meditation. *Frontiers in Neuroscience, 7*, 8.

Maquet, P., Péters, J.-M., Aerts, J., Delfiore, G., Degueldre, C., Luxen, A., & Franck, G. (1996). Functional neuroanatomy of human rapid-eye-movement sleep and dreaming. *Nature, 383*, 163–166.

Maquet, P., Ruby, P., Maudoux, A., Albouy, G., Sterpenich, V., Dang-Vu, T., Desseilles, M., Boly, M., Perrin, F., Peigneux, P., & Laureys, S. (2005). Human cognition during REM sleep and the activity profile within the frontal and parietal cortices: A reappraisal of functional neuroimaging data. In S. Laureys (Ed) *Progress in Brain Research 150.* Elsevier, 219–227.

McCormick, L., Nielsen, T., Ptito, M., Villemure, J.-G., Vera, C., & Montplaisir, J. (1997). REM sleep mentation in right hemispherectomized patients. *Neuropsicologia, 35*, 695–701.

McGeown, W.J., Mazzoni, G., Venneri, A., & Kirsch, I. (2009). Hypnotic induction decreases anterior default mode activity. *Consciousness and Cognition, 18*, 848–855.

Metzinger, T. (2004). *Being No One. The Self-Model Theory of Subjectivity.* Cambridge, MA: MIT Press.

Metzinger, T. (2013). The myth of cognitive agency: Subpersonal thinking as a cyclically recurring loss of mental autonomy. *Frontiers in Psychology, 4*, 931.

Meyer, D.E., & Kieras, D.E. (1997). A computational theory of executive cognitive processes and multiple-task performance: Part 1. Basic mechanisms. *Psychological Review, 104*, 3–65.

Milner, A.D., & Goodale, M.A. (2008). Two visual systems re-viewed. *Neuropsychologia, 46*, 774–785.

Nagel, T. (1974). What is it like to be a bat? *Philosophical Review, 83*, 435–450.

Oakley, D.A., & Halligan, P.W. (2009). Hypnotic suggestion and cognitive neuroscience. *Trends in Cognitive Sciences, 13*, 264–270.

Overgaard, M., Rote, J., Mouridsen, K., & Ramsøy, T.Z. (2006). Is conscious perception gradual or dichotomous? A comparison of report methodologies during a visual task. *Consciousness and Cognition, 15*, 700–708.

Pagnoni, G., Cekic, M., & Guo, Y. (2008). "Thinking about not-thinking": Neural correlates of conceptual processing during Zen meditation. *PLoS ONE, 3*(9), e3083.

Pantani, M., Tagini, A., & Raffone, A. (2018). Phenomenal consciousness, access consciousness and self across waking and dreaming: Bridging phenomenology and neuroscience. *Phenomenology and the Cognitive Sciences, 17*, 175–197.

Pia, L., Neppi-Modona, M., Ricci, R., & Berti, A. (2004). The anatomy of anosognosia for hemiplegia: A meta-analysis. *Cortex, 40*, 367–377.

Raffone, A., & Pantani, M. (2010). A global workspace model for phenomenal and access consciousness. *Consciousness and Cognition, 19*, 580–596.

Raffone, A., & Srinivasan, N. (2009). An adaptive workspace hypothesis about the neural correlates of consciousness: Insights from neuroscience and meditation studies. In N. Srinivasan (Ed.) *Progress in Brain Research: Attention,* Vol. 176. Amsterdam: Elsevier, 161–180.

Raffone, A., & Srinivasan, N. (2010). The exploration of meditation in the neuroscience of meditation and consciousness. *Cognitive Processing, 11*, 1–7.

Raffone, A., & Srinivasan, N. (2017). Mindfulness and cognitive functions: Toward a unifying neurocognitive framework. *Mindfulness, 8*, 1–9.

Raffone, A., & Wolters, G. (2001). A cortical mechanism for binding in visual working memory. *Journal of Cognitive Neuroscience, 13*, 766–785.

Raffone, A., Srinivasan, N., & van Leeuwen, C. (2014). The interplay of attention and consciousness in visual search, attentional blink and working memory consolidation. *Philosophical Transactions of the Royal Society of London. Series B: Biological Sciences, 369*, in press. doi:10.1098/rstb.2013.0215.

Raffone, A., Marzetti, L., Del Gratta, C., Perrucci, M.G., Romani, G.L., & Pizzella, V. (2019). Toward a brain theory of meditation. *Progress in Brain Research, 244*, 207–232.

Raichle, M., MacLeod, A.M., Snyder, A.Z., Powers, W.J., Gusnard, D.A., & Shulman, G.L. (2001). A default mode of brain function. *Proceedings of the National Academy of Sciences USA, 98*, 676–682.

Rainville, P., Hofbauer, R.K., Buschnell, M.C., Duncan, G.H., & Price, D.D. (2002). Hypnosis modulates activity in brain structures involved in the regulation of consciousness. *Journal of Cognitive Neuroscience, 14*, 887–901.

Raz, A., & Shapiro, T. (2002). Hypnosis and neuroscience: A crosstalk between clinical and cognitive research. *Archives of General Psychiatry, 59*, 85–90.

Revonsuo, A. (2006) *Inner Presence: Consciousness as a Biological Phenomenon.* Cambridge, MA: MIT Press.

Revonsuo, A., & Tarkko, K. (2002). Binding in dreams. *Journal of Consciousness Studies, 9*, 3–24.

Roelfsema, P.R., Lamme, V.A.F., & Spekreijse, H. (1998). Object-based attention in the primary visual cortex of the macaque monkey. *Nature, 395*, 376–381.

Salzman, C.D., & Fusi, S. (2010). Emotion, cognition, and mental state representation in amygdala and prefrontal cortex. *Annual Review of Neuroscience, 33,* 173–202.

Schulz-Stubner, S., Krings, T., Meister, I.G., Rex, S., Thron, A., & Rossaint, R. (2004). Clinical hypnosis modulates functional magnetic resonance imaging signal intensities and pain perception in a thermal stimulation paradigm. *Regional Anesthesia and Pain Medicine, 29,* 549–556.

Schwartz, B.L. (1999). Sparkling at the end of the tongue: The etiology of tip-of-the-tongue phenomenology. *Psychonomic Bulletin & Review, 6,* 379–393.

Siegel, D.J. (2007). *The Mindful Brain.* New York: Norton.

Simione, L., Raffone, A., Wolters, G., Salmas, P., Nakatani, C., Belardinelli, M.O., & van Leeuwen, C. (2012). ViSA: A neurodynamic model for visuo-spatial working memory, attentional blink, and conscious access. *Psychological Review, 119,* 745–769.

Slagter, H.A., Lutz, A., Greischar, L.L., Francis, A.D., Nieuwenhuis, S., Davis, J.M., & Davidson, R.J. (2007). Mental training affects distribution of limited brain resources. *PLoS Biology, 5,* e138.

Smallwood, J., & Schooler, J.W. (2006). The restless mind. *Psychological Bulletin, 132,* 946–958.

Solms, M. (1997). *The Neuropsychology of Dreams: A Clinico-Anatomical Study.* Hillsdale, NJ: Lawrence Erlbaum Associates.

Solms, M. (2000). Dreaming and REM sleep are controlled by different brain mechanisms. *Behavioral and Brain Science, 23,* 843–850.

States, B.O. (2000). Dream bizarreness and inner thought. *Dreaming, 10,* 179–192.

Strik, W.K., & Lehmann, D. (1993). Data-determined window size and space-oriented segmentation of spontaneous EEG map series. *Electroencephalography and Clinical Neurophysiology, 87,* 169–174.

Sumedho, Ajahn (2004) *Intuitive Awareness.* Hemel Hempstead (UK): Amaravati Buddhist Monastery.

Tagini, A., & Raffone, A. (2010). The 'I' and the 'Me' in self-referential awareness: A neurocognitive hypothesis. *Cognitive Processing, 11,* 9–20.

Tang, Y.Y., Holzel, B.K., & Posner, M.I. (2015). The neuroscience of mindfulness meditation. *Nature Reviews Neuroscience, 16,* 213–225.

Terhune, D.B., Cardena, E., & Lindgren, M. (2011). Differential frontal-parietal phase synchrony during hypnosis as a function of hypnotic suggestibility. *Psychophysiology, 48,* 1444–1447.

Tononi, G., & Edelman, G.M. (1998). Consciousness and complexity. *Science, 282,* 1846–1851.

van Aalderen, J.R., Donders, A.R., Giommi, F., Spinhoven, P., Barendregt, H.P., & Speckens, A.E. (2011). The efficacy of mindfulness-based cognitive therapy in recurrent depressed patients with and without a current depressive episode: A randomized controlled trial. *Psychological Medicine, 42*(5), 1–13.

van den Hurk, P.A.M., Giommi, F., Gielen, S.C., Speckens, A.E.M., & Barendregt, H.P. (2010). Greater efficiency in attentional processing related to mindfulness meditation. *Quarterly Journal of Experimental Psychology, 63,* 1168–1180.

VanRullen, R., & Koch, C. (2003). Is perception discrete or continuous? *Trends in Cognitive Sciences, 7,* 207–213.

Varela, F.J. (1995). Resonant cell assemblies: A new approach to cognitive functions and neuronal synchrony. *Biological Research, 28,* 81–95.

Varela, F., Lachaux, J.-P., Rodriguez, E., Martinerie, J. (2001) The brainweb: Phase synchronization and large-scale integration. *Nature Review Neuroscience, 2,* 229–239.

von Rospatt, A. (1995). *The Buddhist Doctrine of Momentariness: A Survey of the Origins and Early Phase of This Doctrine Up to Vasubandhu.* Stuttgart: Franz Steiner Verlag.

von Stein, A., Chiang, C., & Koenig, P. (2000) Top-down processing mediated by interareal synchronization. *Proceedings of the National Academy of Sciences USA, 97,* 14748–14753.

Voss, U., & Hobson, A. (2015). What is the state-of-the-art on lucid dreaming? – Recent advances and questions for future research. In T. Metzinger & J.M. Windt, Eds. *Open MIND.* Frankfurt am Main: MIND Group.

Voss, U., Holzmann, R., Hobson, A., Paulus, W., Koppehele-Gossel, J., Klimke, A., & Nitsche, M.A. (2014). Induction of self-awareness in dreams through frontal low current stimulation of gamma activity. *Nature Neuroscience, 17,* 810–812.

Wallace, A. (1999). The Buddhist tradition of Samatha: Methods for refining and examining consciousness. *Journal of Consciousness Studies, 6,* 175–187.

Welford, A.T. (1952). The psychological refractory period and the timing of high-speed performance: A review and a theory. *British Journal of Psychology, 43,* 2–19.

Windt, J.M., & Metzinger, T. (2007). The philosophy of dreaming and self-consciousness: What happens to the experiential subject during the dream state? In D.E. Barrett & P. McNamara (Eds.) *The New Science of Dreaming: Volume 3. Cultural and Theoretical Perspectives. Praeger Perspectives.* Westport, CT: Praeger Publishers/Greenwood Publishing Group, 193–247.

Wolfe, J.M. (2007). Wolfe guided search 4.0: Current progress with a model of visual search integrated models of cognitive systems. In W. Gray (Ed.) *Integrated Models of Cognitive Systems.* New York: Oxford, 99–119.

Woody, E.Z., & Bowers, K.S. (1994). A frontal assault on dissociated control. In S.J. Lynn & J.W. Rhue, Eds. *Dissociation: Clinical and Theoretical Perspectives.* New York: Guilford Press, 52–79.

Zeidan, F., Martucci, K.T., Kraft, R.A., Gordon, N.S., McHaffie, J.G., & Coghill, R.C. (2011). Brain mechanisms supporting the modulation of pain by mindfulness meditation. *The Journal of Neuroscience, 31,* 5540–5548.

Zeki, S. (2003) The disunity of consciousness. *Trends in Cognitive Sciences, 7,* 214–218.

Zylberberg, A., Dehaene, S., Roelfsema, P.R., & Sigman, M. (2011). The human Turing machine: A neural framework for mental programs. *Trends in Cognitive Sciences, 15,* 293–300.

7

A HIGHER-ORDER FACULTY AND BEYOND

Asger Kirkeby-Hinrup

Introduction

A common strategy to explain the difference between conscious and unconscious mental states is by deploying the notion of intentionality. One group of theories argues that what provides an individual with a conscious experience of a mental state $p1$ is the presence of another mental state $p2$ that has $p1$ as its intentional object. Because $p2$ is itself a mental state and is about another mental state, $p2$ is called a higher-order state. Consequently, theories deploying this framework to explain consciousness are called higher-order theories. In most cases, a higher-order state will have as its intentional object a first-order state, for instance, a sensation. However, higher-order states may also have other higher-order states as their object, thus yielding introspective consciousness.

Higher-order theories come in different shapes and sizes, but they have in common the idea that a first-order state by itself is not sufficient for consciousness to occur. The presence of a higher-order state about the first-order state is necessary. This means that with respect to the neural correlates of consciousness (NCC), *ex hypothesi*, we should expect patterns of neural activations corresponding to the two elements (the first-order state and the higher-order state) when subjects are in conscious states. As we shall see below, while roughly representative, this expectation does not generalize completely because some strains of higher-order theory allow for consciousness occasionally to obtain as a result of the presence of a higher-order state only. However, for the present purposes, we can be satisfied with the characterization that higher-order theories normally can be viewed as so-called two-stage models.

Two-stage models commonly are viewed as an alternative to (one-stage) models which posit that first-order states by themselves can yield consciousness, and hence the presence of a higher-order state is not necessary (except on some models for introspection). Within the philosophical domain, one-stage models have prominent proponents and have been cashed out in varying theoretical terms (e.g. Block, 1996, 2005; Dretske, 1993, 1997; Kriegel, 2007b, 2008; Tye, 1997), occasionally invoking a range of empirical evidence in their favor (e.g. Block, 2007; D'Aloisio-Montilla, 2017; Lamme, 2003, 2004; Lamme & Roelfsema, 2000). In addition to representational models, i.e. models conceiving of the mechanism underpinning consciousness in terms of representational states and representational relations, there are models which highlight functional aspects, such as informational integration or availability to cognitive consumer systems to be the driving factors of conscious experience (e.g. Baars, 1996; Dehaene & Naccache, 2001; Tononi, 2005).

Thus, one overarching question about consciousness is what kind of model accurately describes how it is implemented in the brain, i.e. whether two-stage, one-stage or one or the other functional models are correct. The debate pertaining to this question is still ongoing, and turns on the theoretical and empirical merits of the various models on offer. Considerations about what empirical data is predicted by the different models and how this may allow us to distinguish between them are also becoming available (e.g. Lau & Rosenthal, 2011). While it is a necessary precondition, answering the overarching question about what kind of model is correct only takes us halfway toward understanding consciousness. Within each group of models, there are disagreements over details that need to be worked out. Therefore, a secondary question pertains to the merits of the specific theories within a given group of models. In this chapter, I will treat this secondary question to assess how we may distinguish between distinct models within a group based on their expected neural signatures. To do this, I will leave aside the primary question, and assume that some variant of a two-stage model correctly reflects how human consciousness arises from neural processes in the brain. This sets the stage for considerations of how to distinguish between different varieties of two-stage models. However, even when restricting the investigation to two-stage models, we are still left with a significant set of specific and distinct theories, such as the HOROR theory (Brown, 2015), HOGS theory (Van Gulick, 2004), QHOT theory (Coleman, 2015) and Dispositional HOT theory (Carruthers, 2003), among others. Distinguishing, assessing and comparing all two-stage models are not feasible within the scope of this text. Therefore, it is necessary to further narrow down the kind of two-stage models under consideration. Specifically, I consider three variants of HOT theory proposed by David Rosenthal, Hakwan Lau and Rocco Gennaro, respectively. On the bases of their theoretical frameworks, I identify how to distinguish between the different variants of HOT theory, depending on the way the cards fall with respect to the NCC.

One critical point where the three variants of HOT theory differ is the possibility of higher-order misrepresentation. As I will suggest, this difference is likely to show up in the neural signatures, thereby allowing us to distinguish between the theories, *post hoc* to discovery of the NCC. Before turning to the issue of misrepresentation and how this combined with the NCC may allow us to narrow down the kind of HOT theory most likely to accurately reflect how consciousness arises from neural processes, some groundwork is needed. This groundwork consists in laying out the variations of HOT theory under consideration, and assessing the state of the current debate regarding the empirical merits of HOT theory.

Three variants of HOT theory

As higher-order models, the HOT theories endorse the view that being conscious of something requires the presence of a higher-order mental state. The presence of the higher-order state makes the individual aware of herself as being in the mental state the higher-order state is about. As suggested by the higher-order *thought* moniker, the HOT theories hold that the higher-order state is a *thought-like* state. HOT theories are representational theories of consciousness (Carruthers, 1998; Lycan, 2015; Seager, 2002), because the way the higher-order state gets to be *about* another state is conceived of as *representing* it in some suitable manner. Thus, HOT theories posit that the way an individual becomes aware of herself as being in a given state is by having a thought-like higher-order state representing herself as being in the state in question. This leads back to what is often called the "transitivity principle" (see e.g. Berger, 2017; Brown, 2015; Coleman, 2015; Gennaro, 2016b; Gottlieb, 2018; Matey, 2006; Rosenthal, 1997; Weisberg, 2010) that defines a conscious state as a *state the individual is aware of herself as being in*.

Furthermore, most proponents of HOT theory believe that the mind can be naturalized. What "naturalized" implies is captured well by Jean Petitot et al. when they say: "By 'naturalized' we mean integrated into an explanatory framework where every acceptable property is made continuous with the properties admitted by the natural sciences" (Petitot, Varela, Pachoud, & Roy, 1999, pp. 1–2). The central idea behind representational theories, with respect to the naturalization project, is that the notion of representation can serve as a bridge concept between mental terms (e.g. thoughts and percepts) and neural terms (e.g. activation patterns and firing rates). The naturalization project aims to explain conscious phenomena in terms of representations and representational structures, and explain representations and representational structures in terms of processes in the brain.

While the three variants of HOT theory discussed in this chapter differ in various ways, I will consider here just one issue suitable for bringing to light how the three variants may differ with respect to their putative NCCs. The issue is the possibility of higher-order misrepresentation. In the rest of this section, I introduce the three variants of HOT theory and how they each deal with misrepresentation. This provides the groundwork necessary for a brief presentation of the debates on empirical evidence proposed in favor of HOT theory and the possibility of misrepresentation.

Actualist HOT theory

One of the most prominent variants of HOT theory is the one developed by David Rosenthal. This is also one the oldest branches of HOT theory, having been around for more two decades (see e.g. Rosenthal, 1997, 2002). Because the higher-order thought must be an actually occurring state (as opposed to, for instance, merely a dispositional state, see e.g. Carruthers, 1998), Rosenthal's variant of HOT theory is sometimes called *Actualist* HOT theory. There are several riders as to the nature of the HOT for it to make an individual conscious of being in a given mental state. For instance, the HOT must be assertoric and indexical to make the individual *believe* (assertion) that *she* (indexicality) is in the state in question. As mentioned above, the HOT must itself be an unconscious state, except in introspection where it itself is the target of an (unconscious) HOT. Finally, the HOT must not come about as the result of conscious inference, i.e. I sometimes can have thoughts about my own mental states, for example, based on observations of my own behavior, but these do not qualify as HOTs of the kind we are interested in.

Bayesian HOT theory

Hakwan Lau (2007) has proposed a Bayesian version of HOT theory. Lau frames this version of HOT theory as a formal theory of perceptual consciousness based on signal detection theory. As an example, Lau deploys a forced choice visual detection tasks and suggests that the strength of the visual signal can be interpreted as a probability distribution. To decide whether to answer "yes" or "no" in the forced choice detection task, the subjects must match the probability distribution of the signal strength against a subjective decision criterion. Lau argues that interpreting internal signals (e.g. activations from visual stimuli) as probability distributions are necessary because the brain is essentially a noisy system. According to Lau, because the brain is a noisy environment, signal strengths vary; therefore, operating on probability distributions may provide the detection mechanism a dynamic way to determine whether an internal signal actually carries information or is just noise. Lau frames his higher-order Bayesian decision theory as a variant of the higher-order thought theories of consciousness, and have elsewhere (Lau & Brown, 2019; Lau & Rosenthal, 2011) argued for higher-order models. His suggestion is that higher-order representations are the results of interpretations of incoming signals, and the occurrence or non-occurrence of a higher-order representation depends on whether the subjective decision criterion determines an incoming signal carries information or whether it is just noise. With respect to the possibility of misrepresentation, the possibility of false positives, i.e. cases where the subjective decision criterion erroneously classifies noise as containing information, readily allows for misrepresentation to occur. Lau points to these kinds of false positives as a possible cause of hallucinations (Lau, 2007, p. 41).

The wide intrinsicality view

As the name indicates, the wide intrinsicality view (WIV) proposed by Rocco Gennaro posits that conscious states should be individuated *widely*. This means that a conscious state contains more than the state the individual is aware of herself as being in. According to Gennaro, conscious states are complex mental states (CMS) with two proper parts. Gennaro says:

> A mental state M of a subject S is conscious if and only if S has a suitable (unconscious) metapsychological thought, M★ […], directed at M, such that both M and M★ […] are *proper parts of* a complex conscious mental state, CMS.
> *(Gennaro, 2012, p. 104. Italics from original)*

Thus, on the WIV, one part (M) of the CMS is world-directed (what is usually called a first-order state). The other part of the CMS is a higher-order element M★ representing M. Because Gennaro argues that the higher-order content M★ in the CMS must be *thought like*, Gennaro conceives of the WIV as a variant of HOT theory. In contrast to the Actualist HOT theory, Gennaro holds that the higher-order content M★ is not in itself sufficient for consciousness. On the WIV, both M and M★ *and* the right kind of relation between the two are needed for the CMS to yield a conscious state (Gennaro, 2004, 2006). Importantly, a CMS makes an individual aware of herself as being in only its lower-order state M. This might suggest that we should conceive of just M as the conscious state. However, Gennaro argues that because conscious states are CMS that we individuate widely, the conscious state is really the whole of the CMS rather than just the world-directed part M. I.e., the conscious state includes more than the part of which the individual is immediately consciously aware.

Furthermore, because the metacognitive thought M★ (the HOT) is only one proper part of the conscious state, what makes a conscious state conscious is intrinsic to the state. The intrinsic relation between the higher- and lower-order content means discrepancies are unlikely to occur. Importantly, Gennaro does not claim that discrepancies *cannot* occur, but only that if there were to be a discrepancy, the result would not be a conscious state (A view Gennaro has argued in a reply to criticism by Pereplyotchik, see Gennaro, 2015.)

Higher-order misrepresentation

The question of misrepresentation is the question of what happens if there are discrepancies between a higher-order state and its target lower-order state. In its earliest iterations, the possibility of misrepresentation and the challenges this poses were raised by Karen Neander (1998), Kati Balog (2000) and Joseph Levine (2001). Neander in particular has been instructive in highlighting the issues raised by misrepresentation. In her seminal paper, she presents the following case (rephrased slightly here; for the original phrasing, see Neander, 1998, p. 420), that is useful as an introduction to the issue of misrepresentation. Imagine three situations in which an individual differs with respect to the first-order state she is in. In the first situation, the individual has a sensory first-order state of a green patch. In the second situation, the individual has a sensory first-order state of a red patch. In the third situation, the individual has no first-order state at all. Now suppose that in all three situations the individual has identical higher-order states with the content "I am seeing a green patch". The question now is: What will the individual consciously experience? This is the question about the respective roles of higher- and lower-order states in the production of consciousness. There is nothing in the general higher-order idea that tells us how to answer this question. The general higher-order idea simply informs us of two things. First, a conscious state is a state an individual is aware of herself as being in, and second that the way an individual becomes conscious of herself as being in a state is by having a higher-order mental state representing her as being in the state in question. Opponents of higher-order theories have seized on the possibility of misrepresentation to argue against the higher-order model on several grounds. While these objections are peripheral to the central issue in this chapter, they are worth summarizing because they provide context and perspective to the theoretical debate that in turn may bleed into the empirical considerations.

Two classical objections to misrepresentation

One prominent and extensively discussed objection (e.g. Balog, 2000; Block, 2011a, 2011b; Matey, 2011; Neander, 1998; Rosenthal, 2004b, 2012; Shepherd, 2013; Weisberg, 2008, 2010, 2011) turns on the concept of phenomenality, i.e. the subjective feel of conscious states. The idea of subjectivity as an essential part of consciousness is usually attributed to Thomas Nagel (1974), who famously proposed that there must be something *it is like* for an individual to be in a conscious state. With respect to the misrepresentation debate, the question then is whether *what it is like* to be in a conscious state is determined by the higher-order representation or the first-order state. The objection is supposed to present a dilemma. One the one hand, if phenomenality is determined by (or the stronger claim: is intrinsic to) first-order states, then phenomenality (and with it consciousness as it is usually conceived of) cannot occur absent a first-order state as suggested by the possibility of misrepresentation. On the other hand, it is suggested that representational content cannot provide the same richness of experience, as for instance analogue visual content, therefore it is implausible that higher-order representations can account for our vivid and complex conscious experiences.

Another widely discussed objection (e.g. Berger, 2014, Block, 2011a, 2011b; Matey, 2006; Pereplyotchik, 2015; Rosenthal 2011b, 2012, Weisberg, 2010; Wilberg, 2010) to the possibility of misrepresentation suggests that if a mental state is conscious, this seems to entail that it exists. Therefore, allowing consciousness to occur absent a first-order state that is conscious (e.g. the third individual in Neander's example above) is incoherent.

Proponents of the possibility of misrepresentation have provided various rebuttals to the two objections. I shall not rehearse them all in detail here, but merely summarize central points. Regarding phenomenality, the proponents of higher-order theories have (rightly, I think) pointed out that while they agree that there is *something it is like* to be conscious of something, they interpret the notion of *what it is likeness* differently than their objectors. In the words of Rosenthal (2011b, p. 434): "The phrase 'what it's like' is not reliable common currency". From this, proponents of misrepresentation contend, there are ways to cash out this notion that does not lead to the problems suggested by the objectors. As for the question of whether a state being conscious entails that the state exists, proponents of the possibility of misrepresentation have argued that when they use terms such as "conscious state" or "state consciousness" are merely manners of speaking, and that consciousness is a property of individuals not mental states. This view also is reflected in the transitivity principle (see above) defining conscious states as states *an individual* is aware of herself as being in.

Three views on misrepresentation

Rosenthal along with Joshua Weisberg (2010, 2011), another proponent of Actualism, have been among the most ardent defenders of the possibility of misrepresentation. The possibility of misrepresentation, according to Rosenthal and Weisberg, is built into the concept of representation, because representing something does not entail the existence of the represented object.

Thus, they hold that all three individuals in Neander's scenario above will be conscious of whatever states an occurring HOT represents them as being in. According to Rosenthal and Weisberg, from the first person perspective it does not matter if the HOT does not reflect accurately an existing first-order state, or if there is no first-order state at all. To boot, Rosenthal has argued that the distinction between so-called mild misrepresentation (the second individual in Neander's scenario) collapses into radical misrepresentation (the third individual in Neander's scenario). He says (Rosenthal, 2004b, p. 32):

> Suppose my higher-order awareness is of a state with the property P, but the target isn't P, but rather Q. We could say that the higher-order awareness misrepresents the target, but we could equally well say that it's an awareness of a state that doesn't occur. The more dramatic the misrepresentation, the greater the temptation to say the target is absent.

As for what brings about HOTs, Rosenthal remains agnostic, but posits that a HOT can occur "without its target state" (Rosenthal, 2004b, p. 40). For instance, he says:

> [...] requiring, that the mental state be the principal factor in causing the HOT is very likely too strong. [...] In these cases some causal factor other than the

> mental state must figure in explaining why the HOT does or does not occur. [...] we can remain noncommittal about the causal history of HOTs.
>
> *(Rosenthal, 1997, p. 744)*

To summarize, according to Actualism, a HOT by itself is sufficient for conscious experience, a corresponding first-order state is not necessary for the individual to be conscious of being in that state. In the normal case, there *will* be a first-order state that becomes the target of a HOT, thereby rendering the individual conscious of being in that state. However, this normal case has exceptions, because the higher-order machinery may produce HOTs by itself without having been fed a first-order state to represent.

With respect to Bayesianism, it is worth noting that Lau seemingly rejects the philosophical notion of misrepresentation by reformulating the respective roles of the higher-order representations and the signals they interpret. He says:

> the higher order representation represents a scale by which the first-order representation (the internal signal) could be interpreted. The internal signal carries no fixed meaning unless one is to have some access to the higher order representations [...]. Similarly, the higher order representations do not make sense outside of the context of the internal signal. This way, a mismatch [...] is simply not possible: their content cannot directly contradict, because they are never meant to duplicate each other.
>
> *(Lau, 2007, pp. 46–47)*

Be that as it may, the fact that the Bayesianism allows for erroneous interpretations of noise (false positives) to yield conscious experiences (e.g. Hallucinations) maps plausibly onto Neander's example (see e.g. Coleman, 2018, for a similar interpretation of Lau's account).

Gennaro espouses a variant of the no-consciousness reply to misrepresentation that some higher-order theorists (e.g. Wilberg, 2010) have proposed. The no-consciousness reply claims that if discrepancies obtain between the higher-order content and its lower-order target, then this prevents the occurrence of a conscious state. Gennaro argues for his version of the no-consciousness reply with reference to the intrinsic relation that necessarily must hold between M⋆ and M for the CMS to be a conscious state. The intrinsic relation guarantees correct representation of the lower-order state by the metacognitive thought; otherwise, no conscious state occurs. The upshot is that, as conceived by Gennaro, misrepresentation is impossible on the WIV.

Autonomous HOTs and misrepresentation

In the above, I have briefly presented three variants of HOT theory. While the three views differ significantly with respect to their framing and detail, I have focused on identifying their divergence concerning the possibility of misrepresentation

TABLE 7.1 Distinguishing between variants of higher-order theory on the bases of their position on the autonomy of HOTs and the possibility of misrepresentation

	HOTs are autonomous	*Misrepresentation is possible*
Actualism	Yes	Yes
Bayesianism	No	Yes
Wide intrinsicality	No	No

and the autonomy of HOTs. The divergence can be mapped according to their stance on these two issues. The first issue is whether HOTs are autonomous, i.e. if HOTs depend on anything external to themselves or can occur in isolation. The second issue is whether misrepresentation is possible (Table 7.1).

To summarize, according to Rosenthal's Actualist HOT theory, a HOT by itself is sufficient for the occurrence of a conscious state. Ordinarily, the HOT will target lower-order states that originate from standard processes (e.g. sensations), but this is not necessary and there is no commitment to any necessary causal ancestry of HOTs. A HOT may come about entirely on its own, with no relations to other states and yet yield a conscious state (i.e. make the individual aware of herself as being in some state). This means that according to Actualism, misrepresentation is possible, and obtains whenever a HOT occurs in the absence of a target first-order state. According to Hakwan Lau's Bayesianism, HOTs are generated from a heuristic subjective decision criterion that attempts to determine whether an incoming signal carries information or is just noise. Occasionally, this decision mechanism may yield false positives, i.e. classify noise as a proper information-carrying signal yielding a HOT interpreting it as if it was information. This idea produces two upshots. The first is that a HOT cannot occur in the absence of an incoming signal, because according to Lau, HOTs are meaningless without any signal to interpret. The second upshot is that misrepresentation is possible and occurs as a result of false positives, where a HOT represents a signal that is erroneously interpreted as carrying information when it is, in fact, just noise. Finally, the WIV, as proposed by Rocco Gennaro, claims that conscious states must be individuated widely as CMS containing both a HOT and a lower-order state as their proper parts. According to Gennaro, in conscious states an intrinsic relation exists between the higher- and lower-order content that guarantees a correct representational relation. If this relation does not hold, the result is not a conscious state. Therefore, on the WIV, a conscious state will always contain a HOT that correctly represents some lower-order state, and misrepresentation is therefore impossible. Similarly, HOTs are not autonomous on the WIV because they are merely proper parts of a CMS.

Empirical perspectives

Proponents of higher-order theories have been involved extensively in what has become known as the "empirical turn" within the philosophy of mind. The two main assumptions of the empirical turn are first that the explanatory and predictive powers of a theory with respect to empirical evidence are a key indicator of plausibility. And, second that empirical arguments for and against theories are at least as valuable and decisive as the classical philosophical practices of conceptual analysis, thought experiments and other so-called armchair philosophy (see e.g. Weisberg, 2014). Proponents of HOT theories have proposed various empirical findings in support of their theories, both on a general level and within discussions of specific aspects (e.g. misrepresentation). In sections "Charles Bonnet syndrome and misrepresentation" and "Change blindness and misrepresentation", I will start by summarizing the two most discussed empirical arguments in the misrepresentation debate. In section "The neural correlates of higher-order thought", I present the view (currently) most commonly favored regarding the NCC with respect to higher-order theories.

Charles Bonnet syndrome and misrepresentation

Charles Bonnet syndrome normally occurs from ocular pathology resulting in sudden and profound loss of vision. The symptoms are characterized by visual hallucinations that are formed, complex, persistent and stereotyped. Interestingly, sufferers of Charles Bonnet syndrome are otherwise cognitively normal and retain insight into the nature of the hallucinations, making them trustworthy subjects. However, ocular pathology is not the only possible cause. As Gold and Rabins (1989) note, individuals occasionally may develop Charles Bonnet syndrome from damage to one or more cortical areas, primarily the parietal, occipital and temporal lobes. Two such cases have been singled out as evidence of misrepresentation. The two cases are Patient FA, an 81-year-old female, reported by Duggal and Pierri (2002), and an unnamed 74-year-old male, reported by Ashwin and Tsaloumas (2007). What makes these two cases special is that the cortical damage that underlies the Charles Bonnet syndrome is located in the visual cortex, more specifically in V1. To mount the argument for the occurrence of misrepresentation, the lack of V1 functionality, along with the (trustworthy) reports of conscious visual awareness, is combined with findings from Victor Lamme's lab about the role of V1 in conscious visual awareness (Lamme, 2003, 2004). Lamme argues that feedback to V1 plays a crucial role in conscious visual awareness. In the argument, Lamme's characterization of the pre-conscious activations in the visual cortex, and especially the crucial role of V1, is interpreted as evidence of the point of origin of first-order visual states. The interpretation goes roughly as follows: V1 is the starting point of the feedforward sweep. The feedforward sweep is the initial pattern of neural activity from the onset of a visual stimulus. Activity in V1 starts roughly after 40 ms from stimuli onset and spreads to all cortical areas, even those responsible for high-level information, discrimination and selective behavioral responses (Lamme 2004, p. 867). Because activations during the feedforward sweep can guide apparently unconscious behavior, the interpretation suggests a distinction between (unconscious) first-order states generated by the feedforward sweep and conscious states depending on subsequent processes (recurrent processing according to Lamme). So, by transitivity, if V1 is a necessary component in the feedforward sweep, it is also necessary for the creation of first-order visual states. Now, according to HOT theory, the "subsequent processing" that conscious states depend on is, *ex hypothesis*, the generation of a HOT. Because the two sufferers of Charles Bonnet syndrome deployed in the argument had visual hallucinations, this suggests that the HOTs underpinning the conscious awareness should be about first-order visual states. But according to the interpretation of Lamme's findings, these individuals cannot due to the lack of V1 activity generate first-order visual states. Therefore, the proponents of the possibility of misrepresentation conclude that the HOTs must be occurring without first-order states (Lau & Brown, 2019; Lau & Rosenthal, 2011). It is worth noting that the underlying logic of this argument has been disputed (Kirkeby-Hinrup, 2014), but because the purpose here is merely to provide a brief overview, the details of this debate, while interesting, are not necessary here.

Change blindness and misrepresentation

Change blindness is a phenomenon of visual perception characterized by the failure to detect changes in a stimulus array while actively exploring it. There is a wide range of paradigms that can evoke the change blindness effect (see e.g. Beck, Rees, Frith, & Lavie, 2001; Busch, Fründ, & Herrmann, 2009; Rensink, O'Regan, & Clark, 1997; Simons & Ambinder, 2005; Simons & Rensink, 2005).

Because most change blindness paradigms readily allow for alternative interpretations of the data (for instance, the so-called "no comparison" interpretation, see e.g. Kirkeby-Hinrup, 2016), the change blindness paradigm usually leveraged as evidence of misrepresentation is the *saccade-induced change blindness* experiments by John Grimes (1996). Saccade-induced change blindness depends on the fact that during saccades the subject is effectively blind. Grimes exploits this by using eye-tracking to determine the onset of saccades and time the switch in visual stimulus to occur during saccades. Because the stimulus change is not synced to their saccades, to outside observers the changes to the visual stimuli are salient, but to the subject they are very hard to detect. It is the cases where subjects fail to detect the changes to their visual stimulus that are argued to be examples of the occurrence of misrepresentation. The reasoning proceeds from the fact that the content of the HOT, *ex hypothesis*, is fixed by the state the individual is aware of herself as being in. Therefore, if we are to avoid discrepancies between the HOT and its target state, the content the relevant first-order state must be what the individual actually experiences herself as seeing. In the cases where the subjects do not detect the changes, subjects experience themselves as seeing the pre-change visual stimulus. To boot, Rosenthal argues that the pre-change visual signal is either severely degraded or extinguished. He says: "Because retinal input to visual cortex resumes after saccades, first-order states in visual cortex presumably did change in ways that reflected the change in display, despite participants' reporting no awareness of such change" (Rosenthal, 2012, p. 8). The idea is that because input to the retina has resumed, this has either overwritten the pre-change visual trace or displaced it to rapidly decaying memory buffers. In either case, if the subject experiences herself as being in the pre-change state, the HOT will not accurately reflect the state. Moreover, because Rosenthal argues the distinction between the second and third individual in Neander's case collapses, the upshot is that the subjects are aware of themselves as being in a state that (strictly speaking) does not exist.

Observe that it has been contested (Brinck & Kirkeby-Hinrup, 2017; Kirkeby-Hinrup, 2016) whether this interpretation of the change blindness data is the most plausible one. However, the details of these objections are not critical to the current chapter.

The neural correlates of higher-order thought

If the HOT hypothesis is correct, to identify the NCC amounts to identifying the neural correlates of higher-order thoughts. That is, because on the higher-order thought models conscious states derive from HOTs, the neural underpinnings of HOTs are, *ex hypothesis*, identical to the NCC. Thus, the assumption is that there is a mechanism in the brain responsible for the generation of HOTs, I will call this the "higher-order faculty" (HOF). The exact function and location of the HOF currently is undetermined, but candidates have been proposed and the topic is enjoying increased attention in the ongoing debate within consciousness studies.

The consensus, *albeit* one not accepted by Gennaro (see e.g. 2016a), is that the brain region most likely to be the host of the HOF is the prefrontal cortex (PFC). The PFC is considered the most plausible location of HOF because there is a wealth of empirical data documenting its role in a wide range of other metacognitive processes seemingly related in kind to higher-order thoughts (Beeckmans, 2007; Brown, 2012; Kozuch, 2014; Kriegel, 2007a; Lau, 2007; Lau & Brown, 2019; Lau & Rosenthal, 2011).

For instance, the PFC appears to be involved heavily in self-monitoring and judgements of performance (Fleming & Dolan, 2012), cognitive control and planning (Lau, 2011) and theory of mind (Frith & Frith, 2006). Let us briefly unpack what similarities these processes share with the conception of higher-order thoughts deployed by the HOT theories. HOTs are assumed to be essentially indexical (Rosenthal, 2003, 2004a, 2011a), i.e. picking out the individual tokening the HOT, something that also appears necessary to the concept of self-monitoring. Similarly, judgements of performance imply the concept of belief. Like HOTs, beliefs are assertoric in nature. Planning future courses of action requires entertaining counterfactual scenarios, in order to assess their outcomes. Entertaining counterfactual scenarios pertaining to one's future action requires representing oneself as being in particular (counterfactual) states, which bears some similarity to representing oneself as being in actual states. Whether this process is most similar to introspection or "ordinary" consciousness rendering higher-order thoughts is up for debate. Finally, in theory of mind, an individual represents the cognitive, emotional or perceptual states of another individual. That is, the individual entertains higher-order representation of mental states. The main difference seems to be that in theory of mind, the higher-order representations are not essentially indexical, but perhaps merely *faux* indexical, in the sense that they are entertained *as if* they belonged to the individual engaging in theory of mind. Importantly, the reasoning from similarity does not suggest (let alone entail) that the HOF necessarily is comprised of these mechanisms, overlaps with their cortical areas or even recruits (some of) the same processes. The reasoning merely suggests that because the PFC is engaged in processes similar to how we conceive of the processes of the HOF, it is likely the HOF is also found in the PFC.

In the domain of (conscious) visual perception, Hakwan Lau and associates have produced evidence for a possible location for the HOF. In one study, using functional magnetic resonance imaging, Hakwan Lau and Richard Passingham (2006) found that the dorsolateral PFC (dlPFC/Broodman area 46) appears to be involved in the generation of conscious visual awareness. Using a meta-contrast masking paradigm, the study sought to dissociate task performance from conscious perception, attempting to keep performance stable while varying perceptual awareness. Lau and Passingham found that activity in the dlPFC was associated with increased frequency in subjects' reports of conscious awareness of the identity of the visual stimulus (Lau & Passingham, 2006, pp. 18765–18766). In a subsequent study, subjects performed a visual discrimination task while being subjected to transcranial magnetic stimulation (TMS). When applied to the dlPFC, TMS was found to change the subjective reports of awareness of a visual stimulus (Rounis, Maniscalco, Rothwell, Passingham, & Lau, 2010). On the basis of these studies, reasoning from the association between activity in the dlPFC and higher-levels of subjective awareness, the dlPFC has been proposed as a candidate for the generation of HOTs (Lau & Rosenthal, 2011, pp. 367–368).

While there has been a lot of focus on the PFC, it is an open question whether the HOF is distributed topographically across one or more brain regions. For instance, Lau and Rosenthal sometimes include parietal areas (Lau & Rosenthal, 2011). Gennaro, as alluded to above, thinks the PFC is an unlikely candidate, and suggests parietal areas along with the cingulate cortex (Gennaro, 2016a). Josh Weisberg sees multiple topographical and functional candidates for the HOF, including various locations in the PFC as well as the anterior cingulate cortex (Weisberg, 2014).

For the purposes of this chapter, we can remain agnostic about whether the HOF is topographically distributed or not. The assumption that the concept of a HOF maps reasonably onto discrete neural processes is all that is needed for the present purposes. This assumption depends on the two assumptions stated in the introduction: first that the mind can be naturalized, and second that some form of two-stage (higher-order thought) model correctly reflects how consciousness arises from neural processes. Of course, it may be argued that it is possible that there is no one way to (or one process or faculty that) generate HOTs. Perhaps HOTs are generated differently depending on their content or perhaps there is no fixed way at all, and no process, brain area or function is necessary. If the latter is the case, then all bets are off with respect to identifying the NCC. If the former is the case, then the process of identifying the NCC of HOTs will require identifying the necessary components of each way a HOT can be generated, and possibly realign our concept of the HOF to any necessary component shared between the different ways.

Benjamin Kozuch (2014) has suggested that in this last case it is reasonable to assume that some processes in the PFC are a shared necessary component for the production of HOTs. The proposal that the PFC is necessary for HOTs has led opponents of HOT theories to argue that HOT theories are empirically implausible. The arguments turn on cases of conscious experience where PFC activity is absent for one reason or another, thereby suggesting the claim that the PFC is necessary for HOTs is inconsistent. For instance, Miguel Ángel Sebastián (2014) proceeds from the premise that dream experiences are akin to waking experiences, at least in so far they both seem to include phenomenally conscious visual experiences. Sebastián then points to findings to the effect that during REM sleep, where dream experience is prevalent, the dlPFC, parietal cortex as well as the posterior cingulate cortex and precuneus are the least active brain regions (e.g. Maquet et al., 2005, p. 220). Therefore, the dlPFC, a prime candidate for the HOF, it seems, cannot underpin conscious visual experience. The upshot, Sebastián suggests, are that either (1) the dlPFC cannot underpin the conscious experiences during dreams, or (2) one would have to deny that dreams contain phenomenally conscious visual experiences. According to Sebastián, neither is appealing. He argues that if the dlPFC does not sustain conscious visual experience during dreams, it is unlikely to do so for ordinary conscious visual experiences. Denying the presence of visual phenomenology during dreams conflicts with our first person experiences, common sense and supposedly is contradicted by the lucid dreaming phenomenon. In Weisberg's reply to Sebastián (Weisberg, 2014) he counters much of the underlying rationale for Sebastián's conclusion. I shall not rehash it all here, but merely note that with respect to the dlPFC, Weisberg maintains an agnostic stance as to whether it is the prime (or the only) candidate for the HOF and highlights other possible locations to be investigated.

Another objection to the higher-order theories, and in particular the assumption that the PFC is necessary for the generation of HOTs, has been made on the bases of lesion studies. Benjamin Kozuch (2014) has mounted one such objection. He argues that if some higher-order theory is true, prefrontal lesions should produce detectable deficits in consciousness. That is, if the HOF is located in the PFC, and the HOF is critical to consciousness, then lesions to the PFC should affect consciousness. Kozuch concludes from surveys of prefrontal lesions that there appears to be no correlation between prefrontal lesions and dramatic effects on consciousness. Kozuch then argues the claim that if there is a HOF, then it should at least partly include the PFC, and lesions to the PFC should affect its efficacy in generating HOTs. Therefore, Kozuch concludes, the lesion studies are noteworthy evidence against the HOT theories. The role of the PFC in consciousness is a subject to ongoing debate (e.g. Boly et al., 2017) that goes beyond just lesion studies. However, with respect to lesion evidence in particular, proponents of a role for the PFC have replied along three lines (Odegaard, Knight, & Lau, 2017). The first is that in much of the surveyed evidence, the lesions to the PFC leave parts of the PFC intact. The second is that the number of cases surveyed is relatively small. The third is that methodological issues undermine much of the evidence. Ultimately, because the debate on whether the PFC is necessary for consciousness is still ongoing, the question of whether the HOF is located in the PFC is yet to be answered. Evidence proposed in favor of the dlPFC as a good candidate for the HOF will need further corroboration to convince its objectors. However, even if the dlPFC ultimately is debunked as the host of the HOF, there are other plausible candidates to investigate.

Beyond the neural correlates of higher-order thought

In this section, I will show how the way the pieces fall with respect to the localization and the functional profile of the HOF may inform the theoretical debate. Because of the differing predictions yielded by variants of HOT theory, we may be able to decide between them based on the how each corresponds to the functional profile of the HOF. I will consider only one way the identification of the HOF may allow us to arbitrate between competing variants of HOT theory. The way I propose to do this turns on the differing stances on the possibility of misrepresentation and autonomy identified in section "Autonomous HOTs and misrepresentation" above. I leave it open that there are may be other (and possibly more straightforward) ways to assess the variants of HOT theory on the basis of the HOF.

As we saw in section "Higher-order misrepresentation", Actualism, Bayesianism and the WIV differ with respect to how they conceive of the possibility of misrepresentation. Actualism holds that a HOT in itself may yield conscious experience, and that the HOT can do this independently of anything external, i.e. in the absence of a first-order state. This means that on Actualism misrepresentation is possible and can occur out of the blue, as it were. Bayesianism holds that HOTs are generated as interpretations of incoming signals. Occasionally, incoming signals are interpreted as containing information even though they are actually just noise. When this happens, misrepresentation occurs. Finally, the VIW claims that HOTs are proper parts of a larger CMS. If there is any discrepancy between the HOT and its target (the other proper part of the CMS), no conscious state results. This means that on the VIW, consciousness yielding HOTs will always be integrated with their target and misrepresentation yielding conscious states is impossible.

The way I propose to deploy the NCC to distinguish between the three HOT theories rests on the assumption that the differing stances on the possibility of misrepresentation allows different empirical predictions about the conditions under which the HOF may generate HOTs, in particular, different predictions regarding the causal origins of consciousness yielding HOF activity. By virtue of relying on yet to be discovered neural implementations of consciousness, the following conjectures are highly speculative, but such is the nature of reasoning *beyond* the NCC, as is the task in this volume. I will speculate that the theoretical feature allowing us to distinguish between the three HOT theories is their respective predictions on (a) whether an external signal is necessary for the generation of a HOT, and (b) the nature of the external signal in case one is necessary. Below, I will briefly sketch how possible differences in the neural characteristics of the HOF when combined with (a) may allow us to distinguish Actualism from Bayesianism and the VIW, and when combined with (b) may allow us to distinguish between Bayesianism and the VIW.

Distinguishing actualism from Bayesianism and the VIW

As we saw above, according to Actualism, a HOT is by itself sufficient to generate conscious experience. Furthermore, Actualism allows that the state the HOT makes the individual conscious of being in is a state the individual is not actually in. Thus, to reiterate, according to Actualism misrepresentation is possible, and the HOF does not require any external input to generate a HOT. HOTs may occur out of the blue, as it were. One possible interpretation of these claims is that local spontaneous activity in the HOF may generate HOTs and thereby yield conscious states. From the assumption that we have identified the NCC, i.e. *ex hypothesis* the neural implementation of the HOF, we may be then able to detect such spontaneous activity and correlate it with subjective reports. How exactly to conceive of such spontaneous activity is an open question. *Prima facie*, because the activity must be local, i.e. constrained to the HOF, it is presumably not part of the default mode network or resting state activity (albeit there may be some wiggle room, see e.g. Tozzi, Zare, & Benasich, 2016). An alternative is to conceive of the spontaneous activity along the lines of the functional abnormalities found in epileptic seizures. An experimental possibility would be attempt to introduce spontaneous activity artificially through TMS or electrode stimulations. Last, another possible way to investigate the occurrence of spontaneous activity in the HOF would be to correlate conscious states with input to the HOF. Conscious states occurring without the HOF having received any input would indicate that the HOF had generated HOTs without any target state. Importantly, this latter possibility rests on the assumption that signals streaming into the HOF are gated by some mechanism. Some sort of gating seems plausible, since we seem to have very few HOTs (conscious thoughts) at any given point in time. This could make sense from an evolutionary point of view because attention and action would likely be impaired if our streams of consciousness were to host a multitude of synchronous or competing conscious states.

Thus, speculatively, we may be able to conclude that the HOT theory that best describes (human) consciousness is Actualism under the following conditions: (1) We identify the NCCs/HOF and (2) Conscious states can occur either from local spontaneous activity (either endogenous or artificially introduced) in the HOF, or in the absence of any signal passing through a hypothetical gating mechanism or both. Whether or not answering these questions will be feasible, even after discovering the NCCs, remains to be seen. However, conceptually at least, the possibilities are in play.

Distinguishing between Bayesianism and the VIW

Having sketched a preliminary principled way of distinguishing Actualism from the other two options, we can now turn to how to distinguish between Bayesianism and the WIV. Essentially, distinguishing between the two effectively consists in ruling out Bayesianism. Remember, according to Bayesianism misrepresentation occurs when the HOF erroneously interprets an incoming signal as carrying information, when it is in fact just noise. This means it should be possible to test Bayesianism by flooding the gate of the HOF with noise, for instance using TMS (or some future sophisticated treatment with similar effect). If the subject reports (unusual?) conscious experiences when we know that only noise entered the HOF, this indicates that the subject is misrepresenting the noise as actual information carrying signals, and hence that Bayesianism best describes (human) consciousness as opposed to the WIV. If subjects fail to have conscious experiences when the only input to the HOF is noise, this may indicate that there are certain requirements to the kind of signals the HOF can interpret. This would point toward the some version of higher-order theory that rules out misrepresentation, such as the WIV. I here write "some version" because the possibility is left open that the signal merely needs to exhibit certain properties that noise is lacking. In other words, there may exist some features a signal entering the HOF needs to exhibit in order for the HOF to be able to parse it properly and generate a consciousness yielding HOT. Thus, while the failure of the HOF to generate HOTs when the input is only noise does not conclusively establish that the signal necessarily must be a fully formed first-order state with an intrinsic relation to the HOT, as posited by Gennaro's version of the WIV, it would go some way toward establishing the parameters of a proper higher-order theory by ruling out Actualism and Bayesianism.

Concluding remarks

In the above, I have sketched a principled way of empirically distinguishing between three versions of higher-order theory. The proposed way to distinguish between the theories is derived from their differing commitments with respect to the possibility of misrepresentation and the autonomy of the HOF. Actualism, as defended by David Rosenthal, holds that misrepresentation is possible and that the HOF is autonomous, in the sense that it does not, in principle, require an incoming signal to generate HOTs, even if in the most normal case an incoming signal is present. Bayesianism, as proposed by Hakwan Lau, suggests that misrepresentation is possible and that the HOF is not autonomous, because an incoming signal is necessary for the generation of HOTs. Finally, the WIV, defended by Rocco Gennaro, denies the possibility of misrepresentation (in the strong sense, where misrepresentation yields conscious states) and holds that the HOF is not autonomous. These differences I deployed to identify, first, a way to separate Actualism from Bayesianism and the WIV and second, a way to separate Bayesianism from the WIV. Admittedly, the proposals in this chapter are highly speculative. However, given the purpose of this volume, i.e. to go beyond the NCC and consider possible theoretical consequences, speculation is warranted in this case. Yet, it is worth bearing in mind the significant unargued assumptions deployed in the above. First of all, it was assumed that some version of higher-order thought theory was correct. This in itself is not problematic, since it usually is necessary to whittle down the amount of theories under consideration. Another significant assumption concerns the presence of what I have called the HOF. From the assumption that some version of HOT theory is correct, coupled with the assumption that consciousness in some substantive way depends on the brain, it follows that something in the brain realizes higher-order thoughts. Apart from this assertion, I have remained agnostic about the nature of the HOF, for instance, regarding whether it is distributed cortically or not and whether there may be several distinct HOFs, each handling specific types of content or sensory modalities. However, the exact nature of the HOF (or HOFs) may have implications for the reasoning deployed above. In particular, the above relies extensively on our ability to measure, verify and manipulate the signals flowing into the HOF, and the ability to correlate these with conscious experiences, something that is not currently feasible for several reasons, the most significant of which is that the HOF has not yet been located in the brain. In this regard, I will again remind the reader that because the task in this volume is to assume that the NCCs (i.e. the HOF) have been identified, these uncertainties are to be expected. Whether future discoveries will discover the presence of a HOF, and subsequently allow for the requisite measurements and manipulations, is necessarily an open question (otherwise, they would be present discoveries).

Acknowledgments

AKH is funded by the Swedish Research Council (grant 2018-06595).

References

Ashwin, P. T., & Tsaloumas, M. D. (2007). Complex visual hallucinations (Charles Bonnet syndrome) in the hemianopic visual field following occipital infarction. *Journal of the Neurological Sciences, 263*(1–2), 184–186.

Baars, B. J. (1996). Understanding subjectivity: Global workspace theory and the resurrection of the observing self. *Journal of Consciousness Studies, 3*(3), 211–216.

Balog, K. (2000). Comments on David Rosenthal's "Consciousness, content, and metacognitive judgments". *Consciousness and Cognition, 9*(2 Pt 1), 215–219; discussion 231–242.

Beck, D. M., Rees, G., Frith, C. D., & Lavie, N. (2001). Neural correlates of change detection and change blindness. *Nature Neuroscience, 4*(6), 645–650.

Beeckmans, J. (2007). Can higher-order representation theories pass scientific muster? *Journal of Consciousness Studies, 14*(9–1), 90–111.

Berger, J. (2017). How things seem to higher-order thought theorists. *Dialogue: Canadian Philosophical Review, 56*(3), 503–526.

Block, N. (1996). Mental paint and mental latex. *Philosophical Issues, 7,* 19–49.

Block, N. (2005). Two neural correlates of consciousness. *Trends in Cognitive Sciences, 9*(2), 46–52.

Block, N. (2007). Consciousness, accessibility, and the mesh between psychology and neuroscience. *Behavioral and Brain Sciences, 30*(5–6), 481–499; discussion 499–548.

Block, N. (2011a). The higher order approach to consciousness is defunct. *Analysis, 71*(3), 419–431.

Block, N. (2011b). Response to Rosenthal and Weisberg. *Analysis, 71*(3), 443–448.

Boly, M., Massimini, M., Tsuchiya, N., Postle, B. R., Koch, C., & Tononi, G. (2017). Are the neural correlates of consciousness in the front or in the back of the cerebral cortex? Clinical and neuroimaging evidence. *Journal of Neuroscience, 37*(40), 9603–9613.

Brinck, I., & Kirkeby-Hinrup, A. (2017). Change blindness in higher-order thought: Misrepresentation or good enough? *Journal of Consciousness Studies, 24*(5–6), 50–73.

Brown, R. (2012). The brain and its states. In S. Edelman, T. Fekete, & N. Zach (Eds.), *Being in Time: Dynamical Models of Phenomenal Experience* (Vol. 88, pp. 211–238): John Benjamins, Amsterdam, NL.

Brown, R. (2015). The HOROR theory of phenomenal consciousness. *Philosophical Studies, 172*(7), 1783–1794.

Busch, N., Fründ, I., & Herrmann, C. (2009). Electrophysiological evidence for different types of change detection and change blindness. *Journal of Cognitive Neuroscience 22*(8), 1852–1869.

Carruthers, P. (1998). Natural theories of consciousness. *European Journal of Philosophy, 6*(2), 203–222.

Carruthers, P. (2003). *Phenomenal Consciousness: A Naturalistic Theory*: Cambridge University Press, Cambridge, UK.

Coleman, S. (2015). Quotational higher-order thought theory. *Philosophical Studies, 172*(10), 2705–2733.

Coleman, S. (2018). The merits of higher-order thought theories. *Trans/Form/Ação, 41*(SPE), 31–48.

D'Aloisio-Montilla, N. (2017). Imagery and overflow: We see more than we report. *Philosophical Psychology, 30*(5), 545–570.

Dehaene, S., & Naccache, L. (2001). Towards a cognitive neuroscience of consciousness: Basic evidence and a workspace framework. *Cognition, 79*(1–2), 1–37.

Dretske, F. (1993). Conscious experience. *Mind, 102*(406), 263–283.

Dretske, F. (1997). *Naturalizing the Mind*: MIT Press, Massachusetts, US.

Duggal, H. S., & Pierri, J. N. (2002). Charles bonnet syndrome: neurobiological insights. *Indian Journal of Psychiatry, 44*(3), 289–292.

Fleming, S. M., & Dolan, R. J. (2012). The neural basis of metacognitive ability. *Philosophical Transactions of the Royal Society of London B: Biological Sciences, 367*(1594), 1338–1349.

Frith, C. D., & Frith, U. (2006). The neural basis of mentalizing. *Neuron, 50*(4), 531–534.

Gennaro, R. J. (2004). Higher-order thoughts, animal consciousness, and misrepresentation. In R. J. Gennaro (Ed.), *Higher-Order Theories of Consciousness: An Anthology* (pp. 45–68): John Benjamins, Amsterdam, NL.

Gennaro, R. J. (2006). Between pure self-referentialism and the (extrinsic) HOT theory of consciousness. In U. Kriegel, & K. Williford (Eds.), *Self-representational Approaches to Consciousness*: MIT Press, Cambridge, MA, US.

Gennaro, R. J. (2012). *The Consciousness Paradox: Consciousness, Concepts, and Higher-Order Thoughts*: MIT Press, Cambridge, MA, US.

Gennaro, R. J. (2015). Misrepresentation, empty HOTs, and intrinsic HOTs: A reply to Pereplyotchik. *Philosophical Psychology, 28*(3), 449–451.

Gennaro, R. J. (2016a). Higher-order thoughts, neural realization, and the metaphysics of consciousness. In P.S. Satsangi, S. Hameroff, V. Sani & P. Dua (Eds.) *Consciousness: Integrating Eastern and Western Perspectives* (pp. 83–102): New Age Publishers, Delhi, India.

Gennaro, R. J. (2016b). HOT theory, concepts, and synesthesia: A reply to Adams and Shreve. *Symposion, 3*(4), 443–448.

Gold, K., & Rabins, P. V. (1989). Isolated visual hallucinations and the Charles Bonnet syndrome: A review of the literature and presentation of six cases. *Comprehensive Psychiatry, 30*(1), 90–98.

Gottlieb, J. (2018). Verbal disputes in the theory of consciousness. *Ergo, 5*, 319–347.

Grimes, J. A. (1996). On the failure to detect changes in scenes across saccades. In K. Akins (Ed.), *Perception* (pp. 89–110): Oxford University Press, Oxford, UK.

Kirkeby-Hinrup, A. (2014). Why the rare Charles Bonnet cases are not evidence of misrepresentation. *Journal of Philosophical Research, 39*, 301–308.

Kirkeby-Hinrup, A. (2016). Change blindness and misrepresentation. *Disputatio, 8*(42), 37–56.

Kozuch, B. (2014). Prefrontal lesion evidence against higher-order theories of consciousness. *Philosophical Studies, 167*(3), 721–746.

Kriegel, U. (2007a). A cross-order integration hypothesis for the neural correlate of consciousness. *Consciousness and Cognition, 16*(4), 897–912.

Kriegel, U. (2007b). The same-order monitoring theory of consciousness. *Synthesis Philosophica, 22*(2), 361–384.

Kriegel, U. (2008). Self-representationalism and phenomenology. *Philosophical Studies, 143*(3), 357–381.

Lamme, V. A. F. (2003). Why visual attention and awareness are different. *Trends in Cognitive Sciences, 7*(1), 12–18.

Lamme, V. A. F. (2004). Separate neural definitions of visual consciousness and visual attention; a case for phenomenal awareness. *Neural Networks, 17*(5–6), 861–872.

Lamme, V. A. F., & Roelfsema, P. R. (2000). The distinct modes of vision offered by feedforward and recurrent processing. *Trends in Neurosciences, 23*(11), 571–579.

Lau, H. (2007). A higher order Bayesian decision theory of consciousness. *Progress in Brain Research, 168*, 35–48.

Lau, H. (2011). Theoretical motivations for investigating the neural correlates of consciousness. *Wiley Interdisciplinary Reviews: Cognitive Science, 2*(1), 1–7.

Lau, H., & Brown, R. (2019). The emperor's new Phenomenology? The empirical case for conscious experiences without first-order representations. In A. Pautz, & D. Stoljar (Eds.), *Blockheads! Essays on Ned Block's Philosophy of Mind and Consciousness* (pp. 171–197): MIT Press, Cambridge, MA, US.

Lau, H., & Passingham, R. (2006). Relative blindsight in normal observers and the neural correlate of visual consciousness. *Proceedings of the National Academy of Sciences, 103*(49), 18763–18768.

Lau, H., & Rosenthal, D. (2011). Empirical support for higher-order theories of conscious awareness. *Trends in Cognitive Sciences, 15*(8), 365–373.

Levine, J. (2001). *Purple Haze: The Puzzle of Consciousness*: Oxford University Press, Oxford, UK.

Lycan, W. (2015). Representational theories of consciousness. In E. N. Zalta (Ed.), *The Stanford Encyclopedia of Philosophy* (Summer 2015 ed.): Metaphysics Research Lab, Stanford University. https://plato.stanford.edu/

Maquet, P., Ruby, P., Maudoux, A., Albouy, G., Sterpenich, V., Dang-Vu, T., … Peigneux, P. (2005). Human cognition during REM sleep and the activity profile within frontal and parietal cortices: A reappraisal of functional neuroimaging data. *Progress in Brain Research, 150*, 219–595.

Matey, J. (2006). Two HOTs to handle: The concept of state consciousness in the higher-order thought theory of consciousness. *Philosophical Psychology, 19*(2), 151–175.

Matey, J. (2011). Reduction and the determination of phenomenal character. *Philosophical Psychology, 24*(3), 291–316.

Nagel, T. (1974). What is it like to be a bat. *Philosophical Review, 83*(4), 435–450.

Neander, K. (1998). The division of phenomenal labor: A problem for representational theories of consciousness. *Philosophical Perspectives, 12*, 411–434.

Odegaard, B., Knight, R. T., & Lau, H. (2017). Should a few null findings falsify prefrontal theories of conscious perception? *Journal of Neuroscience, 37*(40), 9593–9602.

Pereplyotchik, D. (2015). Some HOT family disputes: A critical review of The Consciousness Paradox by Rocco Gennaro. *Philosophical Psychology, 3*(28), 434–448.

Petitot, J., Varela, F., Pachoud, B., & Roy, J.-M. (1999). *Naturalizing Phenomenology: Issues in Contemporary Phenomenology and Cognitive Science*: Stanford University Press, Stanford, CA, US.

Rensink, R. A., O'Regan, J. K., & Clark, J. A. (1997). To see or not to see: The need for attention to perceive changes in scenes. *Psychological Science, 8*(5), 368–373.

Rosenthal, D. M. (1997). A theory of consciousness. In N. Block, O. Flanagan, & G. Güzeldere (Eds.), *The Nature of Consciousness: Philosophical Debates* (pp. 729–753): MIT Press, Massachusetts, MA, US.

Rosenthal, D. M. (2002). Explaining consciousness. In D. Chalmers (Ed.), *Philosophy of Mind: Classical and Contemporary Readings* (pp. 406–421): Oxford University Press, Oxford, UK.

Rosenthal, D. M. (2003). Unity of consciousness and the self. *Proceedings of the Aristotelian Society, 103*(1), 325–352.

Rosenthal, D. M. (2004a). Being conscious of ourselves. *Monist, 87*(2), 159–181.

Rosenthal, D. M. (2004b). Varieties of higher-order theory. In R. J. Gennaro (Ed.), *Higher-Order Theories of Consciousness: An Anthology* (pp. 19–44): John Benjamins Publishers, Amsterdam, NL.

Rosenthal, D. M. (2011a). Awareness and identification of self. In J. Liu & J. Perry (Eds.), *Consciousness and the Self: New Essays* (pp. 22–50): Cambridge University Press, Cambridge, UK.

Rosenthal, D. M. (2011b). Exaggerated reports: Reply to block. *Analysis, 71*(3), 431–437.

Rosenthal, D. M. (2012). Higher-order awareness, misrepresentation and function. *Philosophical Transactions of the Royal Society of London B: Biological Sciences, 367*(1594), 1424–1438.

Rounis, E., Maniscalco, B., Rothwell, J. C., Passingham, R. E., & Lau, H. (2010). Theta-burst transcranial magnetic stimulation to the prefrontal cortex impairs metacognitive visual awareness. *Cognitive Neuroscience, 1*(3), 165–175.

Seager, W. (2002). *Theories of Consciousness: An Introduction*: Routledge, New York, NY, US.

Sebastián, M. Á. (2014). Not a HOT dream. In R. Brown (Ed.), *Consciousness Inside and Out: Phenomenology, Neuroscience, and the Nature of Experience* (Vol. 6, pp. 415–432): Springer, Heidelberg, NL.

Shepherd, Joshua. (2013). Why block can't stand the HOT. *Journal of Consciousness Studies, 20*(3–4), 183–195.

Simons, D. J., & Ambinder, M. S. (2005). Change blindness: Theory and consequences. *Current Directions in Psychological Science, 14*(1), 44–48.

Simons, D. J., & Rensink, R. A. (2005). Change blindness: Past, present, and future. *Trends in Cognitive Sciences, 9*(1), 16–20.

Tononi, G. (2005). Consciousness, information integration, and the brain. In L. Steven (Ed.), *Progress in Brain Research* (Vol. 150, pp. 109–126).

Tozzi, A., Zare, M., & Benasich, A. A. (2016). New perspectives on spontaneous brain activity: Dynamic networks and energy matter. *Frontiers in Human Neuroscience, 10*, 247.

Tye, M. (1997). *Ten Problems of Consciousness: A Representational Theory of the Phenomenal Mind*: MIT Press, Cambridge, MA, US.

Van Gulick, R. (2004). Higher-order global states (HOGS) an alternative higher-order model. In: R. Gennaro (Ed), *Higher-Order Theories of Consciousness: An Anthology* (pp. 67–93), John Benjamins, Amsterdam, NL.

Weisberg, J. (2008). Same old, same old: The same-order representation theory of consciousness and the division of phenomenal labor. *Synthese, 160*(2), 161–181.

Weisberg, J. (2010). Misrepresenting consciousness. *Philosophical Studies, 154*(3), 409–433.

Weisberg, J. (2011). Abusing the notion of what-it's-like-ness: A response to block. *Analysis, 71*(3), 438–443.

Weisberg, J. (2014). Sweet dreams are made of this? A HOT response to Sebastián. In R. Brown (Ed.), *Consciousness Inside and Out: Phenomenology, Neuroscience, and the Nature of Experience* (Vol. 6, pp. 433–443): Springer Heidelberg, NL.

Wilberg, J. (2010). Consciousness and false HOTs. *Philosophical Psychology, 23*(5), 617–638.

8

AN INTEGRATIVE VIEW OF THE NEURAL CORRELATES OF CONSCIOUSNESS (NCC) – REORGANIZATION OF THE CONNECTIVITY BETWEEN ELEMENTARY FUNCTIONS AS A COMMON MECHANISM OF MENTAL PROCESSES

Jesper Mogensen and Morten Overgaard

The need to address NCC in the context of a neurocognitive model

We have previously argued that the neural correlate of consciousness (NCC) is best understood as an integral aspect of the neural correlates of mental processes in general (e.g. Mogensen & Overgaard, 2017; Overgaard & Mogensen, 2014). In the present chapter we will present the NCC in the context of a general and integrative neurocognitive model.

Studies addressing NCC typically utilize many of the same methods (e.g. neuroimaging, various electrophysiological methods and studies of the consequences of focal brain injury) as those utilized in the attempts to "localize" a broad spectrum of (other) cognitive functions. Although the focus of such "cognitive localizations" is not on identification of NCC, they may still aim to identify neural systems with varying degrees of association to conscious processes. Such examples are the distinction between neural mechanisms mediating "explicit" (and assumed consciously available) memory and implicit memory (assumed not to be available to consciousness) (e.g. Goldfarb et al., 2016; Hannula & Greene, 2012; Shanks & Berry, 2016; Ullman, 2016) and models emphasizing the neural substrate of explicit and implicit regulation of emotions, respectively (e.g. Braunstein et al., 2017; Lane et al., 2015).

Studies of the neurocognitive organization of the brain are performed in animal models as well as in humans. Both of these research domains face significant methodological problems and shortcomings. Human studies, for instance, frequently have to compromise regarding experimental precision and control (e.g. regarding how homogeneous patient groups and to what extent adequate control groups can be formed). In contrast, animal models typically allow a higher level of control and optimal experimental designs. Animal models, however, are obviously addressing non-human species and thereby not the humans which are of primary interest. Additionally, certain cognitive dimensions such as grammar- and concept-based advanced languages and subjective consciousness cannot be directly addressed in non-human species. An extensive literature specifically deals with methodological problems regarding neurocognitive research in humans (e.g. Genon et al., 2018) and animal models (e.g. Mogensen, 2011b; Mogensen & Malá, 2009, 2019), respectively.

The challenges to neurocognitive models

While studies of the neurocognitive organization may at first glance reveal a relatively straightforward "localization" of various cognitive functions, a more detailed scrutiny of such a localization points to the need for a neurocognitive re-conceptualization. A few examples within the domains of language, spatial orientation and visuospatial problem solving will illustrate this.

Numerous studies utilizing neuroimaging techniques and/or the symptoms associated with focal brain injury demonstrate focal specialization of the brain regarding language-associated processes (e.g. an involvement of the Broca area in the mediation of language production and grammar) (e.g. Ansaldo & Arguin, 2003; Ansaldo et al., 2002; Baumgaertner et al., 2005; Ishkhanyan et al., 2017; Meinzer et al., 2007, 2008; Perani et al., 2003; Specht et al., 2009; Szaflarski et al., 2011; Thomas et al., 1997; Thulborn et al., 1999). The idea of the traditional neocortical "language areas", the Broca and Wernicke areas, as relatively homogenous entities is, however, contradicted by studies in which neuroimaging results are subjected to meta-analysis (e.g. Liebenthal et al., 2014; Vigneau et al., 2006). The Broca area has, for instance, been demonstrated to have a number of subareas with functional specializations (e.g. Fedorenko et al., 2012; Sahin et al., 2009). In contrast to the traditional models arguing for a relatively limited number of "language modules", some newer models argue that language-related processes such as grammar are mediated by a more widespread circuitry (e.g. Kaan & Swaab, 2002; Poeppel, 2014).

The assumption that the "language areas" such as the Broca area specifically mediate linguistic processes is being challenged by the observations of a significant overlap between the neural substrates of language and music (e.g. Ishkhanyan et al., 2017; Koelsch et al., 2002, 2005; Levitin & Menon, 2003; Maess et al., 2001; Patel et al., 2008; Schulze & Koelsch, 2012; Schulze et al., 2011a, 2011b; Tillmann et al., 2003).

Dimensions of music also seem to be involved in another set of findings that point to a more general role of what has previously been believed to be language-specific areas (Sluming et al., 2007). Sluming et al. (2007) demonstrated that the Broca area participates in mediation of a visuospatial (mental rotation) task in orchestral musicians, while not doing so in a control group. These results not only indicate the possibility that a "language area" mediates non-linguistic cognitive processes, it also (and equally importantly!) emphasizes that the functional roles of the Broca area may be experience-dependent.

One of the arguments in favour of a regional functional specialization for language is the fact that focal injury to the presumed language-mediating brain regions leads to a more or less complete loss of linguistic abilities (aphasias). While neuroimaging results only demonstrate that a given brain structure is activated during cognitive performance (e.g. language production), the loss of the ability to produce a linguistic output (expressive aphasia) after lesions of a given structure points to that structure being necessary for language production. The general relevance of such arguments, however, is brought into question by the fact that cognitive functions originally lost to focal brain injury (e.g. linguistic abilities) may in many cases be more or less completely regained via posttraumatic training (e.g. Ansaldo & Arguin, 2003; Ansaldo et al., 2002; Baumgaertner et al., 2005; Crosson et al., 2009; Meinzer et al., 2007, 2008; Perani et al., 2003; Specht et al., 2009; Thomas et al., 1997; Thulborn et al., 1999). Apparently, a "language-mediating" structure is necessary for linguistic processes on a short-term basis, while eventually such cognitive functions may be mediated by other brain regions.

Thus, cognitive functions that have been lost to focal brain injury may subsequently be mediated by alternative neural substrates. Such a conclusion may, however, be questioned with reference to the possibility that the neural trauma constitutes a "subtotal lesion". Such a subtotal lesion could, for instance, be that the Broca area has been significantly damaged (enough to cause symptoms to occur), but not completely removed. The present format does not allow a discussion of potential methods addressing such issues in human subjects. But the most compelling arguments in favour of the neurocognitive reorganizations as the mechanism of posttraumatic recovery come from animal models. In animal models, technical and ethical advantages allow lesions to be complete and eventually demonstrated to be so. Research programs addressing aspects of spatial orientation and problem solving in rats have provided such documentation and will be briefly reviewed below.

Both allocentric spatial orientation of the mapping type (Mogensen et al., 2004), egocentric spatial orientation (Mogensen et al., 2005) and spatial delayed alternation (Mogensen et al., 2007) were found to be significantly impaired in rats subjected to bilateral lesions of either the hippocampus or the prefrontal cortex. In all of these tasks and in both the hippocampally and prefrontally lesioned animals, the task performance did, however, posttraumatically return to either a completely normal proficiency or at least a level close to such normality – although the possibility of subtotal lesions was precluded in these studies. Utilizing various "organic challenge" methods – e.g. additional lesions and pharmacological blockade of neurochemical systems – the neural substrate of such functional recovery processes can be identified (e.g. Mogensen, 2011b;

Mogensen & Malá, 2009, 2019). For instance, after hippocampal lesions, the recovery of allocentric spatial orientation of the mapping type is primarily mediated by prefrontal cortical mechanisms. If, however, the prefrontal cortex is not available after a hippocampal lesion (due to the use of combined lesions), a complete functional recovery does still occur – mediated by the parietal association cortex (Mogensen et al., 2004).

In contrast to allocentric spatial orientation of the mapping type, allocentric spatial orientation of the non-mapping type remained unimpaired by both bilateral lesions of the hippocampus (Wörtwein et al., 1995) and systemic administration of the muscarinic receptor antagonist scopolamine (Mogensen et al., 2002). Being an acetylcholine antagonist, scopolamine leaves the hippocampal system as well as other cholinergic-dependent neural systems dysfunctional. The lack of impairment after hippocampal lesions and hippocampal disturbance by scopolamine could easily lead to the conclusion that (in contrast to the mapping type variant) the allocentric spatial orientation of the non-mapping type does not receive significant contributions to its mediation from the hippocampal formation. Such a conclusion would, however, be premature. Further scrutiny (utilizing organic challenges) demonstrated that normally non-mapping type allocentric spatial orientation does receive significant hippocampal contributions to its mediation. But when these hippocampal mechanisms are not available, alternative neural substrates are able to immediately and fully "compensate" for the missing hippocampal processes. While mostly an initial trauma-related impairment is seen and then followed by a recovery process, in the present examples the "recovery"/"compensation" processes was so immediate and complete that no initial impairment was observed. The alternative neural substrate has in these instances been demonstrated to include dopaminergic and prefrontal cortical mechanisms (Mogensen et al., 2002; Wörtwein et al., 1995). It may be added that the non-mapping allocentric spatial orientation is significantly impaired in rats subjected to bilateral lesions of the prefrontal cortex, although the task performance of such animals does eventually recover fully (Mogensen et al., 1995).

Addressing spatial reversal in rats subjected to either bilateral prefrontal cortical ablations or bilateral hippocampal lesions (Malá et al., 2015) results somewhat resembling those just described regarding allocentric spatial orientation of the non-mapping type emerged. Neither lesions of the prefrontal cortex nor hippocampal lesions resulted in significant impairments of the spatial reversal task. Further scrutiny did, however, demonstrate that in both groups, the absence of significant posttraumatic impairments was obtained via an increased reliance on an alternative neural substrate. In case of hippocampal lesions, this "recovery"/"compensation" was obtained via an increased reliance on prefrontal cortical task mediation, while prefrontally lesioned animals obtained their normal level of task performance via an increased mediation by the hippocampal formation (Malá et al., 2015).

Thus jointly, results obtained in patients and in animal models indicate that even when a given structure is completely absent due to acquired brain injury, a functional recovery process can occur and potentially even reach a "full" recovery defined as a task performance at a normal level of proficiency. Furthermore, the use of various organic challenge techniques allows an identification of the alternative neural substrate developed through the recovery process. It should be noticed that such results do not point to a "backup structure" being available. After a given lesion (e.g. of the hippocampus), the alternative neural substrate mediating the posttraumatic functional recovery differs depending on the task being addressed. That is, the alternative substrate being recruited after a given lesion is task-dependent. If a "backup hippocampus" was available anywhere in the brain, one would expect that structure to constitute the alternative neural substrate regardless of which cognitive task was being addressed. Such issues have been discussed repeatedly (e.g. Mogensen, 2011a, 2015).

When we refer to a "full recovery", we do so indicating that the proficiency of task performance is at a normal level. We do not, however, want to indicate that the neural and/or cognitive mechanisms allowing such a full proficiency of task performance are similar to those of an intact individual. Within some traditions of neurology there is a distinction between recovery and compensation, in which recovery indicates a recreation of the mechanisms occurring in the normal individual, while compensation describes a situation in which the individual regains the ability to perform a particular task without recreation of the normal mechanisms (see e.g. Mogensen, 2015). We, however, use a terminology in which recovery describes any process leading to a full or partial re-establishment of the task performance originally lost to injury (e.g. Mogensen, 2015).

It is also of importance to address the issue of not just how well but also how – in terms of cognitive processes – a given task performance is re-established via a recovery process (Mogensen, 2011a, 2015). Such issues can be addressed utilizing the functional/behavioural/cognitive challenges described elsewhere (e.g. Mogensen, 2011b; Mogensen & Malá, 2009, 2019). Utilizing such functional challenges in animal models as well as in humans (e.g. Ishkhanyan et al., 2017; Mogensen et al., 2004, 2005, 2007), it has repeatedly been demonstrated that even in case of a "full recovery" (as defined above), the recovered, lesioned individuals obtain their proficient task performance via the application of cognitive processes different from those of normal individuals (for reviews, see e.g. Mogensen, 2014, 2015).

In order to be a valid, integrative neurocognitive model, any theory will have to be able to account for all of the above-described phenomena. And consequently, NCC has to be conceptualized within the framework of a neurocognitive model not being contradicted by the following observations (summarizing the phenomena described above):

A   Lesions of a given brain structure is typically associated with relatively uniform patterns of symptoms/impairments across individuals, in both patients and animal models.

B   In spite of even complete loss of a given brain structure, a recovery process is able to restore, at least partly (in some instances completely), the proficiency of cognitive processes to their pretraumatic levels.

C   After such a posttraumatic recovery process, the task performance is mediated by a pattern of brain structure dissimilar to that found when intact individuals are performing a similar task.

D   The pattern of structures mediating the recovery process after lesion of a given structure depends on the task being investigated. Dissimilar neural substrates mediate recovery after various cognitive tasks, in spite of the fact that the injury is identical.

E   The cognitive processes enabling the recovered task solution are different from those of the normal individual. Even when a full recovery (normal proficiency of task performance) has been accomplished, the cognitive processes of task performance are different from those of intact individuals performing the same task at the same proficiency.

Although not all neurocognitive models clearly fall within one of these two groups, such models can generally be grouped into modular or connectionist models. While each of these types of models is able to account for some of the phenomena summarized under A–E, neither type of model is able to fully account for all of these phenomena.

Modular and connectionist models – and the REF framework

Modular theories (e.g. Barrett & Kurzban, 2006; Fodor, 1983, 2000; Pinker, 1999) describe the cognitive functions of the brain as "localized" to specific brain structures that function more or less in isolation. By operating with such a strict localization of cognitive functions, modular theories are well equipped to account for the fact that a given type of brain injury is associated with a predictable pattern of impairments/symptoms (point A above). But by considering cognitive functions to be strictly localized to specific structures, the modular theories cannot account for the fact that after losing a given structure to brain injury, an individual is still able to regain the cognitive "function" in question – to recover after brain injury. Thus, point B (as well as C–E) above cannot be accounted for by modular theories.

Connectionist models (e.g. McClelland et al., 1986; McLeod et al., 1998; Rogers & McClelland, 2014; Rumelhart & McClelland, 1986) describe cognitive functions as being mediated by the functional connectivity among "units" – units that are considered to be functionally neutral. The functionally important patterns of connections between these units are experience-driven via backpropagation mechanisms (e.g. Bryson & Ho, 1969; Parker, 1986; Rumelhart & McClelland, 1986; Werbos, 1974, 1994). The connectionist models emphasize the importance of experience-driven networks, and thereby the possibility that remaining parts of an injured brain are able to restructure in ways that allow mediation of a given task. Thus, these models are able to account for the phenomenon of posttraumatic functional recovery (B in the above list). Since differential experiences may also allow the construction of a variety of specialized networks, points C, D and E above may also be in accordance with the predictions of connectionist models. It is, however, more difficult to reconcile the connectionist models with the phenomenon of a neurocognitive organization that is rather homogenous across individuals (point A above). If cognitive functions are mediated by networks of units which are originally functionally neural, it is difficult to see why a given cognitive function should be mediated by networks with a rather uniform distribution across different individuals. Some connectionist models do operate with a degree of regional specialization (e.g. Jacobs, 1997; Jacobs et al., 1991), but even such exceptions do not appear to be able to account fully for all the above observations.

In an attempt to provide a neurocognitive framework which simultaneously can account for all of the phenomena described under A–E above, the Reorganization of Elementary Functions (REF) framework was developed. The focus of the original REF model (Mogensen, 2011a, 2011c, 2012a, 2012b, 2014, 2015; Mogensen & Malá, 2009) is problem solving as well as the general neurocognitive organization. Since the original model does not explicitly address the mechanisms of perception and consciousness in the form of perceptual awareness, the Reorganization of Elementary Functions and Consciousness (REFCON) model (Overgaard & Mogensen, 2014, 2015) was developed. Practically all domain-specific neurocognitive models (e.g. the original REF model and the REFCON model) will have shortcomings (e.g. underdefined entities). The REFGEN model (Mogensen & Overgaard, 2017, 2018b) was developed to avoid such shortcomings – and to account for the global neurocognitive organization.

The basic structures and processes of the REF framework has been described in detail repeatedly (e.g. Mogensen, 2011a, 2011c, 2012a, 2012b, 2014, 2015; Mogensen and Malá 2009).

The main construct of the REF framework is a three-layered structure in which neural processes are related to mental/behavioural processes via computational processes. Such a structure is related to – but not identical to – the classic levels of analysis developed by Marr and Poggio (1977) and Marr (1982). The importance of relating neural and mental/behavioral processes, respectively, via an "intermediate" computational level has recently been stressed repeatedly (e.g. Carandini, 2012; Mogensen & Overgaard, 2018a; Overgaard & Mogensen, 2011).

Both the uppermost and lowermost of these three layers of analysis represent "functions". Their conceptualizations of the "functions" represented within those two layers are, however, radically different. The uppermost layer is the layer of "Surface Phenomena". These surface phenomena include behavioural manifestations (e.g. the performance of a given task) and all types of mental phenomena, including various kinds of conscious awareness. It is at the level of surface phenomena that the consequences of brain injury manifest themselves (point A in the list above). And it is also at the level of surface phenomena that the posttraumatic recovery described under point B is observed. These surface phenomena are typically conceptualized within the framework of more or less traditional behavioural/cognitive "functions": allocentric spatial orientation, expressive language, working memory etc.

In contrast to the "traditional" conceptualization of functions at the uppermost level, the lowermost level is a level of differently conceptualized functions: the level of Elementary Functions (EFs). The neural substrate of a given EF is strictly localized within a restricted subdivision of a neural structure. Every EF performs a fixed information processing – receiving an input, performing the information processing associated with that EF and transmitting the result as its output. The information processing performed by an individual EF cannot be characterized in the traditional "cognitive" terms. Rather, it can best be described in mathematical terms. The EFs are the "building blocks" of the mechanisms mediating all surface phenomena. But none of the EFs are specifically associated with any of the traditional cognitive functions. And most EFs are simultaneously associated with the mediation of several if not many surface phenomena. The level of information processing performed by a given EF is relatively "low". For illustrational purposes (and without presently going into the validity of the specific theory of visual perception), it can be mentioned that the processing level of the entire "zero-crossing" algorithm described by Marr and Hildreth (1980) is above the level expected to be mediated by an individual EF. Rather, the individual processing steps of the "zero-crossing" process is at the level presently proposed to be mediated by an individual EF. EFs are mediated by neocortical, allocortical as well as other neural structures (including regions of the neostriatum and the amygdala). The neural substrate of an individual EF is comparably small and a structure such as the hippocampus mediates hundreds or thousands of individual EFs.

The "bridge" between the uppermost and lowermost layers – the layer connecting surface phenomena and EFs, respectively – is a layer of Algorithmic Strategies (ASs). An AS is the "mechanism" mediating a given surface phenomenon. Every AS consists of numerous interconnected EFs. The computations mediating a given surface phenomenon is determined by the identity of the EFs constituting the AS in question, and the pattern of interaction between these constituent EFs. The neural substrate of an AS consists of the neural substrates of its constituent EFs plus the interconnections between these neural substrates. Thus, the neural substrate of an AS is highly distributed, since an AS typically includes EFs localized within numerous parts of the brain.

When an individual faces a situation calling for a task solution (in the broadest sense of the term), mechanisms to be described below cause the activation of what is assumed to be the best available AS; that is, the AS that has on previous occasions been able best to provide a satisfactory task solution. Depending on the combined prehistory of the individual and the present situation, the activated AS may be perfectly suited for the present situation or may constitute a "best guess" of lower quality. The obtained outcome is evaluated according to mechanisms described below and the result of such an evaluation ("success", "partial success" or "failure") leads to a number of processes – the reorganizations described below.

These processes constitute reorganizations of the internal connectivity between EFs within ASs. And they are obtained via backpropagation mechanisms. Thus, the outcome of a given attempted task solution will – via backpropagation – potentially modify both the AS that was the mechanism of that task solution and a number of other ASs. Those other ASs include "ordinary" ASs that are related to the task solution but not activated in that instance. However, the backpropagation processes also modify a number of specialized ASs. Those specialized ASs are the Situational Algorithmic Strategy (SAS), the Goal Algorithmic Strategy (GAS) and the Comparator.

SAS is an extremely dynamic and widely distributed AS which represents all aspects of the current situation of the individual, external as well as internal (including mental). SAS includes EFs from virtually all regions of the brain.

GAS (like SAS) is highly distributed and dynamic, but represents the current goals of the individual. The term goal is here used in the broadest sense of the term. It may be the goal of guiding an arm and hand to a cup in order to obtain some tea; or the overall life goals of the individual such as completing an education or contributing something of value to mankind.

Comparator is a specialized AS that constantly compares the current status of SAS and GAS. On the basis of such comparisons, GAS may perform one or more activities:

1 Activate an "ordinary" AS to obtain a given goal. If, for instance, GAS represents a goal of having a cup of tea and SAS represents the situation that such a cup is within reach, GAS may select and activate an AS mediating the task of reaching for that cup.
2 Modify the connectivity between EFs within one or more of the "ordinary" ASs (via backpropagation). This will be as a result of an evaluation of how the activation of a given AS changed SAS: bringing it closer to or further away from the configuration indicated by GAS (i.e. the current goal).
3 Modify Comparator itself (via backpropagation) to represent an increased or decreased likelihood that a given AS is activated in a given situation, based on how SAS is changed (relative to the goals represented in GAS) by activation of that AS.
4 Modify GAS (via backpropagation), in case SAS represents a situation calling for one or another change of goals. If, for instance, SAS indicates that the individual needs liquid, then the modification of GAS will represent a goal of getting something to drink.
5 Modify SAS (via backpropagation) in accordance with the combination of the current status within GAS and SAS, respectively. An example (to be addressed later) is modification of SAS in such a way that specific sensory information (e.g. from a given part of the visual field) is represented more prominently within SAS (i.e. an attentional process).

Thus, the above-mentioned activation of an AS in the attempt to obtain a task solution in a given situation is achieved by Comparator, but on the background of the current configurations within SAS and GAS. The situation in question (external as well as internal) is represented within SAS. And it is a comparison between this SAS configuration and the current goals represented within GAS that leads Comparator to select and activate a given AS. Comparator does so on the background of the configuration of Comparator itself – a configuration that includes representations of the successes and failures of various ASs in comparable situations.

The structure and mechanisms of SAS, GAS and Comparator have been described in more detail in Mogensen and Overgaard (2017, 2018b).

As described in Mogensen (2012a, 2012b), "common areas" between various ASs can obtain a relatively independent status in the form of Algorithmic Modules (AMs). AMs share many features with ASs – e.g. being connectionist "programs" providing cognitively relevant information. But contrary to ASs, AMs cannot in themselves be the mechanism of neither behavioural acts nor mental representations. Rather, AMs are high-level "building" blocks of ASs. The distinction between ASs and AMs can be illustrated by an example from the area of linguistics. The production and interpretation of language, respectively, are mediated by various ASs. Grammar, however, is mediated by an AM (e.g. Ishkhanyan et al., 2017). Grammar is essential to both the production and interpretation of language, but cannot in itself constitute an independent act or mental representation.

NCC as an integral aspect of the REF framework

Perceptual Algorithmic Modules (PAMs) are specialized AMs that represent elements within the broadly defined perceptual process. As described in the REF-CON model (e.g. Overgaard & Mogensen, 2014, 2015), a sensory input activates specialized EFs called Perceptual Elementary Functions (PEFs). The constellation of activated PEFs activates PAMs of the lowest level. And in an interaction between upwards directed activation and downwards directed comparisons between the degrees to which a given PAM is able to account for the constellation of activation at the immediately lower level, the "best suited" PAM is selected. Such a cascade of activation and selection is continued regarding PAMs of progressively higher levels.

PAMs of the lower levels include relatively more PEFs than higher-level PAMs. Additionally, those relatively low-level PAMs will often include PEFs from more than one modality. Thus, even the lower levels of the "PAM-cascades" are frequently multimodal. Within the REF framework, multimodality and other aspects of the "binding problem" are seen as an integral aspect of the distributed structure of PAMs.

Being AMs, PAMs are in themselves not available for conscious awareness or behavioural control. But when the cascade of processing via progressively higher levels of PAMs reaches PAMs of the highest level, then those PAMs will become integrated into SAS. And it is SAS that is the basis for such consciousness-related processes. Being integrated into SAS, a given PAM becomes available for both conscious awareness and behavioural control.

Traditionally, perceptual awareness has been seen as either conscious or completely devoid of consciousness. The use of more refined methods such as the Perceptual Awareness Scale (PAS) (Ramsøy & Overgaard, 2004) has, however, demonstrated that perceptual awareness is better understood as a gradual process reaching from complete absence of consciousness to the situation in which the individual is fully aware of the stimulus (e.g. Koch & Preuschoff, 2007; Overgaard et al., 2006, 2013; Sandberg et al., 2011). In the REF framework, it is the degree of integration into SAS that determines the degree to which a given AM (be it a PAM or other AM; see below) is available for conscious awareness (and behavioural control).

Besides the actual REF models, the REF framework also contains The Integrative Model (TIM) (Overgaard & Mogensen, 2017). The background of the development of TIM was to address the neurocognitive differences between primary consciousness and introspection. Those two types of consciousness differ regarding both cognitive (Sherman et al., 2015; Stefanics et al., 2010; Wyart et al., 2012) and neural (Guggisberg et al., 2011) mechanisms. Most, if not all, alternative models of the relationship between primary consciousness and introspection operate with a serial relationship between the two processes. In contrast, TIM describes the two as mediated by parallel processes. In TIM, the sensory information is elaborated at progressively higher levels, in a process closely resembling what is described in the REFCON model. Eventually, this process will reach the highest level and be available to primary consciousness and behavioural control/action. This happens by integration into what is called Network A (in a parallel to the SAS of the REFCON and REFGEN models). But in parallel to the elaboration towards Network A, the information is also fed into the parallel Network B. And within Network B, the information is available for introspection and introspection-based action. The selection between the two Networks as the basis for mental content and/or behaviour is based in the situational demands (in the terminology of the REFGEN model: the structure of GAS).

Due to the clear parallels between TIM and the REF framework, the distinction between Network A and B, respectively, calls for a similar distinction between two parallel versions of SAS: SAS-A and SAS-B. These implications have been stressed repeatedly (Mogensen & Overgaard, 2017; Overgaard & Mogensen, 2017) and an expanded version of the REFGEN model (including SAS-A and SAS-B) is presently in preparation.

In the expanded REFGEN model, SAS-A mediates all externally oriented processes while SAS-B is the mediator of internally oriented processes. Like in TIM, the information represented in SAS-A is constantly also fed into SAS-B. But rather than just being a copy of SAS-A, SAS-B also has "independent" processes related to mediating of, for instance, thinking and mental imagery. In this expanded version of the REFGEN model, Comparator has also been expanded in ways that it not only compares GAS to SAS-A as well as SAS-B separately, but also SAS-A to SAS-B mutually. Comparator in this version modifies both SAS-A and SAS-B (via backpropagation) as well as activates ASs directed to act on SAS-A and/or SAS-B. Comparator may also initiate processes leading to the integration of AMs in either SAS-A or SAS-B.

Comparator's backpropagation-mediated modification of ASs is also expanded to include such changes based on comparisons between SAS-B and GAS before and after application of such ASs within SAS-B. Thereby, normally externally oriented ASs can potentially be improved by mental rehearsal – application of such ASs on a representation of the external world within SAS-B and a subsequent Comparator-mediated fine-tuning of such ASs (e.g. Dickstein & Deutsch, 2007; Jackson et al., 2001, 2003; Liu et al., 2004a, 2004b; Mulder, 2007; Munzert et al., 2009; Ranganathan et al., 2004; Ryan & Simons, 1981; Sharma et al., 2006; Wohldmann et al., 2008; Woolfolk et al., 1985).

Via integration into either SAS-A or SAS-B (and subsequent backpropagation-mediated modifications), AMs may develop a progressively more "general" nature. Thereby, some AMs may become the representation of rather general "concepts" or "schemata" (e.g. Gobet et al., 2015; Mazzone, 2014).

As described above, many PAMs are multimodal, thereby providing a cross-modal "binding" as an integrated part of the process of the progressive PAM selection. Both PAMs and other AMs acquire their structure and thereby representation via Comparator and experience-mediated reorganizations of the connectivity between EFs. Via such processes, PAMs and other AMs may also come to contain the representation of emotional responses. Such a process may include the integration of EFs directly linked to activations of the autonomous nervous system and endocrine systems (e.g. Frodl & O'Keane, 2013; McEwen et al., 2015). Consequently, the emotional reactions associated with a given external or internal stimulus (e.g. the sight or thought of a given person) are within the REF framework, an integral aspect of the general processing of (other) cognitive information. By presenting the "emotional" and "purely cognitive" processing as aspects of the same process, the REF framework offers an alternative view to the debate regarding whether emotions are always secondary to cognitive processes or can occur independently (e.g. Lazarus, 1984; Lazarus & Smith, 1988; Pessoa, 2008; Zajonc, 1984).

Traditionally, both cognitive psychology and neurocognitive models have operated with the concept of cognitive "functions" as the "building blocks" of various analyses. And when addressing the surface phenomena within the REF framework, it may make sense to do so. "Functions" such as emotions, allocentric spatial orientation, attention and working memory have been developed as meaningful entities at the behavioural and/or mental level. They are, however, according to the REF framework neither to be considered "units" nor "building blocks" in a neurocognitive analysis. As has been stressed repeatedly (Mogensen & Overgaard, 2018b; Mogensen et al., 2018), the REF framework operates with strategies rather than functions.

Since all mental and behavioural phenomena are mediated by an AS – be it "ordinary" ASs or SAS – it is the structure of those ASs that constitutes the mechanism mediating all phenomena at the mental/behavioural level. The structure of those ASs (the included EFs and the interactions of those EFs as determined by their current interconnections) is determined by the experience of the individual. The Ass, activated when crossing a given street, may change significantly after that individual has experienced a situation that included almost being hit by a car. Subsequently, the activated PAMs are likely to include more EFs associated with activations of the autonomous nervous system and endocrine systems (e.g. Frodl & O'Keane, 2013; McEwen et al, 2015) – and consequently experienced fear. There is, however, not any independent "fear AS". After such an incident, the individual may also become far more attentive to approaching cars, but not via any "attention AS". Rather, the experience with the near-miss is likely to have led to modifications within GAS – in such ways that when SAS represents a situation of being about to cross that street, GAS will modify SAS in ways promoting a more extensive integration of PAMs representing approaching cars. The increased integration of those PAMs into SAS will lead to a more extensive integration of car representing PAMs within SAS, and consequently an increased conscious awareness of such cars.

In general, it is (as described above) the level of integration into SAS (be it SAS-A or SAS-B) that determines how available an AM is to consciousness. Consequently, according to the REF framework, the NCC can be described as the connectivity between AMs and SAS. This connectivity is best understood via a focus on the connectivity of the individual EFs.

An EF has a number of different types of synaptic connections. The intrinsic connectivity of the EF is part of the local network which meditates the information processing of that EF. Such synapses are relatively stable and "unchanging". In contrast, the synaptic connections linking a given EF into SAS, GAS and Comparator undergo constant and highly dynamic changes. Every EF has pre-wired "potential connections" linking it into SAS, GAS or Comparator – or any combination thereof. The "on/off" switch determining if a given EF participates in SAS, GAS or Comparator is most likely mediated by "latent" synapses (e.g. Kaas, 1991; Kerchner & Nicoll, 2008). Local GABAergic mechanisms allow such synapses to rapidly switch between an "on" and an "off" state (e.g. Chen et al., 2002; Jones, 1993). Dendritic spine modifications may be an alternative or supplementary mechanism for such rapid oscillations between being connected and disconnected to the mentioned ASs (e.g. Araya et al., 2014; Bosch & Hayashi, 2012; Dent et al., 2011; Holtmaat et al., 2005; Majewska et al., 2006; Pilpel & Segal, 2004; Trachtenberg et al., 2002; Yuste, 2011). The synaptic connectivity linking a given EF into the more "ordinary" ASs mostly consists of the more permanent and stable synapses – although some ASs may also include the described "latent" types of synapses.

The degree to which a given AM is integrated into SAS is determined by how much the individual EFs of that AM are connected to SAS. Thus, it is synaptic mechanisms within the constituent EFs that mediate integration into SAS and consequently the degree of conscious awareness associated with that AM. The implication of this regarding NCC is that the "consciousness-related" neural processes are not restricted to any specific region of the brain. Rather, the "mechanism mediating conscious awareness" is local, synaptic mechanisms within the region or regions of the brain mediating the cognitive process in question.

Regarding conscious perceptual awareness, the implication is that in the early steps of the perceptual process (when relatively low levels of PAMs dominate the process), the mechanisms of perceptual consciousness are expected to be associated with areas within or close to the primary sensory area/areas. In later phases of the perceptual process, consciousness-related activity is expected to be found in, for instance, "association" areas of the brain. Such predictions agree well with the results of Andersen et al. (2016), who found that occipital electrophysiological activity with a latency of less than 300 ms was associated with the level of perceptual awareness of a visual stimulus, while during later phases of the perceptual process (later than 300 ms), the consciousness-associated neural processes were within more anterior as well as more widespread regions.

There are resemblances between these aspects of the REF framework and the Global Workspace Theory (e.g. Baars, 2015; Dehaene, 2015). There are, however, also significant differences. For instance, the REF framework does not include any type of "information broadcast" throughout SAS. Conscious awareness can be achieved via SAS integration into any (in principle extremely restricted) regions of SAS.

The focus on AM integration into SAS as the mechanism of conscious awareness may give the impression that systems such as GAS and Comparator play little or no role in the processes of consciousness. Both GAS and Comparator do, however, frequently contribute significantly in this context. The degree of AM integration into SAS is (at least partly) determined by strategies reflecting the current balance between the constellations within SAS and GAS, respectively. An example from blindsight will illustrate this.

Blindsight (in patients injured within the primary visual processing regions of the cortex) is defined as the ability to "guess" correctly regarding the position or other visually given properties of a visual stimulus presented within the "blind" region of the visual field. Traditionally, it is assumed that blindsight is expressed in the complete absence of consciousness. Such an assumption has, however, been challenged by the fact that most (if not all) blindsight patients do report vague experiences associated with the visual stimuli they are to indicate one or another dimension of (Cowey, 2010; Overgaard, 2011, 2012). The assumption of blindsight in complete absence of conscious experience was further questioned by studies of the blindsight patient GR. When examined with PAS – rather than a dichotomous conscious/not conscious evaluation – GR only demonstrated blindsight in situations where PAS indicated at least a level of conscious awareness (Overgaard et al., 2008).

In the context of the REF framework, the interpretation of such results is that the injury to the visual system prevents PAMs associated with the affected part of the visual field from being elaborated to the highest level – the level at which PAMs will normally be integrated into SAS. Consequently, the patient will normally not have visual experiences (nor be able spontaneously to utilize visual information) within the affected region of the visual field. However, top-down influences in the form of verbal instructions from the experimenter can, under test conditions, provoke the available PAMs of lower levels to be integrated into SAS – allowing both blindsight and the mentioned vague visual experiences (e.g. Mogensen & Overgaard, 2017; Overgaard & Mogensen, 2014, 2015). The mechanism of such a top-down influence is based on an interaction between SAS and GAS, as described by Mogensen and Overgaard (2017). The verbal instructions become represented within SAS (via activation of ASs mediating linguistic interpretation). Via Comparator, the demands to report about visual stimuli are "transferred" from SAS to GAS as a goal representation. As a consequence of this goal representation in GAS, Comparator modifies SAS in such a way that SAS becomes especially "receptive" to even PAMs of the lower levels, if such PAMs represent visual information originating in the affected part of the visual field.

In general, GAS will frequently represent goals regarding the need to prioritize one or another type of incoming information over the rest. That may, for instance, be information from a specific part of the visual field, information of one modality over the others or information regarding moving cars over information regarding stationary objects. Such goals will – via Comparator – modify SAS in ways making it more receptive to PAMs (or other AMs) relevant to what is to be prioritized. As stressed elsewhere (Mogensen & Overgaard, 2017), the GAS/SAS interaction in these ways mediate what would traditionally be termed attention.

The interaction between GAS and SAS also frequently represent "predictions" – e.g. regarding the type of sensory input to be expected or the behavioural performance demanded in a given situation. In these ways the REF framework agrees with the "predictive coding" approach (e.g. Friston, 2005). The PAM-based mechanisms of the REFCON model (e.g. Mogensen & Overgaard, 2017; Overgaard & Mogensen, 2014, 2015) also represent a type of "prediction" process: what is progressively activated are the best fitting PAMs and what is eventually available to conscious awareness and behavioural control is a selected (but pre-existing) PAM of the highest level. Thus, the REF framework agrees – at least partly – with both the predictive coding of Friston (2005) and the concept of Gregory (1974) that what is perceived is a pre-existing "model".

As mentioned, GAS may "predictively" influence SAS (via Comparator) to become more receptive to PAMs or other AMs. But GAS may also directly "pre-activate" PAMs (or other AMs). This may, for instance, happen in situations where the interaction between SAS, GAS and Comparator indicates a high probability of a given future stimulus constellation (e.g. Overgaard & Mogensen, 2014). If GAS (via Comparator) pre-activates PAMs associated with an expected stimulus, such a process is likely to be associated with changed responses in both the "early" regions of perceptual processing (including primary sensory areas) and regions associated with "higher-level processing". Aru et al. (2016) obtained results agreeing with these predictions: Prior experience with a visual stimulus influenced both the conscious experience of the stimulus and the associated electrophysiological responses within a time window of 80–95 ms after stimulus onset. The sources of the electrophysiological effects associated with prior presentation were localized to occipital and posterior parietal cortical regions.

Predictive coding (e.g. Friston, 2005) predicts that prior experience with a given stimulus is associated with a reduced neural response when the stimulus is presented again. There are, however, examples of both such a decreased neural response and an actual increase of the neural response when a stimulus is presented again (Aru et al., 2016). According to the REF framework, such – apparently contradictive – results reflect two different types of "expectancy" and consequent strategies in the interaction between GAS and SAS (Overgaard & Mogensen, 2014). In a process relatively similar to traditional "attention", there may be a rather "general" activation of PAMs – for instance those associated with a given part of the visual field. In such a case, one will expect an increase in neural activity. Or there may be a more specific activation of the pattern of previously activated PAMs, leading to a decreased neural response (relative to that associated with a completely novel stimulus) and thus agreeing with the assumptions of predictive coding.

Perspectives

By approaching NCC within the REF framework, we can account for the consciousness mediating neural processes without having to assign them to a specific region of, for instance, the neocortex. Attempts to "localize" the NCC have led to contradictive results – for instance, emphasizing either the primary sensory areas or the prefrontal cortex (for review, see Koch et al., 2016). Such contradictions are not surprising if viewed in the context of the REF framework. The neural regions of major SAS integration will depend on a multitude of factors – e.g. the task in question, the time point within progressive processes (e.g. PAM elaboration) and the prior experience of the subject.

Ongoing and planned research will expand the REF framework and clarify a number of potential weaknesses of the model. One issue to be addressed is the type of backpropagation being involved. It has been argued (e.g. Mazzoni et al., 1991a, 1991b; Stork, 1989) that the traditional backpropagation algorithms (e.g. Rumelhart et al., 1986; Werbos, 1974, 1994) are not biologically plausible. We have, however, not yet within the REF framework subscribed to any specific backpropagation algorithm (Mogensen & Overgaard, 2017). Some further developments of the original algorithms do seem to be more easily implemented within biologically realistic models (e.g. Durbin & Rumelhart, 1989; Hinton & McClelland, 1988; O'Reilly, 1996, 1998). And Schiess et al. (2016) have shown a backpropagation algorithm to be successfully implemented in a single neuron with non-linear dendritic processing. Such a neuron crossing the layers within a region of the neocortex may play an important role in at least some of the processes of the REF framework.

Some of the backpropagation-related issues – as well as other outstanding issues – are likely to be resolved by the ongoing research into the involved biological processes as well as the mathematical modelling of the REFGEN model (e.g. Mogensen et al., 2018). That includes the improved characterization of individual EFs and further identification of the consciousness-related strategies and localized processes. The latter has (as mentioned above) to include methods focusing on individual and experience-associated factors (e.g. Mogensen et al., 2018).

By addressing NCC within the REF framework, we have stepped beyond the more traditional focus of a more or less singular substrate or process of consciousness. But we have also expanded the REF framework relative to most other neurocognitive models – where consciousness is frequently being either ignored or left with a reference to specific and isolated models of the NCC.

Acknowledgements

Jesper Mogensen was supported by a grant from the Danish Council for Independent Research and by a Programme of Excellence grant from the University of Copenhagen.

References

Andersen, L.M., Pedersen, M.N., Sandberg, K., & Overgaard, M. (2016). Occipital MEG activity in the early time range (<300 ms) predicts graded changes in perceptual consciousness. *Cerebral Cortex, 26,* 2677–2688.

Ansaldo, A.I., & Arguin, M. (2003). The recovery from aphasia depends on both the left and right hemispheres: three longitudinal case studies on the dynamics of language function after aphasia. *Brain and Language, 87,* 177–178.

Ansaldo, A.I., Arguin, M., & Lecours, A.R. (2002). The contribution of the right cerebral hemisphere to the recovery from aphasia: a single longitudinal case study. *Brain and Language, 82,* 206–222.

Araya, R., Vogels, T.P., & Yuste, R. (2014). Activity-dependent dendritic spine neck changes are correlated with synaptic strength. *Proceedings of the National Academy of Sciences USA, 111,* E2895–E2904.

Aru, J., Rutiku, R., Wibral, M., Singer, W., & Melloni, L. (2016). Early effects of previous experience on conscious perception. *Neuroscience of Consciousness, 2016,* niw004.

Baars, B.J. (2015) Global workspace theory of consciousness: towards a cognitive neuroscience of human experience? *Progress in Brain Research, 150,* 45–54.

Barrett, H.C., & Kurzban, R. (2006). Modularity in cognition: framing the debate. *Psychological Review, 113,* 628–647.

Baumgaertner, A., Schraknepper, V., & Saur, D. (2005). Differential recovery of aphasia and apraxia of speech in an adolescent after infarction of the left frontal lobe: longitudinal behavioral and fMRI data. *Brain and Language, 95,* 211–212.

Bosch, M., & Hayashi, Y. (2012). Structural plasticity of dendritic spines. *Current Opinion in Neurobiology, 22,* 383–388.

Braunstein, L.M., Gross, J.J., & Ochsner, K.N. (2017). Explicit and implicit emotion regulation: a multi-level framework. *Social Cognitive and Affective Neuroscience, 12,* 1545–1557.

Bryson, A.E., & Ho, Y-C. (1969). *Applied Optimal Control.* New York: Blaisdell.

Carandini, M. (2012). From circuits to behavior: a bridge too far? *Nature Neuroscience, 15,* 507–509.

Chen, R., Cohen, L.G., & Hallett, M. (2002). Nervous system reorganization following injury. *Neuroscience, 111,* 761–773.

Cowey, A. (2010). The blindsight saga. *Experimental Brain Research, 200,* 3–24.

Crosson, B., Moore, A.B., McGregor, K.M., Chang, Y-L., Benjamin, M., Gopinath, K., Sherod, M.E., Wierenga, C.E., Peck, K.K., Briggs, R.W., Rothi, L.J., & White, K.D. (2009). Regional changes in word-production laterality after a naming treatment designed to produce a rightward shift in frontal activity. *Brain and Language, 111,* 73–85.

Dehaene, S. (2015). *Consciousness and the Brain: Deciphering How the Brain Codes Our Thoughts.* , New York: Penguin Books.

Dent, E.W., Merriam, E.B., & Hu, X. (2011). The dynamic cytoskeleton: backbone of dendritic spine plasticity. *Current Opinion in Neurobiology, 21,* 175–181.

Dickstein, R., & Deutsch, J.E. (2007). Motor imagery in physical therapist practice. *Physical Therapy, 87,* 942–953

Durbin, R., & Rumelhart, D.E. (1989). Product units: a computationally powerful and biologically plausible extension to backpropagation networks. *Neural Computation, 1,* 133–142.

Fedorenko, E., Duncan, J., & Kanwisher, N. (2012). Language-selective and domain-general regions lie side by side within Broca's area. *Current Biology, 22,* 2059–2062.

Fodor, J.A. (1983). *The Modularity of Mind.* Cambridge, MA: MIT Press.

Fodor, J. (2000). *The Mind Doesn't Work That Way: The Scope and Limits of Computational Psychology.* Cambridge, MA: MIT Press.

Friston, K. (2005). A theory of cortical responses. *Philosophical Transactions of the Royal Society B, 360,* 815–836.

Frodl, T., & O'Keane, V. (2013). How does the brain deal with cumulative stress? A review with focus on developmental stress, HPA axis function and hippocampal structure in humans. *Neurobiology of Disease, 52,* 24–37.

Genon, S., Reid, A., Langner, R., Amunts, K., & Eickhoff, S.B. (2018). How to characterize the function of a brain region. *Trends in Cognitive Sciences, 22,* 350–364.

Gobet, F., Lane, P.C.R., & Lloyd-Kelly, M. (2015). Chunks, schemata, and retrieval structures: past and current computational models. *Frontiers in Psychology, 6,* 1785,

Goldfarb, E.V., Chun, M.M., & Phelps, E.A. (2016). Memory-guided attention: independent contributions of the hippocampus and striatum. *Neuron, 89,* 317–324.

Gregory, R.L. (1974). *Concepts and Mechanisms of Perception.* London: Duckworth.

Guggisberg, A.G., Dalal, S.S., Schnider, A., & Nagarajan, S.S. (2011). The neural basis of event-time introspection. *Consciousness and Cognition, 20,* 1899–1915.

Hannula, D.E., & Greene, A.J. (2012). The hippocampus reevaluated in unconscious learning and memory: at a tipping point? *Frontiers in Human Neuroscience, 6,* 80.

Hinton, G.E., & McClelland, J.L. (1988). Learning representations by recirculation. In: D.Z. Anderson (Ed.) *Neural Information Processing Systems: Proceedings of a conference held in Denver, Colorado,* November 1987. New York: Springer Science & Business Media, pp. 358–366.

Holtmaat, A.J., Trachtenberg, J.T., Wilbrecht, L., Shepherd, G.M., Zhang, X., Knott, G.W., & Svoboda, K. (2005). Transient and persistent dendritic spines in the neocortex in vivo. *Neuron,* 45, 279–291.

Ishkhanyan, B., Sahraoui, H., Harder, P., Mogensen, J., & Boye, K. (2017). Grammatical and lexical pronoun dissociation in French speakers with agrammatic aphasia: a usage-based account and REF-based hypothesis. *Journal of Neurolinguistics,* 44, 1–16.

Jackson, P.L., Lafleur, M.F., Malouin, F., Richards, C., & Doyon, J. (2001). Potential role of mental practice using motor imagery in neurologic rehabilitation. *Archives of Physical Medicine and Rehabilitation,* 82, 1133–1141.

Jackson, P.L., Lafleur, M.F., Malouin, F., Richards, C.L., & Doyon, J. (2003). Functional cerebral reorganization following motor sequence learning through mental practice with motor imagery. *NeuroImage,* 20, 1171–1180.

Jacobs, R.A. (1997). Nature, nurture, and the development of functional specializations: a computational approach. *Psychonomic Bulletin and Review,* 4, 299–309.

Jacobs, R.A., Jordan, M.I., & Barto, A.G. (1991). Task decomposition through competition in a modular connectionist architecture: the what and where vision tasks. *Cognitive Science,* 15, 219–250.

Jones, E.G. (1993). GABAergic neurons and their role in cortical plasticity in primates. *Cerebral Cortex,* 3, 361–372.

Kaas, J.H. (1991). Plasticity of sensory and motor maps in adult mammals. *Annual Review of Neuroscience,* 14, 137–167.

Kaan, E., & Swaab, T.Y. (2002). The brain circuitry of syntactic comprehension. *Trends in Cognitive Sciences,* 6, 350–356.

Kerchner, G.A., & Nicoll, R.A. (2008). Silent synapses and the emergence of a postsynaptic mechanism for LTP. *Nature Reviews Neuroscience,* 9, 813–825.

Koch, C., & Preuschoff, K. (2007). Betting the house on consciousness. *Nature Neuroscience,* 10, 140–141.

Koch, C., Massimini, M., Boly, M., & Tononi, G. (2016). Neural correlates of consciousness: progress and problems. *Nature Reviews Neuroscience,* 17, 307–321.

Koelsch, S., Gunter, T.C., v. Cramon, D.Y., Zysset, S., Lohmann, G., & Friederici, A.D. (2002). Bach speaks: a cortical "language-network" serves the processing of music. *NeuroImage,* 17, 956–966.

Koelsch, S., Fritz, T., Schulze, K., Alsop, D., & Schlaug, G. (2005). Adults and children processing music: an fMRI study. *NeuroImage,* 25, 1068–1076.

Lane, R.D., Ryan, L., Nadel, L., & Greenberg, L. (2015). Memory reconsolidation, emotion arousal, and the process of change in psychotherapy: new insights from brain science. *Behavioral and Brain Sciences,* 38, e1.

Lazarus, R.S. (1984). On the primacy of cognition. *American Psychologist,* 39, 124–129.

Lazarus, R.S., & Smith, C.A. (1988). Knowledge and appraisal in the cognition-emotion relationship. *Cognition and Emotion,* 2, 281 300.

Levitin, D.J., & Menon, V. (2003). Musical structure is processed in "language" areas of the brain: a possible role for Brodmann Area 47 in temporal coherence. *NeuroImage,* 20, 2142–2152.

Liebenthal, E., Desai, R.H., Humphries, C., Sabri, M., & Desai, A. (2014). The functional organization of the left STS: a large scale meta-analysis of PET and fMRI studies of healthy adults. *Frontiers in Neuroscience,* 8, 289.

Liu, K.P., Chan, C.C., Lee, T.M., & Hui-Chan, C.W. (2004a). Mental imagery for promoting relearning for people after stroke: a randomized controlled trial. *Archives of Physical Medicine and Rehabilitation,* 85, 1403–1408.

Liu, K.P.Y., Chan, C.C.H., Lee, T.M.C., & Hui-Chan, C.W.Y. (2004b). Mental imagery for relearning of people after brain injury. *Brain Injury,* 18, 1163–1172.

Maess, B., Koelsch, S., Gunter, T.C., & Friederici, A.D. (2001). Musical syntax is processed in Broca's area: an MEG study. *Nature Neuroscience,* 4, 540–545.

Majewska, A.K., Newton, J.R., & Sur, M. (2006). Remodeling of synaptic structure in sensory cortical areas *in vivo. Journal of Neuroscience,* 26, 3021–3029.

Malá, H., Andersen, L.G., Christensen, R.F., Felbinger, A., Hagstrøm, J., Meder, D., Pearce, H., & Mogensen, J. (2015). Prefrontal cortex and hippocampus in behavioural flexibility and posttraumatic functional recovery: reversal learning and set-shifting in rats. *Brain Research Bulletin,* 116, 34–44.

Marr, D. (1982). *Vision: A Computational Investigation into the Human Representation and Processing of Visual Information.* San Francisco, CA: W.H. Freeman.

Marr, D., & Hildreth, E. (1980). Theory of edge detection. *Proceedings of the Royal Society of London B,* 207, 187–217.

Marr, D., & Poggio, T. (1977). From understanding computation to understanding neural circuitry. *Neuroscience Research Program Bulletin,* 15, 470–488.

Mazzone, M. (2014). Crossing the associative/inferential divide: ad hoc concepts and the inferential power of schemata. *Review of Philosophy and Psychology,* 5, 583–599.

Mazzoni, P., Andersen, R.A., & Jordan, M.I. (1991a). A more biologically plausible learning rule for neural networks. *Proceedings of the National Academy of Sciences USA,* 88, 4433–4437.

Mazzoni, P., Andersen, R.A., & Jordan, M.I. (1991b). A more biologically plausible learning rule than backpropagation applied to a network model of cortical area 7a. *Cerebral Cortex,* 1, 293–307.

McClelland, J.L., Rumelhart, D.E., & The PDP Research Group (1986). *Parallel Distributed Processing: Vol. 2. Psychological and Biological Models.* Cambridge, MA: MIT Press.

McEwen, B.S., Bowles, N.P., Gray, J.D., Hill, M.N., Hunter, R.G., Karatsoreos, I.N., & Nasca, C. (2015). Mechanisms of stress in the brain. *Nature Neuroscience,* 18, 1353–1363.

McLeod, P., Plunkett, K., & Rolls, E.T. (1998). *Introduction to Connectionist Modelling of Cognitive Processes.* Oxford: Oxford University Press.

Meinzer, M., Obleser, J., Flaisch, T., Eulitz, C., & Rockstroh, B. (2007). Recovery from aphasia as a function of language therapy in an early bilingual patient demonstrated by fMRI. *Neuropsychologia,* 45, 1247–1256.

Meinzer, M., Flaisch, T., Breitenstein, C., Wienbruch, C., Elbert, T., & Rockstroh, B. (2008). Functional re-recruitment of dysfunctional brain areas predicts language recovery in chronic aphasia. *NeuroImage,* 39, 2038–2046.

Mogensen, J. (2011a). Almost unlimited potentials of a limited neural plasticity: levels of plasticity in development and reorganization of the injured brain. *Journal of Consciousness Studies,* 18, 13–45.

Mogensen, J. (2011b). Animal models in neuroscience. In: J. Hau, & S.J. Schapiro (Eds.) *Handbook of Laboratory Animal Science, Third Edition, Volume II. Animal Models.* Boca Raton, FL: CRC Press LLC, pp. 47–73.

Mogensen, J. (2011c). Reorganization in the injured brain: implications for studies of the neural substrate of cognition. *Frontiers in Psychology,* 2, 7.

Mogensen, J. (2012a). Cognitive recovery and rehabilitation after brain injury: mechanisms, challenges and support. In: A. Agrawal (Ed.) *Brain Injury – Functional Aspects, Rehabilitation and Prevention.* Rijeka: InTech, pp. 121–150.

Mogensen, J. (2012b). Reorganization of elementary functions (REF) after brain injury: implications for the therapeutic interventions and prognosis of brain injured patients suffering cognitive impairments. In: A.J. Schäfer, & J. Müller (Eds.) *Brain Damage: Causes, Management and Prognosis.* Hauppauge, NY: Nova Science Publishers, Inc., pp. 1–40.

Mogensen, J. (2014). Reorganization of elementary functions (REF) after brain injury and in the intact brain: a novel understanding of neurocognitive organization and reorganization. In: J. Costa, & E. Villalba (Eds.) *Horizons in Neuroscience Research. Vol. 15.* New York: Nova Science Publishers, Inc.; pp. 99–140.

Mogensen, J. (2015). Recovery, compensation and reorganization in neuropathology – levels of conceptual and methodological challenges. In: J.I. Tracy, B.M. Hampstead, & K. Sathian (Eds.) *Cognitive Plasticity in Neurologic Disorders.* New York: Oxford University Press, pp. 3–28.

Mogensen, J., & Malá, H. (2009). Post-traumatic functional recovery and reorganization in animal models. A theoretical and methodological challenge. *Scandinavian Journal of Psychology,* 50, 561–573.

Mogensen, J., & Malá, H. (2019). Focal and restricted traumatic injury models in the rodent brain: limitations, possibilities and challenges. In: M. Risling, & J. Davidsson (Eds.) *Animal Models of Neurotrauma.* New York: Springer, pp. 19–46.

Mogensen, J., & Overgaard, M. (2017). Reorganization of the connectivity between elementary functions – a model relating conscious states to neural connections. *Frontiers in Psychology,* 8, 625.

Mogensen, J., & Overgaard, M. (2018a). Neural connections and mental states: the need for a neurocognitive framework. *EC Neurology,* 10, 180–194.

Mogensen, J., & Overgaard, M. (2018b). Reorganization of the connectivity between elementary functions as a common mechanism of phenomenal consciousness and working memory: from functions to strategies. *Philosophical Transactions of the Royal Society of London, Series B: Biological Sciences,* 373, 20170346.

Mogensen, J., Pedersen, T.K., Holm, S., & Bang, L.E. (1995). Prefrontal cortical mediation of rats' place learning in a modified water maze. *Brain Research Bulletin,* 38, 425–434.

Mogensen, J., Christensen, L.H., Johansson, A., Wörtwein, G., Bang, L.E., & Holm, S. (2002). Place learning in scopolamine treated rats: the roles of distal cues and catecholaminergic mediation. *Neurobiology of Learning and Memory,* 78, 139–166.

Mogensen, J., Lauritsen, K.T., Elvertorp, S., Hasman, A., Moustgaard, A., & Wörtwein, G. (2004). Place learning and object recognition by rats subjected to transection of the fimbria-fornix and/or ablation of the prefrontal cortex. *Brain Research Bulletin,* 63, 217–236.

Mogensen, J., Moustgaard, A., Khan, U., Wörtwein, G., & Nielsen, K.S. (2005). Egocentric spatial orientation in a water maze by rats subjected to transection of the fimbria-fornix and/or ablation of the prefrontal cortex. *Brain Research Bulletin,* 65, 41–58.

Mogensen, J., Hjortkjær, J., Ibervang, K.L., Stedal, K., & Malá, H. (2007). Prefrontal cortex and hippocampus in posttraumatic functional recovery: spatial delayed alternation by rats subjected to transection of the fimbria-fornix and/or ablation of the prefrontal cortex. *Brain Research Bulletin,* 73, 86–95.

Mogensen, J., Daugaard, N., Kitsios, S., Pedersen, J.E., & Overgaard, M. (2018). Understanding the neurocognitive organization as strategies rather than functions: implications for neurological research. *EC Neurology,* 10, 1008–1016.

Mulder, T. (2007). Motor imagery and action observation: cognitive tools for rehabilitation. *Journal of Neural Transmission,* 114, 1265–1278.

Munzert, J., Lorey, B., & Zentgraf, K. (2009). Cognitive motor processes: the role of motor imagery in the study of motor representations. *Brain Research Reviews*, 60, 306–326.

O'Reilly, R.C. (1996). Biologically plausible error-driven learning using local activation differences: the generalized recirculation algorithm. *Neural Computation*, 8, 895–938.

O'Reilly, R.C. (1998). Six principles for biologically based computational models of cortical cognition. *Trends in Cognitive Sciences*, 2, 455–462.

Overgaard, M. (2011). Visual experience and blindsight: a methodological review. *Experimental Brain Research*, 209, 4, 473–479.

Overgaard, M. (2012). Blindsight: recent and historical controversies on the blindness of blindsight. *Wiley Interdisciplinary Reviews: Cognitive Science*, 3, 607–614.

Overgaard, M., & Mogensen, J. (2011). A framework for the study of multiple realizations: the importance of levels of analysis. *Frontiers in Psychology*, 2, 79.

Overgaard, M., & Mogensen, J. (2014). Visual perception from the perspective of a representational, non-reductionistic, level-dependent account of perception and conscious awareness. *Philosophical Transactions of the Royal Society B*, 369, 20130209.

Overgaard, M., & Mogensen, J. (2015). Reconciling current approaches to blindsight. *Consciousness and Cognition*, 32, 33–40.

Overgaard, M., & Mogensen, J. (2017). An integrative view on consciousness and introspection. *Review of Philosophy and Psychology*, 8, 129–141.

Overgaard, M., Rote, J., Mouridsen, K., & Ramsøy, T.Z. (2006). Is conscious perception gradual or dichotomous? A comparison of report methodologies during a visual task. *Consciousness and Cognition*, 15, 700–708.

Overgaard, M., Fehl, K., Mouridsen, K., & Cleeremans, A. (2008). Seeing without seeing? Degraded conscious vision in a blindsight patient. *PLoS ONE*, 3, e3028.

Overgaard, M., Lindeløv, J., Svejstrup, S., Døssing, M., Hvid, T., Kauffmann, O., & Mouridsen, K. (2013). Is conscious stimulus identification dependent on knowledge of the perceptual modality? Testing the "source misidentifcation hypothesis". *Frontiers in Psychology: Consciousness Research*, 4, 116.

Parker, D.B. (1986). A comparison of algorithms for neuron-like cells. In J. Denker (Ed.) *Proceedings of the Second Annual Conference on Neural Networks for Computing, Proceedings Vol. 151*. New York: American Institute of Physics, pp. 327–332.

Patel, A.D., Iversen, J.R., Wassenaar, M., & Hagoort, P. (2008). Musical syntactic processing in agrammatic Broca's aphasia. *Aphasiology*, 22, 776–789.

Perani, D., Cappa, S.F., Tettamanti, M., Rosa, M., Scifo, P., Miozzo, A., Basso, A., & Fazio, F. (2003). A fMRI study of word retrieval in aphasia. *Brain and Language*, 85, 357–368.

Pessoa, L. (2008). On the relationship between emotion and cognition. *Nature Reviews Neuroscience*, 9, 148–158.

Pilpel, Y., & Segal, M. (2004). Activation of PKC induces rapid morphological plasticity in dendrites of hippocampal neurons via Rac and Rho-dependent mechanisms. *European Journal of Neuroscience*, 19, 3151–3164.

Pinker, S. (1999). *How the Mind Works*. London: Penguin Books.

Poeppel, D. (2014). The neuroanatomic and neurophysiological infrastructure for speech and language. *Current Opinion in Neurobiology*, 28, 142–149.

Ramsøy, T.Z., & Overgaard, M. (2004). Introspection and subliminal perception. *Phenomenology and the Cognitive Sciences*, 3, 1–23.

Ranganathan, V.K., Siemionow, V., Liu, J.Z., Sahgal, V., & Yue, G.H. (2004). From mental power to muscle power – gaining strength by using the mind. *Neuropsychologia*, 42, 944–956.

Rogers, T.T., & McClelland, J.L. (2014). Parallel distributed processing at 25: further explorations in the microstructure of cognition. *Cognitive Science,* 38, 1024–1077.

Rumelhart, D., & McClelland, J. (1986). *Parallel Distributed Processing.* Cambridge, MA: MIT Press.

Rumelhart, D.E., Hinton, G.E., & Williams, R.J. (1986). Learning internal representations by error propagation. In: D.E. Rumelhart, & J. McClelland (Eds.) *Parallel Distributed Processing: Explorations in the Microstructure of Cognition I.* Cambridge, MA: MIT Press, pp. 318–362.

Ryan, E.D., & Simons, J. (1981). Cognitive demand, imagery, and frequency of mental rehearsal as factors influencing acquisition of motor skills. *Journal of Sport Psychology,* 3, 35–45.

Sahin, N.T., Pinker, S., Cash, S.S., Schomer, D., & Halgren, E. (2009). Sequential processing of lexical, grammatical, and phonological information within Broca's area. *Science,* 326, 445–449.

Sandberg, K., Bibby, B., Timmermans, B., Cleeremans, A., & Overgaard, M. (2011). Task accuracy and awareness as sigmoid functions of stimulus duration. *Consciousness and Cognition,* 20, 1659–1675.

Schiess, M., Urbanczik, R., & Senn, W. (2016). Somato-dendritic synaptic plasticity and error-backpropagation in active dendrites. *PLoS Computational Biology,* 12, e1004638.

Schulze, K., & Koelsch, S. (2012). Working memory for speech and music. *Annals of the New York Academy of Sciences,* 1252, 229–236.

Schulze, K., Mueller, K., & Koelsch, S. (2011a). Neural correlates of strategy use during auditory working memory in musicians and non-musicians. *European Journal of Neuroscience,* 33, 189–196.

Schulze, K., Zysset, S., Mueller, K., Friederici, A.D., & Koelsch, S. (2011b). Neuroarchitecture of verbal and tonal working memory in nonmusicians and musicians. *Human Brain Mapping,* 32, 771–783.

Shanks, D.R., & Berry, C.J. (2016). Are there multiple memory systems? Tests of models of implicit and explicit memory. *Quarterly Journal of Experimental Psychology,* 65, 1449–1474.

Sharma, N., Pomeroy, V.M., & Baron, J-C. (2006). Motor imagery. A backdoor to the motor system after stroke? *Stroke,* 37, 1941–1952.

Sherman, M.T., Seth, A.K., Barrett, A.B., & Kanai, R. (2015). Prior expectations facilitate metacognition for perceptual decision. *Consciousness and Cognition,* 35, 53–65.

Sluming, V., Brooks, J., Howard, M., Downes, J.J., & Roberts, N. (2007). Broca's area supports enhanced visuospatial cognition in orchestral musicians. *Journal of Neuroscience,* 27, 3799–3806.

Specht, K., Zahn, R., Willmes, K., Weis, S., Holtel, C., Krause, B.J., Herzog, H., & Huber, W. (2009). Joint independent component analysis of structural and functional images reveals complex patterns of functional reorganization in stroke aphasia. *NeuroImage,* 47, 2057–2063.

Stefanics, G., Hangya, B., Hernadi, I., Winkler, I., Lakatos, P., & Ulbert, I. (2010). Phase entrainment of human delta oscillations can mediate the effects of expectation on reaction speed. *Journal of Neuroscience,* 30, 13578–13585.

Stork, D.G. (1989). Is backpropagation biologically plausible? *Neural Networks,* 2, 241–246.

Szaflarski, J.P., Eaton, K., Ball, A.L., Banks, C., Vannest, J., Allendorfer, J.B., Pape, S., & Holland, S.K. (2011). Poststroke aphasia recovery assessed with functional magnetic resonance imaging and a picture identification task. *Journal of Stroke & Cerebrovascular Diseases,* 20, 336–345.

Thomas, C., Altenmüller, E., Marckmann, G., Kahrs, J., & Dichgans, J. (1997). Language processing in aphasia: changes in lateralization patterns during recovery reflect cerebral plasticity in adults. *Electroencephalography and Clinical Neurophysiology, 102,* 86–97.

Thulborn, K.R., Carpenter, P.A., & Just, M.A. (1999). Plasticity of language-related brain function during recovery from stroke. *Stroke, 30,* 749–754.

Tillmann, B., Janata, P., & Bharucha, J.J. (2003). Activation of the inferior frontal cortex in musical priming. *Cognitive Brain Research, 16,* 145–161.

Trachtenberg, J.T., Chen, B.E., Knott, G.W., Feng, G., Sanes, J.R., Welker, E., & Svoboda, K. (2002). Long-term in vivo imaging of experience-dependent synaptic plasticity in adult cortex. *Nature, 420,* 788–794.

Ullman, M.T. (2016). The declarative/procedural model: a neurobiological model of language learniong, knowledge, and use. In: G. Hickok, & S.A. Small (Eds.) *The Neurobiology of Language.*New York: Elsevier, pp. 953–968.

Vigneau, M., Beaucousin, V., Hervé, P.Y., Duffau, H., Crivello, F., Houdé, O., Mazoyer, B., & Tzourio-Mazoyer, N. (2006). Meta-analyzing left hemisphere language areas: phonology, semantics, and sentence processing. *NeuroImage, 30,* 1414–1432.

Werbos, P.J. (1974). *Beyond Regression: New Tools for Prediction and Analysis in the Behavioral Sciences.* Harvard University: Applied Mathematics Thesis.

Werbos, P.J. (1994). *The Roots of Backpropagation: From Ordered Derivatives to Neural Networks and Political Forecasting.* New York: John Wiley and Sons.

Wohldmann, E.L., Healy, A.F., & Bourne, L.E. (2008). A mental practice superiority effect: less retroactive interference and more transfer than physical practice. *Journal of Experimental Psychology: Learning, Memory, and Cognition, 34,* 823–833.

Woolfolk, R.L., Murphy, S.M., Gottesfeld, D., & Aitken, D. (1985). Effects of mental rehearsal of task motor activity and mental depiction of task outcome on motor skill performance. *Journal of Sport Psychology, 7,* 191–197.

Wörtwein, G., Saerup, L.H., Charlottenfeld-Starpov, D., & Mogensen, J. (1995). Place learning by fimbria-fornix transected rats in a modified water maze. *International Journal of Neuroscience, 82,* 71–81.

Wyart, V. Nobre, A.C., & Summerfield, C. (2012). Dissociable prior influences of signal probability and relevance on visual contrast sensitivity. *Proceedings of the National Academy of Sciences USA, 109,* 3593–3598.

Yuste, R. (2011). Dendritic spines and distributed circuits. *Neuron, 71,* 772–782.

Zajonc, R.B. (1984). On the primacy of affect. *American Psychologist, 39,* 117–123.

INDEX

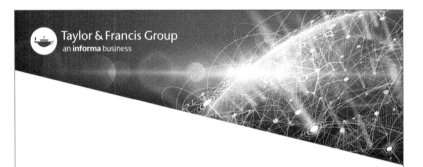

Milton Keynes UK
Ingram Content Group UK Ltd.
UKHW050757190724
445713UK00006B/16